HARCOURT BRACE SPELLING

Thorsten Carlson

Richard Madden

HARCOURT BRACE SPELLING

HARCOURT BRACE & COMPANY

Orlando Atlanta Austin Boston San Francisco Chicago Dallas New York Toronto London

http://www.hbschool.com

Acknowledgments

For permission to reprint copyrighted material, grateful acknowledgment is made to the following sources:

Harcourt Brace & Company: Letter forms from *HBJ Handwriting.* Copyright © 1987 by Harcourt Brace & Company. Definitions and the pronunciation key in the "Spelling Dictionary" are from the *HBJ School Dictionary.* Copyright © 1985, 1977 by Harcourt Brace & Company.

Little, Brown and Company: "Eletelephony" from *Tirra Lirra: Rhymes Old and New* by Laura E. Richards. Copyright 1932 by Laura E. Richards; copyright © renewed 1960 by Hamilton Richards.

Marian Reiner, on behalf of Lillian Morrison: "The Sidewalk Racer" (or "On the Skateboard") from *The Sidewalk Racer and Other Poems of Sports and Motion* by Lillian Morrison. Copyright © 1965, 1967, 1968, 1977 by Lillian Morrison.

PHOTO CREDITS

Key: T, Top; B, Bottom; L, Left; C, Center; R, Right.

Page 18, 22, J. Hoffman Studios; 23, Ingbert Gruttner; 31, Anderson Studios/Derriak Anderson; 36, Clara Alch Photography; 37, Kenneth W. Fink/Bruce Coleman; 39, 40, 42, 44, 57, J. Hoffman Studios; 61, ALL, NASA, 80, Anderson Studios/Derriak Anderson; 86(T), Gabe Palmer/Stock Market; 86(BL), Clara Alch Photography; 88, Victor Beunza/Bruce Coleman; 90, J. Hoffman Studios; 91, Granger Collection; 100, J. Hoffman Studios; 109, Anderson Studios/Derriak Anderson; 112, DPI; 113, John Ficara/Woodfin Camp and Assoc.; 117, 122, 123, 138, 140, 151; J. Hoffman Studios; 165, G.R. Richardson/Taurus; 166, Anderson Studios/Derriak Anderson; 168, J. Hoffman Studios; 169, Anderson Studios/Derriak Anderson; 169, Mount Wilson and Palomar Observatories; 172, J. Hoffman Studios; 173, Anderson Studios/Derriak Anderson; 175, Grant Heilman; 177, 179, J. Hoffman Studios; 180(L), Anderson Studios/Derriak Anderson; 180(L), Anderson Studios/Derriak Anderson; 180(R), Dick Walker/Taurus; 181, 182, Peter Arnold, Inc./G. Ziesler; 184, George Dodge/DPI; 185, 194, J. Hoffman Studios; 196(L), Anderson Studios/Derriak Anderson; 196(R), Runk Schoenberger/Grant Heilman; 201, Alese and Mort Pechter/Stock Market; 202, 203, J. Hoffman Studios.

Printed in the United States of America
ISBN 0-15-313648-0

1 2 3 4 5 6 7 8 9 048 2000 1999

Contents

Study Steps to Learn a Word

 **SAY** the word. Recall when you have heard the word used. Think about what it means.

 **LOOK** at the word. Find any prefixes, suffixes, or other word parts you know. Think about other words that are related in meaning and spelling. Try to picture the word in your mind.

 **SPELL** the word to yourself. Think about the way each sound is spelled. Notice any unusual spelling.

 **WRITE** the word while looking at it. Check the way you have formed your letters. If you have not written the word clearly or correctly, write it again.

 **CHECK** your learning. Cover the word and write it. If you did not spell the word correctly, practice these steps until the word becomes your own.

Skills Check

A. Read the first word in each row. Then write the letter of the word that has the same vowel sound.

1. **strap**   **a.** swift   **b.** brand   **c.** plot
2. **crop**   **a.** fond   **b.** brick   **c.** track
3. **bulb**   **a.** twin   **b.** tube   **c.** month
4. **rice**   **a.** fade   **b.** woke   **c.** tight
5. **cheese**   **a.** pail   **b.** feast   **c.** break
6. **glow**   **a.** groan   **b.** mind   **c.** owl

B. Add *ed* to each word on the left. Add *ing* to each word on the right. Write the words.

ed	ing
7. step	**10.** flap
8. scream	**11.** invite
9. play	**12.** buy

C. Add *ed* and *ing* to each word. Write both words.

13. try

14. worry

D. Write the plural of each word.

15. month   **16.** match

17. story   **18.** stomach

19. loss   **20.** hobby

E. Take away the consonant letter that begins each word. Add a consonant cluster. Write the new word.

21. bend   **22.** hid

23. loan   **24.** meat

F. The words that complete each pair of sentences sound alike, but they are not spelled the same. Complete each sentence with the correct homophone.

25. Our jet ____ took off from O'Hare Airport.

26. It's ____ to see why you want that car.

27. Two of us ate the ____ pizza.

28. We dug a ____ two feet deep.

29. They didn't ____ the jewels.

30. The frame of the building is made of ____ .

31. Please be sure ____ home by five.

32. Here is ____ lunch.

G. Write the word for each pronunciation.

33. /sel'ə·brāt/   **34.** /en'jin/
35. /pich'ər/   **36.** /dez'ərt/
37. /let'is/   **38.** /pur'fikt/
39. /myoo'zik/   **40.** /ō'shən/

H. Write a two-syllable word that means the opposite of each word. Then draw a line between the two syllables.

41. sunrise   **42.** private
43. wide   **44.** remembered
45. worse   **46.** top

I. Add one of these suffixes to each word. Write new words that mean "someone who does something."

-er   -or   -ist

47. act   **48.** science
49. art   **50.** skate
51. sail   **52.** win

best score
F. 8

best score
G. 8

best score
H. 6

best score
I. 6

total
54

3

1 The Sounds /a/, /e/, /i/, /o/, /u/

UNIT WORDS

1. *twist*
2. *shift*
3. *solid*
4. *deaf*
5. *blunder*
6. *dusk*
7. *dwell*
8. *tramp*
9. *smash*
10. *extra*
11. *thunder*
12. *flock*
13. *stock*
14. *snag*
15. *scrap*
16. *drift*
17. *timid*
18. *chest*
19. *threat*
20. *swept*

The Unit Words

The words in this unit have short vowel sounds: /a/, /e/, /i/, /o/, or /u/. The letters that appear between the lines / / represent sounds.

The short vowel sound is spelled with one vowel letter in most of the Unit words.

- The sound /a/ is spelled with **a.**   *snag*
- The sound /e/ is spelled with **e.**   *chest*
- The sound /i/ is spelled with **i.**   *twist*
- The sound /o/ is spelled with **o.**   *solid*
- The sound /u/ is spelled with **u.**   *thunder*

Two of the Unit words have /e/ spelled another way —with **ea** as in *threat.*

4

Spelling Practice

A. Follow the directions using the Unit words.

 1. Write the four words that have the sound /a/.

 2. Write the six words that have the sound /e/. Underline the
    letter or letters that spell /e/ in each word.

B. Write the Unit words that rhyme with each of these words.

 3. lift (two words)

 4. lock (two words)

 5. under (two words)

C. Write the Unit word for each definition.

 6. not hollow   7. bend

 8. twilight   9. shy

10. snow or sand heaped up by the wind

D. Finish these sentences with Unit words.

11. The soccer ball hit Jackie in the _____.

12. The heavy door was made of _____ wood.

13. Maria got _____ pay for working overtime.

14. The _____ of rain made us change our plans.

15. The rushing water _____ the canoe down river.

E. Complete the story with Unit words.

The storm grew worse at __16__. A loud clap of __17__ scared the
__18__ of sheep. The poor, __19__ animals began to bleat loudly.
Were the barn walls __20__ enough to stand up to the wind?
We decided to __21__ the sheep to a safer place.

5

Spelling and Language · Consonant Clusters

Say the word *snag* to yourself. Listen to the consonant sounds /s/ and /n/ at the beginning of *snag*. The letters *sn* in *snag* are a **consonant cluster.** The letters are written together. You hear the two sounds together. Now say *dusk*. The letters *sk* at the end of *dusk* are also a consonant cluster.

Write the Unit words that begin with the same consonant clusters as these words.

1. twin   **2.** flap
3. stamp   **4.** bloom
5. dream   **6.** scream

Write the Unit words that end with the same consonant clusters as these words.

7. west (two words)   **8.** lift (two words)

Writing on Your Own

Write a scary description for your friends. Put your main character on a quiet road at dusk. Then describe the things that frighten him or her. See if you can give your reader goose bumps! Use some of the Unit words to tell what happens.

Using the Dictionary to Spell and Write

The dictionary is a useful tool when you write. To find information in a dictionary, you need to know how it is organized.

The words in a dictionary are listed in **alphabetical order.** To put words in alphabetical order, use the first letter of each word. If the first letters are the same, use the second letter to put words in alphabetical order. If the second letters are the same, use the third letter.

Write each list of words in alphabetical order.

1. swept   **2.** tramp
 scrap   thunder
 snag   threat
 smash   timid

 SPELLING DICTIONARY Remember to use your **Spelling Dictionary** when you write.

Spelling on Your Own

Write sentences using all of the Unit words. Use as many of the words as you can in one sentence, and underline each word. Try to use all of the words in eight sentences. Here's an example: "The *timid flock* ran for cover at the sound of *thunder.*"

MASTERY WORDS

bring
flag
dust
apple
milk
club

Follow the directions using the Mastery words.

1. Write the two words that have the sound /a/.

2. Write the three words that begin with consonant clusters. Circle the word that has /i/.

3. Write the two words that have the sound /u/. Circle the word that ends in a consonant cluster.

Answer the questions using the Mastery words.

4. What American symbol has stars and stripes?

5. What always comes back after you wipe it away?

6. What has green, yellow, or red skin?

7. What drink do you get from cows?

BONUS WORDS

instead
emblem
plaid
sponge
hinder
against
ponder
grudge

1. Write /a/, /e/, /i/, /o/, and /u/ in a column. Next to each vowel sound, write the Bonus words that have that short vowel sound in the syllable said with the most force. Then underline the letter or letters that spell the vowel sound.

2. Write the three words that begin with consonant clusters.

3. Write the Bonus words that are the opposite of *for* and *help*.

4. Write four sentences, using two Bonus words in each sentence.

2 The Sounds /ī/ and /ā/

UNIT WORDS

1. strike
2. fail
3. type
4. reply
5. behave
6. debate
7. entire
8. snail
9. spade
10. waist
11. twine
12. desire
13. flame
14. grave
15. hydrogen
16. deny
17. arrive
18. daily
19. drain
20. style

strike /ī/

The Unit Words

Each Unit word has a long vowel sound—/ī/ or /ā/. The Unit words show two ways to spell /ī/.

- **i**-consonant-**e** as in *strike*
- **y** as in *type*

The Unit words show two ways to spell /ā/.

- **a**-consonant-**e** as in *behave*
- **ai** as in *daily*

entire
/in·tīr/

REMEMBER THIS

Say the word *entire*. The short vowel sound /i/ that you hear at the beginning is spelled **e**. To help you remember how to spell *entire,* use this rhyme:

What you hear in *entire* is not what you see.
Entire begins and ends with an **e.**

Spelling Practice

A. Follow the directions using the Unit words.

1. Write the five words that have /ī/ spelled as it is in *fine*.

2. Write the five words that have /ī/ spelled with *y*.

3. Write the word that sounds like *waste*.

4. Write the other four words that have the sound /ā/ spelled with *ai*.

B. Replace the consonant cluster in each of these words with another cluster to spell a Unit word. Write the words.

5. blame

6. trade

7. brave

8. trail

C. Add a second syllable to each of these syllables. The syllable you add will have one vowel sound. Write Unit words.

9. be

10. en

11. de (three words)

D. Finish the story with Unit words. The vowel sound is given to help you.

Alonso bought a fresh-water /ā/ __**12**__ for his aquarium. He watches it crawl up the side of the glass tank /ā/ __**13**__. Every week, he and his brother /ā/ __**14**__ the water from the tank. Then they add fresh, warm water. If they /ā/ __**15**__ to change the water, the snail could die. They have no /ī/ __**16**__ to see that happen.

9

Spelling and Language · Synonyms

UNIT WORDS

strike
fail
type
reply
behave
debate
entire
snail
spade
waist
twine
desire
flame
grave
hydrogen
deny
arrive
daily
drain
style

Words that have the same or nearly the same meaning are called **synonyms**. For example, the verbs *drain* and *empty* are synonyms. You could use *drain* in place of *empty* in this sentence: "Please *empty* the water out of the sink." The meaning of the sentence does not change.

Write a Unit word that is a synonym for each word.

1. respond   **2.** string   **3.** fashion
4. serious   **5.** argue   **6.** act

Writing on Your Own

Write a paragraph of opinion about a movie. Name the best film you have seen recently. Give at least two reasons why other people should go to see it. Use four or more Unit words in your paragraph. Be sure that you have given good reasons for your opinion.

Using the Dictionary to Spell and Write

If you want to make sure you use a word correctly in your writing, you can look it up in a dictionary. You can use the guide words to help you.

Guide words are the two words found at the top of a dictionary page. The word on the left is the first word on the page. The word on the right is the last word on the page. The rest of the words on the page come between the guide words in alphabetical order.

amusement	attitude

a·muse·ment /ə·myooz'mənt/ *n.*
1 The state of being entertained or amused.

a·rise /ə·rīz'/ *v.* **a·rose, a·ris·en**
/ə·riz'ən/, **a·ris·ing** To get up; to rise.

Write the Unit words that would be on a dictionary page that had each of these pairs of guide words. Write the words in alphabetical order.

1. dabble drama   **2. soak typhoon**   **3. effect ice**

 SPELLING DICTIONARY Remember to use your **Spelling Dictionary** when you write.

Spelling on Your Own

Make a "word puzzle" with the Unit words. Write one word. Use a letter in that word to write another word. Then keep going, writing words across and down. Try to link up all the words.

MASTERY WORDS

myself
snake
bite
paid
line
space

Write the Mastery word that rhymes with each word.

1. race   **2.** made   **3.** fine   **4.** kite

Follow the directions using the Mastery words.

5. Write the two words that begin with consonant clusters.

6. Write the word made up of two smaller words.

Finish the story with Mastery words.

> Today, everything went wrong. I __7__ for some groceries and forgot to take the change. I cut __8__ on the metal fence in the backyard. My __9__ crawled out of its tank, and I couldn't find it. My dog took a __10__ out of my baseball glove. I waited in __11__ for an hour to see a movie. When I got to the front of the line, there was no __12__ left in the theater.

BONUS WORDS

inflate
complain
maintain
ninety
magnify
tyrant
confined
investigate

1. Which Bonus word ends with /ī/?

2. Which word names a number?

3. Which word is the opposite of *released*?

4. Which word has four syllables? Remember that each syllable has one vowel sound.

5. Which word is a synonym for *grumble*?

6. Now write your own clues for the other three words. Begin each clue with "Which word...." Write the answer to each clue.

3 The Sounds /ē/ and /ō/

UNIT WORDS

1. *reveal*
2. *code*
3. *measles*
4. *greetings*
5. *stream*
6. *steel*
7. *vote*
8. *choke*
9. *coast*
10. *grease*
11. *creak*
12. *throat*
13. *screen*
14. *goal*
15. *coal*
16. *cocoa*
17. *squeeze*
18. *grove*
19. *lonesome*
20. *ski*

25 15 21 8 1 22 5
18 5 22 5 1 12 5 4 25 15 21 18
19 11 9 12 12 2 25
2 18 5 1 11 9 14 7
20 8 5 3 15 4 5

The Unit Words

The message above is written in code. Figure out the code. Then replace each number with a letter. Here's a helpful hint: *1* stands for the letter *A* and *26* stands for *Z*.

Each Unit word has a long vowel sound—/ē/ or /ō/. The Unit words show three ways to spell /ē/.

- **ea** as in *stream*

- **ee** as in *greetings*

☐ When /ē/ comes at the end of a word, it is usually spelled **e** as in *he* or **ee** as in *see. Ski* is one of the few English words that has /ē/ spelled **i**.

The Unit words show two ways to spell /ō/.

- **o**-consonant-**e** as in *code*

- **oa** as in *coast*

/ē/

G R E E T I N G S
7 18 5 5 20 9 14 7 19

Spelling Practice

A. Use the number-letter code to complete these exercises.

1. Write this Unit word. $\underline{19}$ $\underline{20}$ $\underline{18}$ $\underline{5}$ $\underline{}$ $\underline{13}$

2. Now write four more Unit words that have /ē/ spelled the same way.

3. Write the four words that have /ē/ spelled $\underline{5}$ $\underline{5}$.

4. Write the word that has /ē/ spelled $\underline{9}$.

5. Use the code to spell this word. $\underline{22}$ $\underline{15}$ $\underline{20}$ $\underline{5}$

6. Now write four more Unit words that have /ō/ spelled this way.

7. Write the five words that have /ō/ spelled $\underline{15}$ $\underline{1}$.

8. Circle the word you wrote for **7** that also has /ō/ spelled with $\underline{15}$.

B. Complete each question with a Unit word. Did you know that . . .

9. iron and ____ are the most useful metals known?

10. the major use of ____ is to produce electricity?

11. women gained the right to ____ in 1920?

12. the length of the Pacific ____ is 55,000 miles?

13. chocolate and ____ are made from cacao beans?

14. the longest ____ jump was 181 meters?

15. the biggest movie ____ is 70 feet by 96 feet?

12 15 14 5 19 15 13 5

13

Spelling and Language · Adding *ed* and *ing*

UNIT WORDS

reveal
code
measles
greetings
stream
steel
vote
choke
coast
grease
creak
throat
screen
goal
coal
cocoa
squeeze
grove
lonesome
ski

You add *ed* to a verb when talking about the past. You add *ing* to a verb when you use it with *am, is, are, was,* and *were.* When a verb ends with *e,* drop the *e* before adding *ed* or *ing.*

Add *ed* or *ing* to the words in ( ) to finish the sentences.

1. The comet is (stream) _____ through the sky.
2. She (squeeze) _____ her way through the crowd.
3. We are (vote) _____ for you for class president.

Add *ed* and *ing* to *ski.* Do not drop the final vowel.

4. ski + ed = _____   5. ski + ing = _____

Writing on Your Own

   Write a message in code to make plans with a friend. Write one or more sentences using as many Unit words as possible. Proofread your message to make sure you have spelled the words correctly. Finally, write your sentences in code and give the message to your friend.

Using the Dictionary to Spell and Write

   Each word explained in a dictionary is called an entry word. The parts of a dictionary **entry** give you information you can use when you write. For example, you can find the correct spelling of a word and the meaning of a word.

   Study the parts of this entry. Then answer the questions.

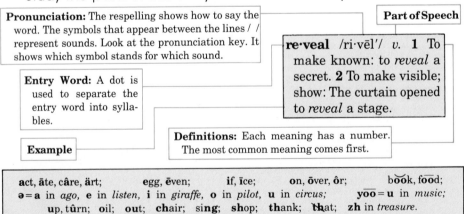

Pronunciation: The respelling shows how to say the word. The symbols that appear between the lines / / represent sounds. Look at the pronunciation key. It shows which symbol stands for which sound.

Part of Speech

re·veal /ri·vēl'/ *v.* **1** To make known: to *reveal* a secret. **2** To make visible; show: The curtain opened to *reveal* a stage.

Entry Word: A dot is used to separate the entry word into syllables.

Definitions: Each meaning has a number. The most common meaning comes first.

Example

act, āte, câre, ärt;   egg, ēven;   if, īce;   on, ōver, ôr;   bŏŏk, fŏŏd;
ə = a in *ago,* e in *listen,* i in *giraffe,* o in *pilot,* u in *circus;*   yŏŏ = u in *music;*
up, tûrn; oil; out; chair; sing; shop; thank; that; zh in *treasure.*

1. How many syllables are in the entry word?
2. Write the pronunciation for *reveal.*
3. Use *reveal* with meaning 1 in a sentence.

14

Spelling on Your Own

Read each word below. Write the Unit word that would come next in alphabetical order. For example, *choke* would follow *chip*.

1. chip
2. thread
3. meadow
4. coarse
5. voice
6. coach
7. ground
8. crank
9. return
10. square
11. cob
12. go
13. scrap
14. straw
15. graze
16. cod
17. steam
18. log
19. skate
20. green

MASTERY WORDS

stove
soak
team
between
joke
asleep

Write the Mastery word for each definition.

1. make wet
2. not awake
3. something funny
4. a group that plays together

Write the Mastery words that rhyme with these pairs of words.

5. wove   cove
6. screen   green
7. scream   dream
8. keep   sweep
9. poke   woke   (two words)

BONUS WORDS

greedy
oppose
erode
easel
coastal
proceed
coax
conceal

Follow the directions using the Bonus words.

1. Write the four words that have the sound /ē/.
2. Write the four words that have the sound /ō/.

Complete the paragraph with Bonus words.

Linda was sure the box contained an __3__ . She could hardly __4__ her excitement. She had been trying to __5__ her parents into buying it. Maybe she could __6__ with her art lessons if her parents didn't __7__ the idea.

15

4 Words with *ed* and *ing*

UNIT WORDS

1. scrubbing
2. extended
3. pointed
4. dropped
5. sounding
6. shouting
7. expected
8. spoiled
9. trotting
10. jammed
11. laughing
12. mailed
13. passing
14. swapped
15. wrapped
16. snapping
17. roasting
18. electing
19. reached
20. grabbing

The Unit Words

Study the pictures above. The position of the flags in each figure's hands stands for a letter in the alphabet. What happens to the final consonant letter in *scrub* when you add *ing*? The letter *b* is doubled— *scrubbing*.

All the words in this unit are verbs. Verbs show action or being. When *ed* and *ing* are added to most verbs, the spelling does not change.

extend + ed = extended
shout + ing = shouting

The spelling does change, however, for words that have a short vowel sound and end with one consonant letter. With words such as *swap* and *grab*, you double the final consonant before you add *ed* or *ing*.

swap + ed = swapped
grab + ing = grabbing

Spelling Practice

A. Add the letters for /a/ or /o/ to the consonants given. Write the base words. Then write the words with the endings shown.

1. j__m + ed   **2.** dr__p + ed

3. wr__p + ed   **4.** sn__p + ing

5. tr__t + ing   **6.** sw__p + ed

B. Take off the ending of each of these words. Then write the word. Underline the consonant cluster that ends the word. Then add *ed* or *ing* and write a Unit word.

7. roasted   **8.** elected   **9.** expecting

10. pointing   **11.** sounded   **12.** extending

C. Write the Unit words for these pronunciations. Then complete **17** and **18.**

13. /skrub'ing/   **14.** /pas'ing/

15. /laf'ing/   **16.** /grab'ing/

17. Circle the word in which the double consonant letters are part of the base word.

18. Underline the word with an unusual spelling for /a/.

D. Now try this "word math."

19. rich − /i/ + /ē/ + ed = ____

20. shut − /u/ + /ou/ + ing = ____

21. mile − /ī/ + /ā/ + ed = ____

22. spill − ill + /oi/ + l + ed = ____

Spelling and Language ·
Capitalization and Punctuation

Read the rules for capitalization and punctuation of sentences.

- Capitalize the first word of a sentence.
- Capitalize the word *I* and the names of people and places.
- Place a period after a sentence that makes a statement or request or gives a command. Place a question mark after a question.

Now rewrite these sentences. Add periods, question marks, and capital letters where they are needed.

1. mail the wrapped packages today
2. are we roasting chicken for dinner

Writing on Your Own

Imagine that you are entering a recipe contest at your school. Write directions for making "The Most Healthful Sandwich in the World." First list the ingredients. Then describe each step in making the sandwich. Use some of the Unit words in the recipe. Think about the punctuation in your sentences.

WRITER'S GUIDE For a sample how-to paragraph, turn to page 268.

Proofreading

Mei wrote this in her journal. She misspelled six words.

1. Read what Mei wrote and find the mistakes.

> When I reeched the ballet studio, the room was jamed with dancers. My teacher, Lena, was snaping at anyone who wasn't pointing her toes. I wrapt my legs in warm-up socks and began to practice. I extendid my right arm forward and my left arm and leg backward. Lena pointid to my left foot. "Very nice," she said. I smiled and continued practicing.

2. Write the six misspelled words correctly.

Spelling on Your Own

UNIT WORDS

Divide the Unit words into two groups. In one group, write all the words that end with *ed*. In the other, write all the words that end with *ing*. Then use each of the words with *ing* in a sentence after *am*, *is*, *are*, *was*, or *were*. For example: "He was *laughing* at my jokes." Write ten sentences.

MASTERY WORDS

Add *ed* or *ing* to each word to spell a Mastery word.

1. skin　　**2.** rest　　**3.** cross
4. tag　　**5.** stop　　**6.** climb

Finish these sentences with Mastery words.

7. Conchita ____ her elbow playing ball.

8. Steve ____ the tree to rescue the cat.

9. Alice is ____ the street to get to my house.

10. Bill ____ to listen to the news report.

11. After the long walk, they ____ in the shade.

12. My younger sister is always ____ after me.

> stopped
> climbed
> tagging
> skinned
> rested
> crossing

BONUS WORDS

Write a Bonus word for each definition.

1. shocked　　　**2.** answered　　　**3.** happened
4. pulled with force　　**5.** liked better

Follow the directions using Bonus words.

6. Write the five words in which the final consonant is doubled before *ed* or *ing* is added.

7. Write the three words that begin with consonant clusters. Circle the word that has the sound /u/.

8. Write the word that has the sound /ā/.

9. Write a story with the title "An Afternoon on a Sailboat." Use as many Bonus words as you can in your story.

> dimming
> hauled
> occurred
> braiding
> knotting
> responded
> preferred
> stunned

5 The Sounds /s/ and /z/

UNIT WORDS

1. bicycle
2. distance
3. sincerely
4. license
5. sense
6. except
7. force
8. peace
9. recite
10. tense
11. service
12. season
13. cozy
14. clumsy
15. chose
16. citizen
17. graze
18. daisy
19. arise
20. closet

The Unit Words

The Unit words have the consonant sounds /s/ and /z/. You hear the sound /s/ at the end of *force.* You hear the sound /z/ at the end of *fours.*

The most common way to spell the consonant sound /s/ is with **s**, as in *season.* The Unit words show three more ways to spell the sound /s/.

- **c** as in *recite*
- **ce** as in *force*
- **se** as in *tense*

There are two common ways to spell the consonant sound /z/.

- **z** as in *cozy*
- **s** as in *closet*

REMEMBER THIS

Here is a tip to help you spell the second syllable in *sin·cere·ly.* The syllable *cere* rhymes with *here* and is spelled with **ere**.

sin cere ly

Spelling Practice

A. *Cell* and *sell* sound alike. They both begin with the sound /s/. But /s/ is spelled with a different letter in each word.

1. Write the six Unit words that have /s/ spelled with *c*, as in *cell*.

2. Write the five Unit words that have /s/ spelled with *s*, as in *sell*.

B. *Ice* and *eyes* have the same vowel sound, /ī/. But they end with different consonant sounds.

3. Say the word *ice*. Listen to the final sound, /s/. Write the seven Unit words that end with this sound.

4. Circle the words you wrote for **3** that have final /s/ spelled *se*.

5. Say the word *eyes*. Listen to the final sound, /z/. Write the three Unit words that end with this sound.

C. Follow the directions using the Unit words.

6. Write the three words that end with /z/ before /ē/.

7. Write the four words in which *c* spells the sound /k/.

8. Write a Unit word that rhymes with each of these words.

lazy	horse
geese	fence
raise	rosy

21

Spelling and Language · Homophones

Q: What dog has money?
A: A bloodhound. It's always picking up *scents*.

The answer to the riddle is a play on words. *Scents,* the smells that bloodhounds can follow, sounds just like *cents,* or coins. Words that sound alike but have different spellings and meanings are called **homophones.**

Write the word that is the correct homophone for the underlined word in each sentence.

1. A bloodhound has a keen <u>cents</u> of smell.
2. There will be <u>piece</u> once the nations sign the treaty.
3. The cattle <u>grays</u> peacefully in the meadow.

Writing on Your Own

Pretend you rode your bicycle in a race yesterday. Write a letter to a relative telling what happened during the race. Tell how far you had to ride, what you felt while you were racing, and who won the race. Use some of the Unit words in your letter.

 WRITER'S GUIDE For a sample friendly letter, turn to page 271.

Using the Dictionary to Spell and Write

Knowing how to pronounce a word can help you remember how to spell the word. A **pronunciation** is given after each entry word in a dictionary. For the word *season,* it looks like this: /sē′zən/. The pronunciation shows you how to say the word. A **pronunciation key** helps you read the pronunciation. It lists the sound symbols and gives a sample word for each sound.

act, āte, cȃre, ärt;	egg, ēven;	if, īce;	on, ōver, ôr;	book, food;
ə = a in *ago,* e in *listen,* i in *giraffe,* o in *pilot,* u in *circus;*				yoo = u in *music;*
up, tûrn;	oil;	out;	chair; sing; shop; thank; that;	zh in *treasure.*

Read the sentences. Write the regular spellings for the words in / /.

1. I closed the letter with "/sin·sir′lē/ yours."
2. Everyone went on the picnic /ik·sept′/ me.
3. Sarah ran a /dis′təns/ of two miles.
4. He became a United States /sit′ə·zən/.

UNIT WORDS

bicycle
distance
sincerely
license
sense
except
force
peace
recite
tense
service
season
cozy
clumsy
chose
citizen
graze
daisy
arise
closet

Spelling on Your Own

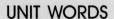

Add the letters that spell /s/ or /z/. Write the words.

1. _in_erely	**2.** _ervi_ _	**3.** li_en_ _	**4.** _ea_on
5. co_y	**6.** ex_ept	**7.** di_tan_ _	**8.** _iti_en
9. ten_ _	**10.** dai_y	**11.** clum_y	**12.** bi_ycle
13. pea_ _	**14.** clo_et	**15.** gra_e	**16.** _en_ _
17. re_ite	**18.** for_ _	**19.** ari_e	**20.** cho_e

MASTERY WORDS

juice
decide
wise
prize
busy
else

Follow the directions using the Mastery words.

1. Write the two words that end with /s/, heard in *ice*.

2. Write the two words that end with /z/, heard in *eyes*.

3. Write another word that has the sound /z/.

Find the two misspelled words in each sentence. Then write the words correctly.

4. A wize person can decid what's right.

5. A glass of cold juise is nice after a buzy day.

6. I hope someone elce wins the prise.

BONUS WORDS

cereal
advice
principal
bazaar
advise
immense
concert
recent

1. Write the six Bonus words that have the sound /s/. Underline the letters that spell /s/ in each word.

2. Write the word that is a homophone for *principle*. Then use both words in a sentence.

3. Write the two words that have a similar meaning. One word ends with /s/, the other with /z/. Then use both words in a sentence.

4. Use the word *bazaar* in a sentence.

Review

Follow these steps when you are unsure how to spell a word.

- **Say** the word. Recall when you have heard the word used. Think about what it means.
- **Look** at the word. Find any prefixes, suffixes, or other word parts you know. Think about other words that are related in meaning and spelling. Try to picture the word in your mind.
- **Spell** the word to yourself. Think about the way each sound is spelled. Notice any unusual spelling.
- **Write** the word while looking at it. Check the way you have formed your letters. If you have not written the word clearly or correctly, write it again.
- **Check** your learning. Cover the word and write it. If you did not spell the word correctly, practice these steps until the word becomes your own.

UNIT 1

scrap
solid
shift
threat
thunder
smash
dwell
drift
dusk
flock

UNIT 1 **Write words from Unit 1 that have the same vowel sound as each of these words.**

1. sun

2. nap

3. nod

4. red

5. twist

UNIT 2

type
waist
behave
deny
arrive
reply
flame
daily
fail
entire

UNIT 2 **Follow directions using words from Unit 2.**

6. Write the three words that have the sound /ī/ spelled *y.* Circle the words that have two syllables.

7. Write the two words that have /ā/ spelled *a*-consonant-*e.*

Finish these sentences.

8. Caroline, Maria's pen pal, would _____ at 5:00 P.M.

9. Caroline's trip would take an _____ day; Maria could not _____ to be at the airport on time.

10. Caroline told Maria that she would wear a white dress with a blue belt around her ____ .

11. Maria had a schedule of ____ events planned.

UNIT 3 Follow the directions using words from Unit 3.

12. Write the three words that have /ō/ spelled as it is in *boat.*

13. Write the five words that have the sound /ē/. Circle the letters that make the long vowel sound.

14. Write the two words that have /ō/ spelled o-consonant-e.

Finish this story. The long vowel sound of each word is given to help you.

    Have you ever spent a vacation camping? Last summer my family camped near a /ē/ __15__ in the mountains. Every night we drank hot /ō/ __16__ while we sat around the campfire. I was /ō/ __17__ for my friends, but I enjoyed that week in the wilderness.

UNIT 4 Follow the directions using words from Unit 4.

Add *ing* to these base words. Circle all double consonants.

18. laugh

19. scrub

20. grab

21. elect

22. trot

Finish these sentences.

23. We had ____ rain for our morning hike, but the sky was bright blue.

24. At this welcome sight, we all started ____ our knapsacks and hiking boots.

25. Kim could not stop ____ at all the gear I wanted to take.

26. Finally we ____ our lunches, packed them, and started off.

UNIT 3
squeeze
throat
stream
lonesome
cocoa
coast
vote
reveal
creak
steel

UNIT 4
electing
laughing
expected
grabbing
scrubbing
wrapped
jammed
trotting
pointed
reached

27. After a long climb, we ___ the top of the mountain.

28. Kim ___ out our starting place far below.

29. That night we all ___ into pup tents and slept at the top of the mountain.

UNIT 5 **Follow these directions using words from Unit 5.**

30. Write the two words that have /s/ spelled *ce*.

31. Write the four words in which /z/ is spelled *s*.

32. Write the two words that have both of these sounds: /s/ and /z/.

Finish these sentences.

33. Carlos walked his ___ uphill.

34. He was a little ___ when he reached the hilltop.

35. He pulled on the helmet that he had found in his ___ .

36. The downhill ride would be three miles in ___ .

37. "To think I ___ this hill myself!" he sighed.

38. During the descent he had a ___ of sitting still while houses and trees flew by.

39. "That was fantastic," thought Carlos at the end of the ride. "I can't wait for racing ___ to begin."

UNIT 5
bicycle
daisy
distance
license
sense
citizen
season
tense
closet
chose

WORDS IN TIME

The word *daisy* comes from two Old English words, *daeges eàge*, meaning "the day's eye," or "the sun." Why do you think people first used the words *daeges eàge* as a name for the daisy?

Spelling and Reading
A Description

Read the following story. Notice the vivid words that describe the scene.

The citizen stood tense and alone by the stream. Her throat was tight and dry. Thunder in the distance and the threat of a storm made waiting on this dark night even harder. "When will they arrive?" she wondered. "I expected them long ago. My people are not the type to behave like this."

Suddenly there was a shift in the wind, and it began grabbing at her clothing. Scraps of paper and leaves swirled around her. She pulled her coat tighter around her waist as she searched the sky. Then a welcome glow appeared high above her. As the light came nearer, the glow took shape, and she could see the ship. Laughing, she waved as the ship touched solid ground. Her lonesome wait was over. With a sigh, she squeezed through the hatch. The ship began to rise. Finally she was going home.

Write the answers to the questions.

1. With what picture does the writer begin this description?
2. What makes waiting even harder for the citizen?
3. Why was the citizen nervous and concerned?
4. The suspense builds as the event is told. Find one or more sentences in the second paragraph that tell you something is about to happen. Write the sentence or sentences.
5. Who do you think the citizen is?

Underline the review words in your answers. Check to see that you spelled the words correctly.

Spelling and Writing
A Description

Words to Help You Write

smash
dusk
behave
arrive
reply
entire
reveal
creak
steel
wrapped
pointed
reached
sense
chose
season

Think and Discuss

A good description creates a vivid picture for the reader. It helps the reader to see, hear, feel, smell, and taste what is being described. A description comes alive when a writer uses details that appeal to the reader's senses. Good writers choose vivid and colorful words to describe what they want the reader to see, hear, feel, smell, and taste.

Look at the picture. Does it show the scene you pictured when you read the story about the citizen on page 27? The writer uses the words *thunder, threat of a storm,* and *dark night* to help the reader see the scene. What other words does the writer use to tell about the scene before the glow appeared in the sky?

What two words does the writer use in the first sentence to tell how the citizen feels? What other words does the writer use to help the reader understand what the citizen is feeling?

Look at the fourth sentence in the second paragraph. What one word does the writer use to tell the reader that the citizen is glad to see the glow in the sky?

Apply

Write a **paragraph of description** for a friend or classmate. Create a sense of mystery or suspense. Use vivid, colorful words. Follow the writing guidelines on the next page.

Prewriting

Think of some scenes that could be mysterious and choose one.

● Make a chart with five columns labeled *see, hear, touch, smell,* and *taste.* List words in each column that describe the scene.

 THESAURUS For help finding vivid, colorful words, turn to page 205.

Composing

Use your chart to write the first draft of your descriptive paragraph.

● Write a topic sentence that clearly tells what your subject is.
● Write detail sentences that describe the scene. Use words that are as vivid and colorful as possible.
● Keep your audience in mind. Use words to make your description mysterious or suspenseful.
● Look back at your prewriting chart. Are there more detail words or sentences you would like to add to your draft?

Revising

Read your paragraph and show it to a classmate. Follow these guidelines to improve your work. Use the editing and proofreading marks on this page to show corrections.

Editing

● Make sure your paragraph describes a mysterious or suspenseful scene.
● Check your details. Add words or phrases that will make the word picture more vivid for your reader.

Proofreading

● Check your spelling and correct any mistakes.
● Check your capitalization and punctuation.

 WRITER'S GUIDE If you need help with capitalization or punctuation, turn to pages 280 and 281.

Copy your paragraph onto a clean sheet of paper. Write carefully and neatly.

Publishing

Ask a classmate to read your paragraph and draw the scene you described. Did your words help the reader "see" the scene?

Editing and Proofreading Marks

≡ capitalize

⊙ make a period

∧ add something

⋏ add a comma

⌄⌄ add quotation marks

⌐ take something away

◯ spell correctly

⊓ indent the paragraph

╱ make a lowercase letter

∿ tr transpose

---

7 The Sounds /k/ and /kw/

UNIT WORDS

1. ticket
2. deck
3. comics
4. quit
5. ache
6. continue
7. collapse
8. anchor
9. chemical
10. quiet
11. quite
12. occupied
13. inquire
14. shock
15. rocket
16. according
17. question
18. square
19. customer
20. pickle

The Unit Words

The Unit words have the consonant sounds /k/ and /kw/.

The sound /k/ is most often spelled with **c,** as in *comics.* The letter *c* begins more English words than any other letter except *s.*

The Unit words show three more ways to spell the sound /k/.

- **ck** as in *ticket*
- **ch** as in *anchor*
- **cc** as in *occupied*

The sounds /kw/ are spelled with **qu,** as in *question.*

Spelling Practice

A. Write the Unit word for each pronunciation. If you need help, use the pronunciation key on page 162.

1. /āk/   **2.** /rok'it/   **3.** /kwīt/

4. /ok'yə·pīd/   **5.** /kwī'ət/   **6.** /kə·laps'/

B. Use the words you wrote for **1–6** to help you complete these activities.

7. What letters spell /k/ in the word you wrote for **1**?

8. Write two more Unit words that have /k/ spelled this way.

9. What letters spell /k/ in the word you wrote for **2**?

10. Write four more Unit words that have /k/ spelled this way.

11. Look at **3** and **5**. What letters spell the sounds /kw/?

12. Write four more Unit words that are spelled with these letters.

13. What letters spell /k/ in the word you wrote for **4**?

14. Write another Unit word that has /k/ spelled this way.

15. How did you spell /k/ in **6**?

16. Write four more Unit words that have this spelling for /k/.

C. Complete each sentence with a word that begins with /kw/.

17. Everyone has _____ working.

18. I am _____ sure they've all gone home.

19. It's been very _____ for the past half hour.

Spelling and Language · Nouns and Verbs

<table>
<tr><td>UNIT WORDS</td></tr>
<tr><td>ticket
deck
comics
quit
ache
continue
collapse
anchor
chemical
quiet
quite
occupied
inquire
shock
rocket
according
question
square
customer
pickle</td></tr>
</table>

Some of the Unit words can be used as both nouns and verbs. A **noun** names a person, place, or thing. A **verb** shows action or being.

Noun	We struggled to lift the heavy *anchor.*
Verb	Shall we *anchor* our boat here?

Complete each pair of sentences with a form of a Unit word. The word will be a noun in the first sentence and a verb in the second.

1. Yoshiro had an ____ in his shoulder.
2. It ____ when he raised his arm.
3. The doctor asked Yoshiro a ____ about his shoulder.
4. She ____ Yoshiro for five minutes.

Writing on Your Own

Imagine that you are an astronaut on a space flight. You keep a daily log to help you remember exactly what happens and what you are thinking about. Write one day's entry in your log. Use some of the Unit words twice to show that they can be used both as nouns and verbs.

▶ **WRITER'S GUIDE** For a sample journal entry, turn to page 273.

Using the Dictionary to Spell and Write

To use a word correctly in your writing, it is important to know the meaning of the word. A **definition** gives the meaning of a word. Many words have more than one definition. Dictionary definitions are numbered. Read the definitions for *shock.*

> **shock** /shok/ **1** *n.* An unexpected, violent shake or blow: the *shock* of an earthquake. **2** *n.* A sudden, violent, or upsetting event: My parrot's death was a great *shock.* **3** *v.* Cause to feel surprise, terror, or disgust: The bus accident *shocked* the community. **4** *n.* What the body feels when an electric current passes through it.

Finish each sentence with *shock.* Then write the definition number.

____ 1. The broken wire gave him a slight ____ .
____ 2. Her bad manners ____ me.
____ 3. The ____ of the explosion threw us down.
____ 4. My report card grades were a ____ to me.

Spelling on Your Own

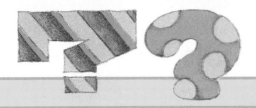

UNIT WORDS

Write the Unit words in alphabetical order. Then use each word that begins with *c* or *q* in a question. Supply answers for your questions. Try to write your questions as riddles. Here's an example: "What gets answered without asking a *question*? A telephone."

lucky
camp
quick
neck
crack
cane

MASTERY WORDS

Follow the directions using the Mastery words.

1. Write the three words that end with /k/.

2. Write another word that has /k/ spelled the same way.

Change the first sound in each word to the sound or sounds given. Write the words.

3. mane /k/   **4.** kick /kw/

5. ramp /k/   **6.** track /k/

Change the last sound in each word to the sound /k/. Write the words.

7. crab   **8.** quit   **9.** net

BONUS WORDS

schedule
biscuit
liquid
character
occupation
monarch
frequent
mechanic

1. Use each of the first three Bonus words in a sentence. Underline the Bonus word. Circle the letter or letters that spell the sound /k/ or /kw/.

Follow the directions using the Bonus words.

2. Write the word that has /k/ spelled with *cc*.

3. Write the four words that have /k/ spelled with *ch*.

4. Write the three words that have /k/ spelled with *c*.

5. Write the two words that have /kw/ spelled with *qu*.

6. Choose a character that you admire from a book you have read. In a paragraph, explain why you admire this person.

8 Plurals

UNIT WORDS

1. shelves
2. movies
3. addresses
4. bakeries
5. batteries
6. bunches
7. chimneys
8. diaries
9. donkeys
10. groceries
11. highways
12. knives
13. loaves
14. scarves
15. stitches
16. taxes
17. trays
18. valleys
19. wives
20. wolves

The Unit Words

Suppose you walked into the General Store and bought one *shelf.* How many would you walk out with?

A plural noun names more than one thing. A singular noun names just one thing. All the Unit words are plural nouns. Here are the common ways to form plurals.

● Add *s.* Most plurals are formed this way.

> chair   chairs   pencil   pencils

● Add *es* to words that end with *ss, x, ch,* or *sh.*

> addresses   taxes   stitches

● For some words ending in *f* or *fe,* change *f* to *v* and add *es.*

> shelf   shelves

● When words end with a consonant + *y,* change *y* to *i* and add *es.*

> bakery   bakeries   diary   diaries

● Add *s* to words that end with a vowel + *y.*

> valleys

REMEMBER THIS

The singular of *movies* does not end with *y.* To make *movie* plural, just add *s.*

Spelling Practice

A. Write the Unit words that follow these patterns for forming the plural.

1. dog   dogs   monkey   monkeys   (six words)

2. beach   beaches   (four words)

3. puppy   puppies   (four words)

4. elf   elves   (six words)

B. Complete this list using the Unit words.

Harold has a habit of buying things he doesn't need. Here's what he ordered from a holiday catalog last fall.

5. one map showing all the roads and _____ in Iowa

6. two _____ of plastic grapes

7. three books on how to clean brick _____

8. four red, white, and blue silk _____

9. five _____ for peeling potatoes

10. six _____ for writing down events for the same year

11. seven _____ for the radio he hoped to get

12. eight _____ for serving milk and cookies

13. nine wooden _____ to hold all he had bought

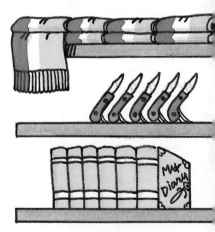

C. Find the misspelled word in each sentence. Write the word correctly.

14. Those were the best movys I've ever seen.

15. At night we could hear wolfs howling.

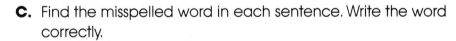

35

Spelling and Language · Subject-Verb Agreement

UNIT WORDS
shelves
movies
addresses
bakeries
batteries
bunches
chimneys
diaries
donkeys
groceries
highways
knives
loaves
scarves
stitches
taxes
trays
valleys
wives
wolves

The subject and verb in a sentence must agree in number. A subject and verb agree if both are singular or both are plural. For example, you would finish the sentence "The ____ above my eye is coming out today" with the singular noun *stitch* because *is* is a singular verb. But you would say "The *stitches* above my eye are coming out today" because *are* is a plural verb.

Complete each sentence. Use a Unit word or the singular form of a Unit word.

1. The ____ of the ____ is 15 Follen Street.
2. I rode my ____ there.
3. I bought two ____ of bread.

Writing on Your Own

Pretend you own the One-of-a-Kind Bakery. Write a two-paragraph advertisement to bring in new customers. Explain the special features of your shop and the wonderful foods you sell. Use as many of the Unit words as you can.

 WRITER'S GUIDE   For help revising your work, turn to the checklist on page 265.

Using the Dictionary to Spell and Write

You can use the **Spelling Dictionary** to check the spelling of plural words that are not formed by adding *s* or *es.* You can also check the plural of words whose spelling changes before *s* or *es* is added.

---

di·a·ry /dī′(ə·)rē/ *n., pl.* **di·a·ries**

shelf /shelf/ *n.,pl.* **shelves** /shelvz/

To find these plurals, you must look up the singular form of each word. Write the word you would look up to find each word.

1. bakeries   2. scarves   3. wives
4. groceries   5. loaves   6. batteries

Write the plural for each of these words. Then check your answers in the **Spelling Dictionary.**

7. daisy   8. country

36

Spelling on Your Own

 UNIT WORDS

Think of an adjective that could be used to describe each Unit word. Then write the adjective and the plural noun together. Remember that adjectives add meaning to nouns. For example, you might write *sharp knives* or *howling wolves*.

 MASTERY WORDS

desks
classes
guesses
buddies
puppies
parents

Write the plural form of each of these words.

1. desk   **2.** parent   **3.** class
4. guess   **5.** buddy   **6.** puppy

Complete the story with Mastery words.

    My __7__ own a pet shop. Last week, they came to school to talk to several fifth-grade __8__ about the care of young animals. They brought with them four eight-week-old __9__. Everyone made __10__ about the puppies' breed. One of my close __11__ said they were collies. Everyone got a chance to pet the animals.

BONUS WORDS

sketches
wristwatches
crutches
allies
flurries
alleys
displays
quantities

Write the Bonus word for each definition.

1. drawings   **2.** supports for walking

3. timepieces   **4.** exhibits

5. amounts   **6.** light snowfalls

Write the Bonus word for each pronunciation.

7. /al′ēz/   **8.** /al′īz/

Follow the directions using the Bonus words.

9. Write the singular form of each Bonus word.

10. Write a story with this title: "The Missing Wristwatches." Use as many Bonus words as you can in your story.

37

9 Clusters and Digraphs

UNIT WORDS

1. clamp
2. stamp
3. splint
4. crust
5. prompt
6. shrub
7. dent
8. draft
9. blast
10. thrift
11. blend
12. crunchy
13. block
14. shrunk
15. gust
16. insect
17. traffic
18. slant
19. crank
20. defend

The Unit Words

Which letters can you combine with *r* to form two- or three-letter consonant clusters? You can combine *t, c, sh, d,* and *p* with *r* to form *tr, cr, shr, dr,* and *pr.*

Each of the words in this unit has at least one consonant cluster. A **consonant cluster** is two or three consonant letters written together. You hear the sounds of all the letters in a consonant cluster. A consonant cluster may come at the beginning or end of a word.

<u>tr</u>affic   gu<u>st</u>   <u>cl</u>a<u>mp</u>

A **consonant digraph** can be part of a consonant cluster. The letter pairs **sh, th,** and **ch** are consonant digraphs. A **consonant digraph** is two consonant letters together that stand for one consonant sound. That sound is different from the sound of either letter alone. In the word *shrub,* the digraph **sh** and the letter **r** make up the consonant cluster **shr.** Say the word *shrub* and listen for the two beginning consonant sounds—/sh/ and /r/.

38

Spelling Practice

A. Add a single consonant to the beginning of each word. Write Unit words. Then underline the consonant cluster that begins each word.

1. lamp   **2.** raft

3. lock   **4.** last

B. Add a consonant cluster to the end of each group of letters. Write Unit words.

5. gu ____   **6.** inse ____

7. de ____   **8.** pro ____

9. cru ____   **10.** thri ____

11. sta ____   **12.** cra ____

C. Follow the directions using the Unit words.

13. Write the three words that begin with two sounds spelled with three letters.

14. Take the ending *-ier* away from *crunchier*. Write the word that is left. Then add the ending *-y* and write a Unit word.

15. Write the four words that end with the sound /k/.

D. Add *t* or *d* to complete each word. Write Unit words.

16. splin ____   **17.** defen __

18. blen ____   **19.** slan ____

E. Finish these riddles with Unit words. The consonant cluster is given in ( ) to help you.

20. What kind of police officers enjoy their work most?

Those that direct (tr) ____. They whistle while they work.

21. What did the envelope say to the (st) ____ ?
Stick with me and we'll go places.

Spelling and Language · Adjective Endings

UNIT WORDS

UNIT WORDS
clamp
stamp
splint
crust
prompt
shrub
dent
draft
blast
thrift
blend
crunchy
block
shrunk
gust
insect
traffic
slant
crank
defend

You can add -y to form adjectives. Remember that an adjective describes a noun.

draft + y = drafty   a *drafty* room

Add -y to each word in ( ). Write the missing words.

1. Sheila loves peanut butter on (crust) ____ bread.
2. Her favorite kind is the (crunch) ____ type.
3. She went shopping for it on a cold, (gust) ____ day.

Writing on Your Own

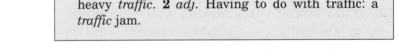

Write two paragraphs for a young child who has never visited a city before. Describe some of the surprising things he or she might see. Use some of the Unit words in your paragraphs. Make your description clear and interesting. Use adjectives to make your writing colorful.

Using the Dictionary to Spell and Write

The dictionary can help you use a word correctly in your writing. Read the dictionary entry for *traffic*. The abbreviations *n.* and *adj.* tell you that *traffic* can be a noun or an adjective.

> **traf·fic** /traf'ik/ **1** *n.* The movement of people, cars, buses, etc., through an area or along a route: heavy *traffic*. **2** *adj.* Having to do with traffic: a *traffic* jam.

Finish each sentence with the word *traffic*. After the word, write *n.* or *adj.* to show how *traffic* is used in the sentence.

1. The ____ slowed down because of a detour on the road.
2. The sudden hail storm caused a major ____ jam.

Look up *slant* in the **Spelling Dictionary.** Write one sentence using the word as a noun and one using it as a verb.

 SPELLING DICTIONARY Remember to use your **Spelling Dictionary** when you write.

Spelling on Your Own

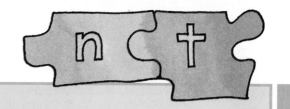

Write all the Unit words that have these kinds of consonant clusters:
(1) final clusters that include *t*; (2) beginning clusters that include *l*;
(3) beginning clusters that include *r*. Then write the two words that
end with *mp* and the two that end with *nd*. Use each of the words
that end with *mp* or *nd* in a sentence together with another Unit word.

dent

bump
task
trick
bend
crop
step

MASTERY WORDS

Write the Mastery words that have the vowel sounds heard in
these words.

1. net (two words) **2.** hat **3.** hit
4. not **5.** nut

Change the vowel letter in each word to spell a Mastery word.

6. band **7.** truck **8.** tusk **9.** stop

Write the Mastery word that has the same consonant cluster as
each of these words.

10. dump **11.** steam **12.** mask
13. mend **14.** crew **15.** trap

BONUS WORDS

1. Write the two Bonus words that have a consonant digraph as
part of a consonant cluster.

2. Write the five other Bonus words that begin with consonant
clusters.

3. Write all the words you can think of that end with *ample, ill,
one,* and *est*. Begin by writing the Bonus word that ends with
each of these spelling patterns.

4. Write the two Bonus words that have these meanings: "step
on heavily" and "travel slowly with effort." Then add *ed* to
each word. The final consonant in one of the words must be
doubled. Use each word in a sentence.

trek
trample
shrill
smudge
throne
fringe
jest
station

10 The Sounds /j/ and /ch/

UNIT WORDS

1. checkers
2. challenge
3. storage
4. ginger
5. hinge
6. future
7. culture
8. agent
9. arrange
10. pasture
11. porch
12. capture
13. imagine
14. range
15. furniture
16. fortune
17. nature
18. manage
19. postage
20. peach

The Unit Words

The words in this unit have the consonant sounds /j/ and /ch/.

The sound /j/ is often spelled with **j,** as in *jacket.* The Unit words show two other ways to spell /j/.

- **g** before **e** or **i** as in *agent* and *imagine*

- **ge** at the end of a word as in *challenge*

The sound /ch/ is usually spelled with the consonant digraph **ch,** as in *checkers.* The Unit words also show another way to spell /ch/.

- **t** before **u** as in *fortune* and *nature*

REMEMBER THIS

Here is a tip to help you spell *storage.* When you add *store + age,* you "put away" the *e* in *store* to form *storage.*

42

Spelling Practice

A. Finish the sentences with Unit words that begin with the sound /ch/.

1. The game of ___ was first played in Egypt thousands of years ago.

2. Today people still enjoy the ___ of the game.

B. Follow the directions using the Unit words.

3. Write the two words that end with the sound /ch/.

4. Write the word that means the opposite of *release*. Underline the consonant letter that spells /ch/.

5. Write the six other words that have /ch/ spelled with this letter.

C. Finish the paragraph with Unit words that end with the sound /j/.

Dominic took his collection of postcards out of __6__. He needed to get them ready for the next day's postcard show at the town hall. He piled them on the dining room table. "I must __7__ them in some order in these shoe boxes," he said to himself. "The __8__ of subjects is so wide. There are street scenes, views of towns and cities, and famous people. I hope I can __9__ to finish the job tonight."

D. Follow the directions using the Unit words.

10. Write the three words ending with /j/ spelled *ge* that you did not use to complete the paragraph in **C.**

11. Write the three words that have /j/ spelled *g* before *i* or *e*.

Spelling and Language · Plurals

UNIT WORDS

checkers
challenge
storage
ginger
hinge
future
culture
agent
arrange
pasture
porch
capture
imagine
range
furniture
fortune
nature
manage
postage
peach

You add *s* to most nouns to make them plural. You add *es* to nouns that end with *ch, ss, x,* and *sh.*

Read each pair of sentences. Write a Unit word to complete one sentence. Write the plural form of the same word to complete the other.

1. Mr. Dunn gave Ricardo ten dollars for painting his ____ . He would be rich if he painted all the ____ in town.
2. Mr. Dunn's rusty door ____ needed to be replaced. So Ricardo helped him replace all the rusty ____ .

Writing on Your Own

Imagine that you are Ricardo's brother or sister. Mr. Dunn has just telephoned to say that he has another job for your brother. Use some of the Unit words to write a telephone message for Ricardo. Include all of the information that he will need: the name of the person who called, the date and time of the call, the phone number Ricardo will need, and the message.

▶ **WRITER'S GUIDE**   For a sample telephone message, turn to page 279.

Using the Dictionary to Spell and Write

When you write, you sometimes need to check the meaning of a word. A dictionary **definition** tells the meaning of a word. Many words have more than one definition. Read the definitions for *fortune.*

> **for·tune** /fôr′chən/ *n.* **1** What is going to happen to a person. **2** Luck or chance. **3** A large amount of money; wealth.

Finish each sentence with *fortune.* Then write the definition number.

1. Bert read his ____ in the newspaper.
2. Robin's grandmother had a ____ in jewels.
3. I had the good ____ to find a dollar.

Use *fortune* with meanings 1 and 3 in two sentences.

Spelling on Your Own

UNIT WORDS

The words below are written in code. To decode the Unit words, look at each letter. Then write the letter that comes just before it in the alphabet. Here's an example: bhfou = agent. The letter *a* comes before *b*, *g* comes before *h*, and so on.

1. sbohf	**2.** qpsdi	**3.** obuvsf	**4.** jnbhjof	**5.** nbobhf
6. bhfou	**7.** hjohfs	**8.** qfbdi	**9.** dbquvsf	**10.** dibmmfohf
11. ijohf	**12.** qptubhf	**13.** gvuvsf	**14.** gpsuvof	**15.** gvsojuvsf
16. qbtuvsf	**17.** bssbohf	**18.** tupsbhf	**19.** difdlfst	**20.** dvmuvsf

MASTERY WORDS

Follow the directions using the Mastery words.

1. Write the three words that have the sound /ch/.

2. Write the three words that have the sound /j/. Underline the letter that comes after *g* in each word.

Write the Mastery words that mean the opposite of these words.

3. safety   **4.** rough

Write the Mastery words that rhyme with these words.

5. match   **6.** stranger   **7.** page   **8.** peach

> teacher
> reach
> age
> gentle
> catch
> danger

BONUS WORDS

Write the Bonus word for each definition.

1. leaves of a tree or plant   **2.** a jelly-like food
3. behavior that can harm   **4.** to satisfy a thirst by drinking

Follow the directions using the Bonus words.

5. Write the words in two groups according to the consonant sounds /j/ and /ch/. Underline the letters that spell /j/ and /ch/.

6. Find the meaning of *salvage* in the **Spelling Dictionary.** Then write a sentence using the word.

> naturally
> gelatin
> salvage
> quench
> genes
> charity
> foliage
> mischief

11 The Sound /sh/

UNIT WORDS

1. *issue*
2. *special*
3. *direction*
4. *social*
5. *shelter*
6. *motion*
7. *shower*
8. *pressure*
9. *action*
10. *selection*
11. *shack*
12. *polish*
13. *ashamed*
14. *assure*
15. *official*
16. *tissue*
17. *ancient*
18. *mention*
19. *fashion*
20. *delicious*

COUNTY SHERIFF ISSUES
SPECIAL DIRECTIONS

The Unit Words

Read the special bulletin on the TV screen. Find the four words that have the sound /sh/. Then decide which letters spell /sh/ in each word.

All the words in this unit have the consonant sound /sh/. The sound /sh/ is usually spelled with the consonant digraph **sh**, as in *shelter.* The Unit words show three other ways to spell /sh/.

- **ss** as in *issue*
- **ci** as in *special*
- **ti** as in *direction*

REMEMBER THIS

Don't leave *off* the *o-f-f* when you write *official.*

Spelling Practice

A. Follow the directions using the Unit words.

1. Write the three words that begin with /sh/.

2. Write the other three words that have /sh/ spelled with a consonant digraph.

3. Write the four words that have the sound /sh/ spelled with *ss*.

B. Finish the sentences with Unit words that have /sh/ spelled with *ti*.

4. He started to _____ to his friend, but she didn't see him.

5. She turned the corner without looking in his _____.

6. The school cafeteria has a large _____ of food.

7. I must _____ this restaurant to my friends.

8. The lifeguard's quick _____ saved the drowning man.

C. Follow the directions using the Unit words.

9. Write the words that end with the adjective suffixes -*al* and -*ous*. Underline the letters that spell /sh/.

10. Write another adjective that has /sh/ spelled the same way.

D. Write the Unit word that is a synonym for each of these words.

11. shine   **12.** gesture   **13.** hut   **14.** style

E. Write the Unit word that rhymes with each pair of words.

15. indention   tension   **16.** vicious   nutritious

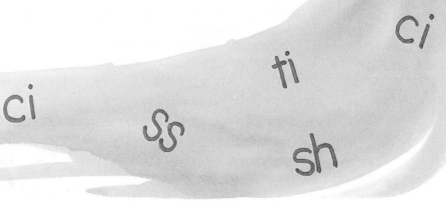

Spelling and Language · Capitalization

You use capital letters when you write book titles. Capitalize the first and last words and all other words in the title except for *a, an, and, the, of, for, to, on,* and *in.* Here are two examples: <u>The Trumpet of the Swan</u> and <u>The Cricket in Times Square.</u>

Rewrite each of these book titles. Use capital letters where they are needed.

1. the best motion pictures of the eighties

2. ancient shelters of the egyptians

Writing on Your Own

Imagine that you are a newspaper reporter. Write the first paragraph of a news story about a famous person who is visiting your area. Use at least five of the Unit words in your paragraph. Write a strong headline for your work.

Using the Dictionary to Spell and Write

Suppose you want to check the spelling of a word in the dictionary. A quick way to find the word is to use the guide words. **Guide words** are the two words at the top of each dictionary page. The word on the left is the first word on the page. The word on the right is the last word on the page. The other words on the page come between the guide words in alphabetical order.

muscle		occupy

mus·cle /mus′əl/ *n.* One of the bundles of stringy tissue in the body that produce the body's movements by tightening and stretching.

nev·er·the·less /nev′ər·thə·les′/ *adv., conj.* In any event; however: The movie had started, but we went *nevertheless.* I hurt my arm; *nevertheless,* I played.

1. Suppose the guide words were *sand* and *stomach.* Which six Unit words would be on the dictionary page? Write them in alphabetical order.

2. Look up *assure* in the **Spelling Dictionary.** Then write the guide words that appear on the page where you found *assure.*

Spelling on Your Own

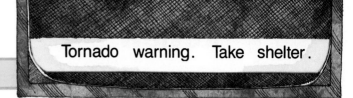

UNIT WORDS

Write sentences using all of the Unit words. Make some of your sentences sound like special bulletins you might see on TV. Use as many of the words as you can in each sentence. Underline each Unit word. Look at the example on page **46.**

MASTERY WORDS

crash
shy
splash
short
vacation
shiny

Follow the directions using the Mastery words.

1. Write the three words that begin with /sh/.

2. Write the two words that end with /sh/.

3. Write the word that has /sh/ spelled as it is in *action*.

4. Write the three words that are adjectives and begin with /sh/. Remember that an adjective describes, or tells more about, a noun.

Use two of the words you wrote for **4** to finish these sentences.

5. Dale put the _____ silver dollar in her bank.

6. The _____ kitten hid under my bed.

BONUS WORDS

permission
possession
patient
cashier
stationery
sherbet
imagination
gracious

Write the Bonus word for each base word. Remember that a base word is a word without an ending.

1. cash   **2.** grace   **3.** imagine   **4.** possess   **5.** permit

Follow the directions using the Bonus words.

6. Read the definitions for *patient* in the **Spelling Dictionary.** Write a sentence for each meaning.

7. Write the word that names a dessert.

8. Write the word that is a homophone for *stationary*. Find the definitions for both words in the **Spelling Dictionary.** Then use each word in a sentence.

49

12 Review

Follow these steps when you are unsure how to spell a word.

- **Say** the word. Recall when you have heard the word used. Think about what it means.
- **Look** at the word. Find any prefixes, suffixes, or other word parts you know. Think about other words that are related in meaning and spelling. Try to picture the word in your mind.
- **Spell** the word to yourself. Think about the way each sound is spelled. Notice any unusual spelling.
- **Write** the word while looking at it. Check the way you have formed your letters. If you have not written the word clearly or correctly, write it again.
- **Check** your learning. Cover the word and write it. If you did not spell the word correctly, practice these steps until the word becomes your own.

UNIT 7

ticket
question
customer
ache
occupied
quit
continue
quiet
quite
according

UNIT 7 Follow the directions using words from Unit 7.

1. Write the words that have /kw/.

Write the words to finish the paragraph.

"The clerk just sold the last **_2_** to the **_3_** in the brown hat. **_4_** to the clerk, all of the seats inside the theater are **_5_** . Do you want to **_6_** to wait in line, just in case? I hope not, since my feet are starting to **_7_** ."

UNIT 8

valleys
addresses
shelves
knives
groceries
movies
diaries
loaves
trays
bunches

UNIT 8 Follow the directions using words from Unit 8.

Write the words that follow these patterns for forming plurals.

8. highway   highways

9. stitch   stitches

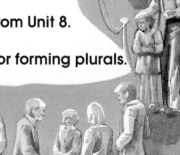

10. battery   batteries

11. wife   wives

Fill in words to tell what you might find where.

12. pages in _____

13. actors in _____

14. _____ in ovens

UNIT 9   **Follow the directions using words from Unit 9.**

15. Write the words that have /t/ in their consonant clusters. Circle all the consonant clusters.

16. Write the two pairs of words that end in the same consonant clusters.

17. Write the word that ends in a three-letter consonant cluster.

18. Write the word that has a consonant digraph as part of a consonant cluster.

UNIT 10   **Follow the directions using words from Unit 10.**

Finish the sentences with words that have /ch/. Circle the consonant letter or letters that spell this sound.

19. Don't forget to polish the _____ in the hall.

20. She made a _____ buying and selling land.

UNIT 9
prompt
stamp
insect
shrunk
traffic
crust
dent
blend
slant
defend

UNIT 10
furniture
fortune
imagine
arrange
checkers
storage
agent
nature
manage
postage

WORDS IN TIME

Postage comes from the Middle French word *poste,* meaning "relay station." Long ago, riders carried mail along a particular route, stopping at each *poste* to change horses. Mail carried by these messengers was said to go by *post.* What does *postage* mean? How do you think *postage* got its name?

21. It is the tiger's ____ to hunt smaller animals.

22. I love to play the game of ____ .

Finish these sentences. Use the words from Unit 10.

23. Mr. Trotter is the ____ for the book company.

24. I cannot ____ what is inside that package.

25. She found the old trunk in the ____ room.

26. That little boy cannot ____ to row the boat himself.

27. ____ for me to sit up front.

28. The package has enough ____ to send it to Peru.

UNIT 11 Follow the directions using words from Unit 11.

29. Write the synonym for *shine.* Circle the letters that spell /sh/.

30. Write the two words in which /sh/ is spelled with a double letter. Circle the double letters.

Finish these sentences.

31. Our clubhouse looks like an ____ building.

32. It faces in a southern ____ .

33. Our club now has an ____ uniform.

34. We like to take ____ and solve community problems.

35. We also hold parties and other ____ events.

36. We usually have ____ food at our parties.

UNIT 11

polish
delicious
direction
tissue
special
social
pressure
official
ancient
action

Spelling and Reading
A Story

Read the following story beginning. Pay special attention to the setting and the main characters.

I can recall vividly the spring day my mother and I drove into the country, searching for our new home.

"If we continue in this direction, I think we will find it," said my mother. "Watch the addresses."

The agent said we were lucky to be able to buy the house. He said it was a special place, hidden in one of the quiet valleys outside of town. Hidden was the word. So far we had not managed to find the house!

My head began to ache. I wished we could quit looking. I tried to imagine going back to our old house, but I knew we could not. The old house was occupied by others now, and all our furniture was in storage.

"Isn't that the address?" My mother's question made me sit up.

I saw an ancient house with crumbling chimneys. It was partly hidden by big bunches of tall weeds. I wished we had that agent with us. He would have had to defend himself against two quite unhappy customers.

Write the answers to the questions.

1. What three characters are mentioned in the story beginning?
2. Why didn't the boy and his mother give up and go back to their old house?
3. What reason did the boy and his mother have for thinking the house would be nice?
4. Was the boy pleased when he saw the house at last? What does the writer say that gives you this idea?

Underline the review words in your answers. Check to see that you spelled the words correctly.

Spelling and Writing
A Story

Words to Help You Write

ache
continue
quiet
quite
shrunk
traffic
defend
furniture
imagine
arrange
nature
manage
direction
ancient
action

Think and Discuss

Most stories have a **beginning,** a **middle,** and an **ending.** In a story beginning, writers usually introduce the main characters. They also describe the setting — the time and place. Look back at the story beginning on page 53. What main characters are in this story? When and where does the writer tell you the story takes place?

In the middle part of a story, writers usually show how their main characters deal with a problem. Often writers give hints about this problem in the beginning of the story. Think about the story beginning on page 53. What can you guess about the problem these characters may face?

In a story ending, writers show what happens to the characters as a result of their problem. Many stories show how the characters finally solve their problem. In other stories, the characters fail to solve their problem in the end. How do you think the story that begins on page 53 will end?

In most good stories, the main characters go through important changes. Their feelings at the end are different from their feelings at the beginning. Look again at the story on page 53. How do the characters feel when the story begins? How might their feelings change by the end?

Apply

Write a **story** for your classmates to enjoy. Use the story beginning on page 53. Write a middle and an ending that show what happens to the boy and his mother. Follow the writing guidelines on the next page.

Prewriting

Make a chart to help you organize your ideas for the story.

- Divide a sheet of paper into three columns.
- On the left, list things that could go wrong in the house.
- In the middle, note what can be done about each problem.
- On the right, note what the action taken by the boy and his mother might lead to. List any new problems that are created.

Composing

Choose the most interesting chain of events in your chart. Write a first draft of your story based on these events.

- Write a story middle that shows what problem the boy and his mother face. Describe how the boy and his mother struggle with the problem.
- Write a story ending that shows how the boy and his mother solve or fail to solve their problem. Try to show readers how the characters feel about this outcome.

 THESAURUS If you need help finding vivid words to make your story come alive, turn to page 205.

- Look back over your prewriting chart. Do you want to add any details to your first draft?

Revising

Read your story. Follow these guidelines to improve your work. Use the editing and proofreading marks on this page to show corrections.

Editing

- Make sure you have written a middle part and an ending for your story.
- Check to see that you have shown how your characters' feelings have changed by the end of the story.

Proofreading

- Check your spelling, capitalization, and punctuation.

Copy your story onto a clean sheet of paper. Write carefully and neatly.

Publishing

Share your story with your classmates. Ask if your story held their interest and if they liked the way it ended.

Editing and Proofreading Marks

≡	capitalize
⊙	make a period
∧	add something
⌄	add a comma
＂＂	add quotation marks
ℰ	take something away
◯	spell correctly
¶	indent the paragraph
/	make a lowercase letter
∿ tr	transpose

55

13 Words with *ed* and *ing*

serv(e)   served

UNIT WORDS

1. served
2. decorating
3. applying
4. delaying
5. employed
6. studying
7. supposed
8. exciting
9. married
10. envied
11. studied
12. lied
13. preying
14. relayed
15. preparing
16. replied
17. doubled
18. noticed
19. promised
20. lying

The Unit Words

The words in this unit are verbs that end with *ed* or *ing*. The spelling of the base word often changes when these endings are added.

Here are some rules that will help you spell the Unit words correctly.

1. When a word ends with *e*, drop the *e* before adding *ed* or *ing*.

> serve + ed = served
> excite + ing = exciting

2. When a word ends with a consonant and *y*, change *y* to *i* before you add *ed*. Keep the *y* when you add *ing*.

> study + ed = studied
> study + ing = studying

3. When a word ends with a vowel and *y*, the spelling of the word does not change.

> employ + ed = employed
> delay + ing = delaying

☐ The word *lying* does not follow the usual rule for adding *ing*. You drop final *e* from *lie* and change *i* to *y* before adding *ing*.

56

Spelling Practice

A. Add *ed* or *ing* to these words to spell Unit words.

1. serve
2. employ
3. notice
4. delay
5. prey
6. suppose
7. relay
8. promise
9. apply
10. double

studying

B. Follow the directions using the Unit words.

11. Write the four words in which *y* is changed to *i* before *ed* is added.

12. Write the three words in which final *e* is dropped before *ing* is added.

C. Finish this "word math." Remember to use *i* and *y* correctly.

13. applied − ed = _____ + ing = _____
14. marrying − ing = _____ + ed = _____
15. replying − ing = _____ + ed = _____
16. studied − ed = _____ + ing = _____
17. lied − ed = _____ + ing = _____
18. envying − ing = _____ + ed = _____

D. Write the word for each of these pronunciations. Then write each word with *ed* and *ing*.

19. /im·ploi'/
20. /sə·pōz'/
21. /lī/
22. /dub'əl/
23. /nō'tis/
24. /prom'is/
25. /ik·sīt'/

57

Spelling and Language · Adding *ed* and *ing*

UNIT WORDS

served
decorating
applying
delaying
employed
studying
supposed
exciting
married
envied
studied
lied
preying
relayed
preparing
replied
doubled
noticed
promised
lying

You add *ed* to make a word that tells about the past. You add *ing* to make a word that can be used with forms of the verb *be* — *am, is, are, was, were, have been,* and *had been*.

Add *ed* or *ing* to the words in ( ) and complete the paragraph.

Ellen and Max had been (prepare) __1__ for their science test. They (study) __2__ their notes on Saturday. Then on Sunday Max quizzed Ellen. Ellen (reply) __3__ with all the correct answers. That afternoon Max (notice) __4__ a rash on his arms. He knew he would be too sick to take the test the next day.

Writing on Your Own

Imagine that a favorite relative of yours has become famous. You have been chosen to write a biography of him or her. Write the first paragraph of the biography. Tell when and where your relative was born. Then give a detail or two about his or her childhood. If you wish, you may make up an imaginary relative. Use at least four of the Unit words in your paragraph. Use some of your verbs with forms of *be*.

 WRITER'S GUIDE For a sample paragraph from a biography, turn to page 274.

Proofreading

Read the announcement. There are six misspelled words. Three words need capital letters.

1. Find each of the errors in this announcement.

> One of our teachers, Ms. Marlene Polacca, is getting marryed next week. Her students are planning a party in her honor on Friday at 3 P.M. we need some help in prepareing for this exiting event.
> - We are decorateing the gym on Thursday at 4 P.M.
> - bruce promiced to serve the punch. he needs some helpers. Any volunteers?
> - We need a volunteer to take pictures. Has anyone studyed photography?

2. Write the six misspelled words correctly. Then write the three words that should begin with capital letters.

Spelling on Your Own

Write the Unit words in alphabetical order. Then find the nine base words that end with *y.* Use each of the nine base words with *ed* or *ing* in a sentence.

MASTERY WORDS

carrying
copied
staying
dancing
worried
changed

Add *ed* or *ing* to these words to spell Mastery words.

1. change **2.** carry **3.** worry
4. stay **5.** dance **6.** copy

Follow the directions using the Mastery words.

7. Write the two words that have double consonant letters.
8. Write the two words that have base words that end with *e.*

Add *ed* or *ing* to the words in ( ). Write Mastery words.

9. I am (worry) ____ about my sick dog.
10. Marisa (change) ____ the flat tire on her bicycle.
11. Connie is (stay) ____ with her cousins this week.
12. She (copy) ____ her homework from the chalkboard.

pry + ed = pried
prey + ed = preyed

BONUS WORDS

struggling
pitied
pried
eyed
satisfying
hesitated
dismayed
varied

Add *ed* or *ing* to each word to spell a Bonus word.

1. hesitate **2.** pry **3.** eye **4.** struggle
5. dismay **6.** pity **7.** vary **8.** satisfy

Follow the directions using the Bonus words.

9. Write the homophones for *I'd* and *pride.* Then try to use all four words in one sentence.
10. Write the two words that have four syllables each.
11. Write a story that begins with this sentence: "I *eyed* the strange-looking box covered with dust." Use as many Bonus words as you can.

14 The Sounds /oi/ and /ou/

UNIT WORDS

1. *voyage*
2. *join*
3. *enjoyable*
4. *loyalty*
5. *fountain*
6. *growl*
7. *coward*
8. *doubt*
9. *county*
10. *oyster*
11. *broil*
12. *soil*
13. *annoy*
14. *powder*
15. *scowl*
16. *towel*
17. *couch*
18. *amount*
19. *poison*
20. *avoid*

The Unit Words

Each Unit word has the vowel sound /oi/ or the vowel sound /ou/.

You hear the vowel sound /oi/ in *join.* This sound is spelled two ways in the Unit words.

- **oi** as in *soil*

- **oy** as in *voyage*

You hear the vowel sound /ou/ in *couch.* The Unit words show two ways to spell the sound /ou/.

- **ou** as in *fountain*

- **ow** as in *growl*

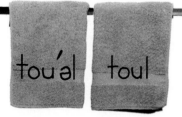

tou'əl   toul

REMEMBER THIS

Do you say *towel* like *growl* and *scowl*? If you do, don't forget to write *e* before *l* in *towel.*

60

Spelling Practice

A. Follow the directions using the Unit words.

1. Write the five words that have /oi/ between two consonant sounds.

2. Write the five words that have /oi/ spelled with *oy*.

B. Finish the sentences with words that have the sound /oi/.

3. In 1961 the first U.S. astronaut, Alan Shepard, found his ride in space exciting and _____.

4. In 1966 U.S. astronauts Armstrong and Scott had a successful _____. They were able to link up, or _____, two vehicles in space.

5. In 1976 a U.S. Viking spacecraft landed on Mars to photograph the planet and scoop up samples of rock and _____.

Alan Shepard

C. Follow the directions using the Unit words.

6. Write the five words that have the sound /ou/ spelled with *ou*.

7. Write the three words with /ou/ that end with *l*.

8. Write the other two words that have /ou/ spelled with *ow*.

D. Finish these sentences with words that have the sound /ou/.

9. U.S. astronauts Cernan and Schmitt spent the greatest _____ of time on the moon: 74 hours, 59 minutes.

10. Americans _____ that life exists on Mars.

11. The soil on the moon is not like fine _____. Instead it is made up of bits of rock and glass.

Eugene Cernan
Harrison Schmitt

Spelling and Language · Synonyms

UNIT WORDS

voyage
join
enjoyable
loyalty
fountain
growl
coward
doubt
county
oyster
broil
soil
annoy
powder
scowl
towel
couch
amount
poison
avoid

Synonyms are words that have the same or nearly the same meaning. For example, *join* and *connect* are synonyms. You could replace *connect* with *join* in this sentence, and the meaning would not change: "You must *connect* these two wires to make the radio work."

Write a Unit word that is a synonym for the underlined word in each sentence.

1. My dogs <u>snarl</u> whenever someone comes to the door.
2. Patty moved quickly to <u>dodge</u> the dogs.
3. She did not have a <u>pleasant</u> time with them.

Writing on Your Own

Write a short story for a school humor magazine about a costume party. Tell what happens to five or six guests at the party. Be sure to write a beginning, a middle, and an ending. Use at least six Unit words in your story.

 WRITER'S GUIDE   For a sample paragraph from a story, turn to page 273.

Using the Dictionary to Spell and Write

Learning the pronunciation of a word can help you remember how to spell a word. In the dictionary, the pronunciation for a word with two or more syllables has an accent mark ('). It shows which syllable is said with the most force. This syllable is called the **accented syllable.** The first syllable in *loyalty* is accented. The other two syllables are unaccented.

loy·al·ty   /loi′əl·tē/

Write the word for each pronunciation. Then underline the letters that spell the accented syllable.

1. /foun′tən/   2. /ois′tər/
3. /poi′zən/   4. /pou′dər/
5. /kou′ərd/   6. /koun′tē/
7. /voi′ij/   8. /tou′əl/

Find three more Unit words that each have two syllables.

9. Write the three words.

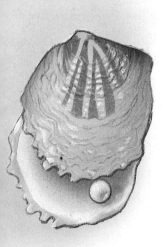

62

Spelling on Your Own

UNIT WORDS

Write the plural of each of the fifteen Unit words that can be nouns. Write the twelve words that can be verbs with *ed* added. The Unit word that remains is an adjective. Use that word in a sentence.

MASTERY WORDS

loud
howl
oil
bounce
loyal
coin

Follow the directions using the Mastery words.
1. Write the three words that have the sound /oi/.
2. Write the three words that have the sound /ou/.
3. Write the word that means the opposite of *quiet.*

Change the beginning consonants and write some Mastery words.
4. proud
6. join
5. royal
7. growl

Add *ed* to each word in ( ). Finish the sentences with the words.
8. I (oil) ____ the gears on my bicycle.
9. The dog (howl) ____ when I stepped on its paw.
10. The ball (bounce) ____ down the stairs.

BONUS WORDS

vow
surround
flounder
fowl
appoint
rejoice
devour
cower

Write the Bonus word for each definition.
1. promise
2. chickens and turkeys
3. struggle clumsily
4. eat up
5. crouch in fear
6. close in on all sides
7. choose someone for a job
8. express joy

Follow the directions using the Bonus words.
9. Read the entries for *flounder*[1] and *flounder*[2] in the **Spelling Dictionary.** Then write a sentence using *flounder*[1]. Write another using *flounder*[2].
10. Write the word that sounds like *foul.* Find the meanings of both words in the **Spelling Dictionary.** Write a sentence using each word.

63

15 The Sounds /o͞o/ and /o͝o/

UNIT WORDS

1. booklet
2. hood
3. understood
4. woolen
5. boost
6. chew
7. gloomy
8. shampoo
9. scoop
10. loose
11. proof
12. renew
13. drew
14. prove
15. jewels
16. crew
17. disapprove
18. crook
19. smooth
20. canoe

The Unit Words

There are two vowel sounds in the Unit words that are spelled with **oo**: /o͝o/, as in *booklet,* and /o͞o/, as in *boost.*

The vowel sounds /o͝o/ and /o͞o/ are usually spelled with **oo.** The Unit words show three ways to spell /o͞o/ besides **oo.**

- **o**-consonant-**e** as in *prove*

- **ew** as in *jewels*

☐ In *canoe* /o͞o/ is spelled with **oe.** There are only a few words in English that have this spelling for /o͞o/. One, however, is very common. Can you name it?

REMEMBER THIS

When a word ends with the vowel sound /o͞o/, it is usually spelled **ew.** Only a very few verbs — like *moo, boo,* and *shampoo* — spell this ending sound with **oo.**

64

Spelling Practice

A. Follow the directions using the Unit words.

1. Write the five words that have the sound /oŏ/, heard in *shook.*

2. Write the word that ends with /oo̅/ spelled *oo.*

3. Write the five other words that end with /oo̅/, heard in *shoe.*

B. Write the Unit words that have these meanings.

4. sad   **5.** not tight   **6.** lift   **7.** gems

C. Follow the directions using Unit words.

8. Write four other words besides the ones you wrote in **4–7** that have /oo̅/ spelled with *oo.*

9. Write the two words that have /oo̅/ spelled with *o-consonant-e.*

D. Finish the story with Unit words that have the sound /oo̅/.

   I pulled my __10__ into the water and began to paddle upstream. It was a dark and __11__ day. The water was not calm or __12__. In my pocket I had the evidence that could __13__ the suspect had stolen the __14__. Suddenly a strong gust of wind rocked the canoe. I was thrown into the water. I swam back to the canoe and climbed in. I paddled as hard as I could. I had to turn my __15__ over to the state police or the suspect would be released from jail.

Spelling and Language · Word Families

UNIT WORDS
booklet
hood
understood
woolen
boost
chew
gloomy
shampoo
scoop
loose
proof
renew
drew
prove
jewels
crew
disapprove
crook
smooth
canoe

A **word family** is a group of words with the same base word. The words *mover, unmovable, movement,* and *remove* all belong to the same word family. They are all formed by adding prefixes and suffixes to the base word *move.*

Each of these words belongs to the same word family as a Unit word. Write the related Unit word.

1. jewelry   **2.** bookcase   **3.** gloom
4. booster   **5.** scoopful   **6.** chewy

Writing on Your Own

Imagine that you are a famous advertisement writer. You have to name a new shampoo and write a magazine ad to convince people to try it. Use at least eight of the Unit words in your ad. You may also want to draw a picture to show how the ad will look.

WRITER'S GUIDE   For help revising your work, turn to the checklist on page 265.

Using the Dictionary to Spell and Write

Learning idioms can make your writing more colorful. An **idiom** is a group of words that has a meaning different from the meanings of the individual words. Look at the dictionary entry for the word *smooth.* At the end of the entry two idioms are given in boldface: *smooth over* and *smooth sailing.*

> **smooth** /smooth/ **1** *adj.* Without rough spots or lumps. **2** *v.* To make something smooth.
> —**smooth over** To make something seem more pleasant; to try to excuse. —**smooth sailing** Progress made without difficulty; a situation without problems.

Complete each sentence with one of the idioms.

1. Rory tried to _____ his argument with Miyako by giving her a present.

2. Once we understood the directions, putting the bike together was _____ .

Spelling on Your Own

UNIT WORDS

Add the letters that spell /ōo/ or /ŏo/. Write the Unit words.

1. gl__ __my
2. disappr__v__
3. ch__ __
4. l__ __se
5. sc__ __p
6. underst__ __d
7. b__ __st
8. can__ __
9. pr__v__
10. j__ __els
11. cr__ __
12. w__ __len
13. h__ __d
14. b__ __klet
15. ren__ __
16. dr__ __
17. shamp__ __
18. pr__ __f
19. sm__ __th
20. cr__ __k

MASTERY WORDS

move
broom
stood
choose
shook
flew

Write a Mastery word to rhyme with each word.

1. prove
2. wood
3. lose
4. blue
5. room
6. took

These verbs tell about the present. Write verbs that tell about the past. Use Mastery words.

7. shake
8. fly
9. stand

Finish these sentences with Mastery words.

10. She ____ up and ____ the blanket.
11. We could have used a ____ to sweep away the ants.
12. She wanted to ____ our picnic.
13. We could ____ from many spots.

BONUS WORDS

neighborhood
withdrew
proofread
overlook
bamboo
maroon
produce
jewelry

1. Write the two Bonus words that have /ŏo/ heard in *stood*.

2. Write the two words that have /ōo/ spelled with *ew*.

3. Write the three words that have /ōo/ spelled with *oo*. Circle the word that is a compound and use it in a sentence.

4. Write the word that has /ōo/ spelled with *u*. Write one sentence using the word as a verb.

16 "Silent" Letters

UNIT WORDS

1. knight
2. kneel
3. wreck
4. wrist
5. honor
6. shepherd
7. castle
8. fasten
9. knowledge
10. wrinkle
11. wreath
12. glisten
13. knotty
14. wrestle
15. rustle
16. knob
17. wring
18. knead
19. honest
20. hour

THE WIZARD OF ID by Brant parker and Johnny hart

Reprinted by permission of Johnny Hart and Creators Syndicate, Inc.

The Unit Words

All the Unit words have letters that are not pronounced. These letters are often called "silent" letters. Hundreds of years ago, "silent" letters were pronounced. The pronunciation has since changed, but the spelling has stayed the same.

The Unit words show four "silent" letters. Be sure to write these letters when you spell the Unit words.

- **k** is silent in *knob* and *kneel*
- **w** is silent in *wreck* and *wrist*
- **h** is silent in *honor* and *shepherd*
- **t** is silent in *castle* and *fasten*

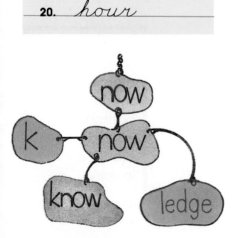

REMEMBER THIS

Add the letter *k* to *now* to make the word *know*. Add *ledge* to *know* to make the word *knowledge*. The vowel sound is different in each of the three words, but the spelling *ow* is the same.

68

Spelling Practice

A. Follow the directions using the Unit words.

1. Write the six words that begin with /r/ spelled *wr.*

2. Write the four words that have the "silent" letter *h* before a vowel.

3. Write the five words that have the "silent" letter *t.*

B. Six Unit words begin with the "silent" letter *k.* Write each word beside the sound that ends it.

4. /j/

5. /t/

6. /ē/

7. /d/

8. /b/

9. /l/

C. Write the Unit words that rhyme with these words.

10. vessel

11. college

12. tower

13. leopard

14. muscle

15. tassel

16. heal

17. deck

D. Complete each sentence with two Unit words. Both words have the same "silent" letter.

18. It is difficult for a _____ to _____ in his suit of armor.

19. My wet shirt will _____ if I _____ out the water.

20. My _____ sister said it was an _____ to be chosen class treasurer.

21. I ran to _____ the door when I heard something _____ in the garden.

Spelling and Language · Homophones

Wrap and *rap* sound alike, but they have different spellings and different meanings. Word pairs such as these are called **homophones.**

These messages might appear on signs. Read each pair. Write the homophones. Circle the one that is used correctly in the sign.

1. Silver rings on sale.   Silver wrings on sale.
2. Saturday Ours: 9 A.M. to 5 P.M.   Saturday Hours: 9 A.M. to 5 P.M.
3. Fly at knight for cheaper fares.   Fly at night for cheaper fares.

Writing on Your Own

Pretend you are a king or a queen who lived during the Middle Ages. What would your knights have to do to prove that they were honest and brave? Make a list of tasks for your knights to perform. Then write five sentences, mentioning one task in each sentence. Use at least fifteen of the Unit words in describing the tasks.

Using the Dictionary to Spell and Write

You can use the dictionary to find the correct spelling of a word. Suppose you want to write the word for this picture. You can hear that the first consonant sound is /r/ and the vowel sound is /e/. You know that /e/ is probably spelled *e,* but you aren't sure how to spell /r/. How can a dictionary help you?

Think of the ways you have learned to spell /r/ at the beginning of a word. The beginning sound /r/ can be spelled **r, rh,** and **wr.** Then look in the **Spelling Dictionary** for the word beginning with *re, rhe,* and *wre.* You will find the correct spelling, *wreck.*

Use the **Spelling Dictionary** to help you find the correct spelling for each pronunciation.

act, āte, câre, ärt;   egg, ēven;   if, īce;   on, ōver, ôr;   b o͝ok, f oō d;
ə = a in *ago,* e in *listen,* i in *giraffe,* o in *pilot,* u in *circus;*   y oō = u in *music;*
up, tûrn;   oil;   out;   chair;   sing;   shop;   thank;   th at;   zh in *treasure.*

1. /res'əl/   2. /ri·plī'/   3. /rek/   4. /rēth/

 SPELLING DICTIONARY   Remember to use your **Spelling Dictionary** when you write.

70

Spelling on Your Own

UNIT WORDS

The "silent" letters have been omitted in these words. Add the missing letters to spell Unit words. Write the words.

1. fasen
2. reath
3. night
4. our
5. nowledge
6. rinkle
7. neel
8. rusle
9. nob
10. sheperd
11. nead
12. onor
13. notty
14. rist
15. resle
16. casle
17. reck
18. onest
19. ring
20. glisen

MASTERY WORDS

written
knock
gnat
knot
wrong
known

Write the Mastery word that rhymes with each of these words. Then underline the "silent" letter in each word.

1. grown
2. song
3. mitten
4. plot

Follow the directions using the Mastery words.

5. Write the word that has the "silent" letter *g*. ____

6. Write the four words that begin with the sound /n/. Circle the word that has the sound /ō/.

7. Write the word that is the homophone for *not*.

BONUS WORDS

rhythm
knuckle
exhaust
knapsack
bristle
debt
mortgage
wriggle

1. Write the Bonus words in alphabetical order. Then underline the "silent" letter in each word.

Follow the directions using the Bonus words.

2. Write the word that comes from the Old French word *dette*, meaning "something owed."

3. Write the five words that have the sound /i/.

4. Write the two words that have the "silent" letter *k*.

5. Write a sentence using the word that is a synonym for *squirm*.

17 Double Letters

UNIT WORDS

1. allow
2. baggage
3. collect
4. dessert
5. difficult
6. dizzy
7. drizzle
8. jazz
9. juggle
10. kennel
11. mammal
12. message
13. office
14. opposite
15. riddle
16. settlers
17. sheriff
18. squirrel
19. stress
20. stubborn

Sweet Stuff

The Unit Words

All the Unit words have double consonant letters. **Double consonant letters** are two letters that are the same and stand for one sound. For example, there are two *z*'s in *dizzy*, but you hear only one sound /z/: /diz'ē/. Usually double consonant letters come after a short vowel sound.

Can you find twelve different sets of double consonant letters in the Unit words?

REMEMBER THIS

The word *dessert* has two *s*'s—two *s*'s for *sweet stuff*.

The word *desert* has one *s*—one *s* for *sand*.

Spelling Practice

A. Add second syllables to these first syllables. Write complete Unit words.

1. rid   **2.** al   **3.** squir

4. ken   **5.** bag   **6.** set

B. Follow the directions using Unit words.

7. Write the two words that have /u/ before double consonant letters.

8. Write the five words that have /i/ spelled *i* before double consonant letters.

C. Add the missing letters to each word. Write Unit words.

9. me _ _ age   **10.** o _ _ osite

11. o _ _ ice   **12.** di _ _ y

13. de _ _ ert   **14.** co _ _ ect

15. ja _ _   **16.** stre _ _

D. Finish these sentences with Unit words.

17. President Jefferson's favorite ____ was ice cream.

18. The largest and heaviest ____ is the blue whale.

19. A red ____ can cut a hundred or more cones from a pine tree in an hour.

20. Do you know this ancient ____? "What flies forever and rests never?"   (The wind)

E. Write the Unit words that rhyme with these words.

21. middle   **22.** struggle

23. busy   **24.** has

Spelling and Language · Synonyms

UNIT WORDS

allow
baggage
collect
dessert
difficult
dizzy
drizzle
jazz
juggle
kennel
mammal
message
office
opposite
riddle
settlers
sheriff
squirrel
stress
stubborn

Synonyms are words that have the same or nearly the same meaning. *Happen* and *occur* are synonyms.

Replace the underlined word in each sentence with a synonym. Write Unit words.

1. We promised to gather wood for the campfire.
2. In *message,* the accent is on the first syllable.
3. Elisa had a hard time removing the old wallpaper.
4. After the airplane landed, we claimed our luggage.
5. The lawman ran the bandits out of Dodge City.

Writing on Your Own

Imagine that you have been on a journey. The first part of your trip went smoothly and easily. The last part was full of problems. Write a short article about your trip for a travel magazine. Describe both parts in detail. Use as many of the Unit words as you can. Replace some of your descriptive words with synonyms that are fresh and vivid.

THESAURUS For help finding synonyms, turn to page 205.

Using the Dictionary to Spell and Write

Suppose you were writing a sentence with the word *dessert.* When you reached the end of the line, you realized there wasn't enough room to write the whole word. What should you do?

Dear Lucy,
Everyone is
bringing refresh-
ments. Can
you bring
a tasty des

1. Look up the word in the dictionary. See how it is divided into syllables. **des·sert**
2. Then go back to writing your sentence. End the line with the syllable *des* and put a hyphen (-) after it. The hyphen shows that the rest of the word will follow on the next line. You can divide a word at the end of a line after any syllable that has more than one letter.

Look up each of these words in the **Spelling Dictionary.** Write the entry word in syllables. Put a hyphen at each syllable break.

1. opposite   **2.** squirrel   **3.** baggage   **4.** difficult

Spelling on Your Own

There are twelve different sets of double consonant letters in the Unit words. Write each set. Under each set write the words that have those double letters.

MASTERY WORDS

Write the Mastery words that have these double consonant letters.

1. dd   **2.** nn   **3.** pp (two words)   **4.** tt (two words)

Write the Mastery word that has nearly the same meaning.

5. oar   **6.** take place   **7.** supper

8. believe   **9.** jug

Finish the conversation with Mastery words.

> Dina: We __10__ to have the same birthday.
> Mike: Do you __11__ we can go bowling for our birthdays?
> Dina: I hope so. Then let's have __12__ at the Coach Inn.
> Mike: I love their warm rolls and homemade __13__ .

butter
bottle
happen
dinner
paddle
suppose

BONUS WORDS

Write each of these misspelled words correctly.

1. succesful   **2.** ballay   **3.** commitee   **4.** cuning

5. embarass   **6.** scisors   **7.** interupt   **8.** assemmbly

Follow the directions using the Bonus words.

9. Write the three words that each have two pairs of double consonant letters.

10. Write story titles using the Bonus words. Use one or two of the words in each title. Here's an example: "A *Successful Assembly.*" Then choose one of your titles and write a story.

committee
scissors
cunning
successful
embarrass
interrupt
assembly
ballet

18 Review

Follow these steps when you are unsure how to spell a word.

- **Say** the word. Recall when you have heard the word used. Think about what it means.
- **Look** at the word. Find any prefixes, suffixes, or other word parts you know. Think about other words that are related in meaning and spelling. Try to picture the word in your mind.
- **Spell** the word to yourself. Think about the way each sound is spelled. Notice any unusual spelling.
- **Write** the word while looking at it. Check the way you have formed your letters. If you have not written the word clearly or correctly, write it again.
- **Check** your learning. Cover the word and write it. If you did not spell the word correctly, practice these steps until the word becomes your own.

UNIT 13

noticed
lying
replied
promised
exciting
studying
supposed
studied
lied
applying

UNIT 14

towel
poison
annoy
amount
enjoyable
join
doubt
soil
couch
county

UNIT 13 Follow the directions using words from Unit 13.

1. Write the five words that drop *e* when *ed* or *ing* is added.

2. Write the two words that do not change their spelling when *ing* is added.

3. Write the two words that change the *y* to *i* when *ed* is added.

4. Finish this spelling problem to show which letters the word *lie* lost and gained.

   lie − ( ) + ( ) + ing = lying

UNIT 14 Follow the directions using words from Unit 14.

Finish this paragraph with words that have the same vowel sound as *cow*.

Today I am going to the __5__ picnic. I remembered to take my __6__ from the __7__ so that I could go swimming in the lake. I __8__ that I brought the right __9__ of sandwiches to last me all day, though.

Finish these sentences with words that have the same vowel sound as *boy*. Use words from Unit 14.

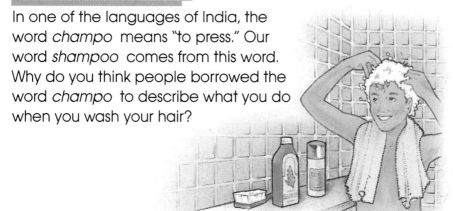

10. Keep ____ away from children and animals.

11. The ____ around this plant is dry.

12. Our trip to the park was ____ .

13. Would you like to ____ in our game?

14. Talking can ____ people trying to work.

UNIT 15 Follow the directions using words from Unit 15.

15. Write the words that have the /o͝o/ heard in *booklet*.

Each sentence has two or more misspelled words. Underline the misspelled words and then write them correctly.

16 After I shampew my hair, I like to leave it lose.

17. I disaproove of letting the dog choo on that new wollen scarf.

18. I can proove that I drue that picture myself.

19. We paddled our canoo across the smoothe lake.

UNIT 16 Follow the directions using words from Unit 16.

20. Write three words that have a silent *w*.

UNIT 15
canoe
smooth
drew
disapprove
understood
woolen
chew
shampoo
loose
prove

WORDS IN TIME

In one of the languages of India, the word *champo* means "to press." Our word *shampoo* comes from this word. Why do you think people borrowed the word *champo* to describe what you do when you wash your hair?

UNIT 16
honor
wrist
wrestle
knowledge
honest
fasten
rustle
knob
wring
hour

Finish these sentences. Circle the silent letter in each word. Use the words from Unit 16.

It was an __21__ to be trusted to guard the treasure map. After I had been at my post for an __22__ , I thought I heard the __23__ of someone's clothes. Then I saw the door __24__ slowly turn. Who else had the __25__ that the map was here? Captain Burns did, but he was too __26__ to try to steal it. Had I remembered to __27__ the bolt that locked the door? I would find out in another minute.

UNIT 17 Follow the directions using words from Unit 17.

UNIT 17
message
difficult
opposite
collect
dessert
allow
mammal
office
settlers
stubborn

Write the words that are spelled with these double consonant letters.

28. *ss* (two words)

29. *ll* (two words)

30. *ff* (two words)

31. *mm*   **32.** *bb*

33. *pp*   **34.** *tt*

35. Find the misspelled words in this paragraph. Then write them correctly.

I got Ben's mesage to hurry to the kennel oposite the park. As I went in, Ben burst out of his offise. He was very angry. "I hope you've come to colectt that . . . ," he stopped. It seemed dificcult for him to find the word he wanted. ". . . that mammel!" he finished. I guess Tramp was being stuborn again. If Ben will not alow me to keep my dog there, I don't know what I'll do.

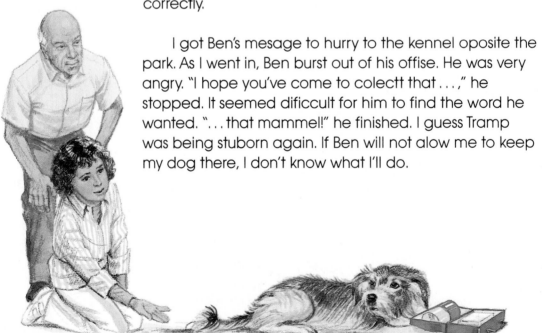

Spelling and Reading
A Business Letter

Read the following business letter. Notice the six parts of the letter.

748 Jessie St.
Monterey, CA 93940
February 21, 19 —

Heading

Ms. Judy Garcia
County Office for Better Business
Greenwood, CA 94008

**Inside
Address**

Dear Ms. Garcia:

Greeting

    I recently bought a product that did not work the way it was supposed to. The product is Hi-lite dog shampoo. The clerk promised that the shampoo would leave my dog Harpo's hair soft and smooth.

    I studied the directions carefully. First I put the green liquid on, and then I started applying the yellow liquid. The smell wasn't enjoyable, and it seemed to annoy Harpo. After I had finished and dried Harpo with a towel, I noticed that his hair wasn't soft at all. It was quite the opposite! He looked like the old woolen hat that I had given to the cat to chew. The enclosed pictures prove it.

    The clerk said I must not have understood the directions. I do not agree. Can you help me get a refund?

Body

Sincerely,
Allan Taylor
Allan Taylor

**Closing
Signature**

Write the answers to the questions.

1. To which person and which office has the writer written this business letter?
2. What kind of product is the writer complaining about?
3. Do you think Allan is right to complain? Why or why not?
4. What do you think Ms. Garcia might do about Allan's complaint? Why do you think so?

Underline the review words in your answers. Check to see that you spelled the words correctly.

Spelling and Writing
A Business Letter

Think and Discuss

People write many types of letters, some to friends and relatives and others to businesses and government offices. Letters to businesses or offices are different from letters to friends. A **business letter** is usually to someone you don't know. It is written to ask for help or information, or to praise or complain about a product. A business letter has six parts. It has the five parts of a friendly letter, and it also has a part called the **inside address.** The inside address is the same as the receiver's address. Look at the business letter on page 79. On which part of the page is the inside address written?

When you write a business letter, you begin the **body** of your letter by stating your reason for writing. In the business letter on page 79, what is Allan's reason for writing? Notice that he has given all the information needed to make his complaint understood. What product is he complaining about? What was the product supposed to do? What did it do instead?

In a letter of complaint you must also explain who caused the problem. You must show that you did not cause the problem. What does Allan say to show that the shampoo was to blame for what happened to his dog?

Apply

Write a **business letter** to the manager of an imaginary company. Complain about a product the company has made. Follow the writing guidelines on the next page.

Prewriting

Think up an imaginary product to complain about in a business letter. If you need help thinking of an idea, imagine you are one of the people in these pictures. What might you have to complain about? Copy the following list of questions. Next to each question, write notes about your answer.

- Where did you buy the product?
- What was the product supposed to do?
- What happened when you used the product?
- How do you want to solve the problem?

Composing

Use your notes to help you write the first draft of your business letter.

- State your complaint clearly and explain who caused the problem. Tell the manager how you would suggest solving the problem.
- Look back at your prewriting notes. Have you left out any points you wanted to make?

Revising

Read your letter and show it to a classmate. Follow these guidelines to improve your work. Use the editing and proofreading marks on this page to show corrections.

Editing

- Make sure you included all six parts of a business letter.
- Make sure your letter clearly describes your problem.
- Check that you have explained what you want done about your problem.

Proofreading

- Check your spelling and correct any mistakes.
- Check your capitalization and punctuation.

Copy your letter onto a clean sheet of paper. Write carefully and neatly.

Publishing

Show your letter to several classmates. Ask them how they would respond or solve your problem if they were the company manager.

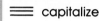

Editing and Proofreading Marks	
≡	capitalize
⊙	make a period
∧	add something
⋏	add a comma
ⱴ ⱴ	add quotation marks
ℓ	take something away
◯	spell correctly
⊬	indent the paragraph
/	make a lowercase letter
∿ tr	transpose

UNIT WORDS

1. argue
2. award
3. carpet
4. carton
5. carve
6. charm
7. garden
8. harvest
9. quarter
10. regard
11. reward
12. starve
13. swarm
14. tardy
15. toward
16. warmth
17. warning
18. wharf
19. guard
20. sergeant

Garden Harvest Awards

The Unit Words

Say the words *award, charm, swarm,* and *wharf.* You hear the sounds /ôr/ or /är/ in each word.

The words *award, swarm,* and *wharf* have the sounds /ôr/. The word *charm* has the sounds /är/. Each Unit word has one of these vowel sounds with **r**—/ôr/ or /är/. Both sound combinations are spelled **ar** in most of the Unit words.

☐ Now say the word *sergeant.* You hear the sounds /är/, heard in *charm.* In this Unit word /är/ is spelled with **er.**

REMEMBER THIS

In the word *guard,* the *gu* is pronounced like the /g/ in the word *gate.*

Spelling Practice

A. Follow the directions using the Unit words.

1. Add letters to *warm*. Spell two Unit words.

2. Write the three words that include *ward*.

3. Write the two words that begin with *re-*.

4. Add letters to the end of *car*. Write three Unit words.

5. Write the two words that begin with the sounds /gär/.

6. Add letters to the beginning of *arm*. Write two Unit words.

7. Write the only word that doesn't spell /är/ with *ar*.

B. Write the Unit word that is a synonym for each of these words.

8. alarm   **9.** dock

C. Write the base word for each of these words. Write Unit words.

10. tardiness   **11.** argument

12. quarterly   **13.** starvation

D. Finish the paragraph with Unit words.

　　Manuel and I walked __14__ the vegetable __15__ feeling so proud. The corn was ready to be picked. This would be our first __16__. In the __17__ of the sun, we picked several dozen ears of corn. It would be a fine __18__ for a summer of hard work. I patted our scarecrow on the back. "You made an excellent __19__," I said. "You frightened away the birds just as we had hoped."

Spelling and Language · Analogies

"Reply is to *answer* as *tardy* is to *late."* This is an analogy. *Reply* has the same relationship to *answer* as *tardy* has to *late.* Both pairs of words are synonyms.

Read each of these analogies. See how the first two words are related. Finish the analogy with a Unit word.

1. *Error* is to *mistake* as *medal* is to _____ .
2. *Smooth* is to *rough* as *punish* is to _____ .
3. *Shelf* is to *shelves* as _____ is to *wharves* .

Writing on Your Own

Pretend you are the director of a summer camp planning the Last Day Celebration. What awards will your campers receive? You can make the prizes funny or serious. List the titles of three awards. Then write several sentences to explain why each award is given. Use at least one Unit word in each award name and sentence.

 WRITER'S GUIDE   For help revising your sentences, turn to the checklist on page 265.

Proofreading

This is part of a letter Jeff wrote. He misspelled six words. Two words are divided incorrectly at the end of a line.

1. Read what Jeff wrote and find each misspelled word.

> Uncle Henry sent me a cartin of old nature magazines and news-papers. I decided to try to sell them for a qworter apiece at the flea market next weekend. I'll put the money I earn tord the purch-ase of a new bowling ball.
>
> This has been an exciting day. My principal gave me an aword for being an excellent school crossing gard. Also, my father said I could work with him this summer on the worf. I'll help him unload his fishing boats. I'm looking forward to it.

2. Write the six misspelled words correctly.

3. Write the two words that were each divided incorrectly at the end of a line. Use the **Spelling Dictionary** to see how they should have been divided. Add hyphens at the syllable breaks.

Spelling on Your Own

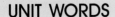
Use all the words to make a word search puzzle. You can write the words across or down. Fill in the empty spaces with other letters. When you finish your puzzle, let someone else solve it.

```
S  C  H  A  R  M  P
B  A  H  C  O  D  I
E  R  E  G  A  R  D
M  V  O  O  R  T  S
T  E  N  W  E  P  E
```

MASTERY WORDS

park
farm
barber
bark
hardly
card

Write a Mastery word that rhymes with each pair of words.

1. harm   charm   **2.** yard   guard   **3.** dark   mark

Follow the directions using the Mastery words.

4. Write the word that means "not quite."

5. Write the four words that end with consonant clusters.

6. Finish the sentence. Use a Mastery word.

Mr. Torres is the _____ who cuts my father's hair.

BONUS WORDS

archery
partial
guardian
argument
dwarf
forewarn
apartment
wart

Write the Bonus words that have these base words.

1. guard   **2.** argue   **3.** part (two words)

Follow the directions using the Bonus words.

4. Write the three words that have the sounds /ôr/, heard in *wharf*. Circle the word in which /ôr/ is spelled two different ways.

5. Write the two words that begin with the sounds /är/, heard in *carve.*

6. Write the three other words that have the sounds /är/.

7. Write analogies for four of the words. Leave a blank where the Bonus word should go. Study the examples on page 84. When you finish, ask a classmate to complete the analogies.

20 The Sounds /ûr/

UNIT WORDS

1. verse
2. swerve
3. curve
4. whirl
5. worship
6. hurdle
7. curb
8. purchase
9. thirsty
10. flirt
11. preserve
12. herb
13. nerve
14. swirl
15. worm
16. turkey
17. blur
18. refer
19. herd
20. worst

ON THE SKATEBOARD

Skimming
an asphalt sea
I swerve, I curve, I
sway; I speed to whirring
sound an inch above the
ground; I'm the sailor
and the sail; I'm the
driver and the wheel;
I'm the one and only
single engine
human auto
mobile.

LILLIAN MORRISON

The Unit Words

Each Unit word has the vowel sound /û/ before the letter **r**—/ûr/.

The sounds /ûr/ are spelled four different ways in the Unit words.

- **ur** as in *curve*
- **er** as in *verse*
- **ir** as in *whirl*
- **or** as in *worst*

REMEMBER THIS

Remember to write the *h* in *herb* even if you do not pronounce it.

Spelling Practice

A. Follow the directions using the Unit words.

1. Write the six words that have the sounds /ûr/ spelled with *ur.*

2. Write the three words that have /ûr/ spelled with *or.*

B. Add the letters that spell /ûr/. Write Unit words.

3. pres___ve

4. v___se

5. th___sty

6. ref___

7. h___dle

8. fl___t

C. Complete each pair of sentences with Unit words. The words used in each pair must rhyme.

9. She didn't have the ____ to play the tennis champ.

10. I saw Anita ____ to avoid hitting the runner.

11. We parked our car close to the ____.

12. My mother often cooks with the ____ parsley.

13. Betty watched the water ____.

14. Tim saw Jan ____ when he called her name.

D. *Herd* and *heard* are homophones. Finish the funny conversation using *herd* and *heard* correctly.

City Man: Look at that bunch of cows.

Cowboy: Not bunch — **15** .

City Man: Heard of what?

Cowboy: **16** of cows.

City Man: Sure, I've **17** of cows.

Cowboy: No! A cow **18** .

City Man: Why should I care what a cow **19** ?
               I've got no secrets from a cow.

Spelling and Language · Adding *ed* and *ing*

UNIT WORDS

verse
swerve
curve
whirl
worship
hurdle
curb
purchase
thirsty
flirt
preserve
herb
nerve
swirl
worm
turkey
blur
refer
herd
worst

Verbs with *ed* added tell about the past. Verbs with *ing* can be used with a form of the verb *be.* Remember to drop the final *e* before you add *ed* or *ing.*

Add *ed* or *ing* to the words in boldface. Write the verbs to finish the sentences.

swirl 1. The wind is _____ the leaves in the yard.
curve 2. The road _____ to the left.
whirl 3. The fan _____ the dust around in the air.
flirt 4. The boys were _____ with my sister.

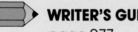
Writing on Your Own

Write a poem for a school literary magazine about how it feels to run, bike, or skateboard. Choose words that capture the sounds you hear and the feelings you have as you move. Use some of the Unit words in your poem. Use some verbs with *ing.*

> **WRITER'S GUIDE** For a sample poem, turn to page 277.

Using the Dictionary to Spell and Write

Many words have several definitions. When you write, you should be familiar with these definitions. In a dictionary, each definition is numbered. Read the entry for *preserve.*

> **pre·serve** [pri·zûrv′] *v.* **pre·served, pre·serv·ing,** *n.* **1** *v.* To keep from danger. **2** *v.* To prepare food so it can be kept without spoiling. **3** *v.* To keep from spoiling: to *preserve* a specimen. **4** *n.* An area set aside for the protection of plants and animals.

Complete each sentence with *preserve.* Then write the number that tells which definition of *preserve* is used.

1. My mother taught me how to _____ tomatoes.
2. Animals are safe from hunters on a game _____ .
3. A thick coat of wax will _____ the wood.
4. The ice in the cooler will _____ our picnic lunch.

Spelling on Your Own

UNIT WORDS

Complete the chart. Write the Unit words that have /ûr/ spelled with these letters. Then use two words from each column in a sentence. Write four sentences.

er	ir	ur	or

MASTERY WORDS

church
fern
worry
further
stir
skirt

Write the Mastery words that have the sounds /ûr/ spelled with these letters.

1. er   **2.** or   **3.** ir (two words)   **4.** ur (two words)

Write the Mastery word that rhymes with each of these words.

5. shirt   **6.** furry   **7.** burn   **8.** search

Follow the directions using the Mastery words.

9. Write the plural of *church*. _____

10. Write the present tense of the verb *worried.* Then use the word in a sentence.

11. Use the word that rhymes with *purr* in a sentence.

BONUS WORDS

circuit
university
concern
urgent
worthwhile
nervous
surplus
murmur

1. Write the Bonus words in four groups according to the letters that spell the sounds /ûr/ in each word.
2. Write the plural of *university.*
3. Write the Bonus words that are synonyms for *uneasy* and *excess.* Then use both words in a sentence.
4. The word *concern* can be used as a noun and as a verb. Write one sentence using it as a noun. Write another using it as a verb.
5. Write a story with the title "An Urgent Message." Use as many Bonus words as you can in your story.

21 The Sounds /ər/

UNIT WORDS

1. tailor
2. humor
3. clever
4. collar
5. mayor
6. dealer
7. swimmer
8. jogger
9. cellar
10. pillar
11. proper
12. saucer
13. editor
14. tutor
15. lunar
16. armor
17. polar
18. speaker
19. inventor
20. horror

The Unit Words

Say the word *tailor*, and listen for the two syllables. Each syllable has one vowel sound. Then decide which syllable is said with greater force. The syllable said with greater force is the **accented syllable.** In *tailor*, the first syllable is the accented syllable. The unaccented syllable has a weak vowel sound called a **schwa.** This is the sign for schwa: /ə/.

You can hear the sound schwa with /r/ at the end of each Unit word. The Unit words show three ways to spell /ər/.

- **er** as in *clever*
- **or** as in *tailor*
- **ar** as in *collar*

REMEMBER THIS

When a word has a short vowel sound and ends with one consonant letter, you double the final consonant before adding *er.*

jog — jogger   swim — swimmer

Spelling Practice

A. Follow the directions using the Unit words.

1. Write the four words that begin with consonant clusters. Then write the letters that spell /ər/ in the words.

2. Write the three words that begin with vowel sounds.

3. Write the five other words that spell /ər/ with *or*.

B. Write the Unit words with beginnings that rhyme with these words.

4. soon   **5.** peel

6. doll   **7.** spell

8. bowl   **9.** cross

C. The sounds /ər/ can be added to a verb to make a noun that means "someone who does something." Finish each sentence below.

10. Someone who jogs is a ____.

11. Someone who speaks is a ____.

12. Someone who invents is an ____.

13. Someone who edits is an ____.

14. Someone who swims is a ____.

Thomas Edison

D. Write the Unit word that is a synonym for each underlined word.

15. My math <u>teacher</u> works with me every Thursday at 4 P.M.

16. Kiyo has his trains set up in the <u>basement</u>.

17. This is the <u>correct</u> way to tie a knot.

18. Nadia has a <u>bright</u> idea for decorating the gym.

19. She took my picture in front of the stone <u>column</u>.

20. We watched with <u>dread</u> as the lion attacked the zebra.

Spelling and Language · Possessive Nouns

To make a singular noun show ownership or possession, you add 's. To make a plural noun that ends with s show possession, you just add an apostrophe (').

dealer's   dealers'

Finish each sentence with the possessive form of the noun in ( ).

1. The (tailor) _____ shop is around the corner.
2. The (swimmer) _____ goggles protect his eyes.
3. Daily runs are part of many (joggers) _____ routines.
4. That (inventor) _____ machine changed the way we heat our homes.

Writing on Your Own

Pretend you are the mayor of your city or town. You want your community to build a new sports center. Write an opinion paragraph explaining your reasons for considering it a good idea. Use at least six Unit words. Use some possessive forms of both singular and plural nouns.

 WRITER'S GUIDE   For a sample opinion paragraph, turn to page 269.

Proofreading

Read Lin's story. She misspelled six words. She also forgot three capital letters and two question marks.

1. Find each of Lin's errors.

> Sometimes i dream of the future. What if I were a clevor inventer   I could build a machine that gives dogs a shampoo. what if I were an explorer like Admiral Perry   I could lead a polor expedition. What if I were in politics? Maybe I could be the most popular mayer the city ever had. if I were an astronaut, I could go to the moon. I could build a space station on the lunor surface. Maybe an editar of a magazine would ask me to write about my journey. Just maybe, one of these dreams will come true.

2. Write the six misspelled words correctly. Then write the three words that should begin with capital letters.

 WRITER'S GUIDE   See the editing and proofreading marks on page 266.

Spelling on Your Own

UNIT WORDS

Write all of the Unit words in alphabetical order. Then underline the words that name people. Use the possessive form of each of these singular nouns in a sentence. Here's an example: "The *tutor's* pupil works hard."

MASTERY WORDS

Add the letters that stand for /ər/. Write the Mastery words.

1. supp___   **2.** sug___   **3.** mot___
4. own___   **5.** fav___   **6.** cov___

Write the words that have these vowel sounds.

7. /ā/   **8.** /ō/ (two words)

Finish the sentences with Mastery words.

9. Eddie forgot to ___ the peanut butter jar.
10. My favorite ___ is meatballs and spaghetti.
11. Jill doesn't put ___ on her grapefruit.

Rewrite these sentences. Correct the misspelled words.

12. The ownar forgot to covor the suger bowls.
13. I did Mom a faver and made suppar.

cover
motor
supper
sugar
owner
favor

BONUS WORDS

1. Write the Bonus words in three groups. List them according to the letters that spell final /ər/.
2. Write the two words that have the sounds /ûr/.
3. Use the word that begins with a consonant cluster in a sentence.
4. Write the four words that each name a person. Then use each of these nouns and another Bonus word in a sentence. For example, "The *author* was careful about *grammar.*"

particular
grammar
operator
hamburger
consumer
labor
burglar
author

93

22 The Sounds /əl/ and /ən/

UNIT WORDS

1. hospital
2. ankle
3. pupil
4. apron
5. burden
6. sandal
7. pedal
8. label
9. certain
10. swollen
11. evil
12. general
13. peddle
14. whistle
15. curtain
16. pardon
17. medal
18. barrel
19. captain
20. saddle

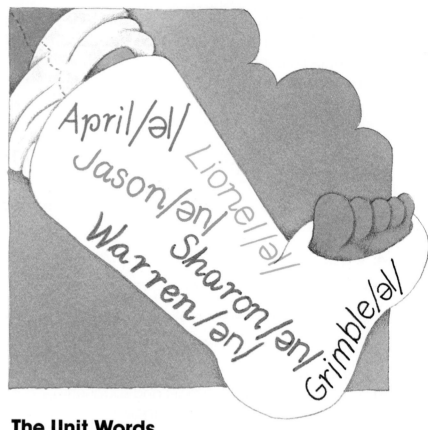

April /əl/
Lionel /əl/
Jason /ən/
Sharon /ən/
Warren /ən/
Grimble /əl/

The Unit Words

In Unit 21 you studied words with /ər/ in the final, unaccented syllables. In this unit, you will study words that have /ə/ before /l/ or /n/.

The Unit words show four ways to spell /əl/.

- **le** as in *ankle*
- **al** as in *hospital*
- **el** as in *barrel*
- **il** as in *pupil*

The Unit words show three ways to spell /ən/.

- **en** as in *swollen*
- **on** as in *apron*
- **ain** as in *certain*

94

Spelling Practice

A. Follow the directions using the Unit words.

1. Write the two words with /əl/ spelled *al* that rhyme.

2. Write the three other words that have /əl/ spelled the same way.

3. Find the three words that have /ən/ spelled *ain*. Write the words in alphabetical order.

4. Write the four words that have double consonant letters.

5. Write the two words that sound alike but are spelled differently.

6. Write the word that rhymes with each of these words.

paddle   stolen

table   handle

B. Write the word for each definition.

7. forgive   **8.** student   **9.** a load   **10.** wicked

11. something worn to protect clothing

C. Finish the sentences with Unit words that end in /əl/.

12. Beth sprained her _____ skating.

13. I read the washing instructions on the shirt _____ .

14. The driver stopped when he heard the officer's _____ .

15. The leather strap on my summer _____ is torn.

16. Alton visited his sick friend in the _____ .

17. Mrs. Smith pickled cucumbers in a _____ .

95

Spelling and Language · Homophones

UNIT WORDS

hospital
ankle
pupil
apron
burden
sandal
pedal
label
certain
swollen
evil
general
peddle
whistle
curtain
pardon
medal
barrel
captain
saddle

Words that sound alike but have different spellings and different meanings are called **homophones.** For example, *pedal* and *peddle* are homophones.

Say the word *petal.* It sounds almost like *pedal* and *peddle.* But it is not a true homophone for these words.

Finish this paragraph with *pedal, peddle,* or *petal.*

This summer my sisters are going to __1__ flowers in the square. They will wrap the flowers carefully to make sure not a single __2__ falls off. Then they will put the flowers in their bike baskets and __3__ to the square.

Writing on Your Own

Write a paragraph telling a friend how to whistle, ride a bike, or do something else. Make sure you clearly explain all the steps. Use some of the Unit words.

 WRITER'S GUIDE For a sample how-to paragraph, turn to page 268.

Using the Dictionary to Spell and Write

Dictionaries provide many kinds of information that can help you when you write. Some of the entries in the **Spelling Dictionary** include word histories. A **word history** tells you the origin of a word, or where a word comes from. Sometimes it also shows you how the meaning of a word has changed over time. A word history follows the definitions in an entry. This symbol ▶ indicates a word history.

Find these five words in the **Spelling Dictionary.** Read the word history. Then write the word for each origin.

> **captain   general   burden   pedal   apron**

1. Old English word meaning "to carry"
2. Latin root meaning "foot"
3. Latin word meaning "kind"
4. Middle French word meaning "a small cloth"
5. Latin word meaning "head"

 SPELLING DICTIONARY Remember to use your **Spelling Dictionary** when you write.

Spelling on Your Own

UNIT WORDS

Complete the chart. In each column, write the Unit words that have /əl/ or /ən/ spelled with these letters. Then write silly sentences using all the words in each column that end with these letters: *ain, le,* and *on.* Here's an example: "The *captain* is behind the *curtain,* I'm *certain.*"

le	al	on	en	il	el	ain

MASTERY WORDS

Write the Mastery words that end with these letters.

1. el   **2.** al   **3.** en   **4.** on
5. le (two words)

Write the words that have these vowel sounds.

6. /u/ (two words)   **7.** /ē/ (four words)

Finish the sentences with Mastery words.

8. There were eight ____ on a bus. Two got off at the first stop.

An ____ number of people were left.

9. You must ____ 3 to get 6.

10. Three plus two plus seven is ____ to twelve.

> even
> tunnel
> double
> reason
> equal
> people

BONUS WORDS

1. Write the Bonus word that is the homophone for *medal.*
2. Write the Bonus word that has three syllables.
3. Write the Bonus word that is a synonym for *package.*
4. Write the two Bonus words that have double consonant letters.
5. Use the **Spelling Dictionary** to find out where the word *slogan* comes from. Write a sentence about the history of the word.
6. Now write three clues for the Bonus words you did not write. Begin each clue "Write the word…" Then write the three Bonus words.

> missile
> slogan
> rural
> meddle
> parcel
> civil
> abandon
> bargain

23 Compound Words

UNIT WORDS

1. *horseback*
2. *weekend*
3. *cartwheel*
4. *airline*
5. *windmill*
6. *flashlight*
7. *itself*
8. *everywhere*
9. *whenever*
10. *ourselves*
11. *anymore*
12. *cupboard*
13. *barefoot*
14. *nevertheless*
15. *nearby*
16. *waterproof*
17. *underwater*
18. *cloudburst*
19. *notebook*
20. *wherever*

CLOVER LAKE STABLES
❧ 210 Clover Rd., Scottsdale ❧

Horseback Riding Lessons
Weekend Rates $8.50 per hour
Weekday Rates $7.00 per hour
Hours 10-4   456-8907

The Unit Words

Each Unit word is a compound word. A compound word is made up of two or more words. The words are usually written together as one word.

horse + back = horseback
never + the + less = nevertheless

Compound words are easier to spell if you remember the smaller words that make up each compound. Usually, the spellings of the smaller words do not change when they are combined. Sometimes, however, a letter is dropped.

☐ where + ever = wherever

REMEMBER THIS

Cupboard is made up of the words *cup* and *board*. When the two words are combined to form the compound, the pronunciation changes.

cup /kup/   board /bôrd/
cupboard /kub′ərd/

98

Spelling Practice

A. Follow the directions using the Unit words.

1. Add a word from the box on the left and a word from the box on the right to make a compound word. Write six compound words.

water	cloud	cup
our	cart	flash

wheel	board	light
burst	selves	proof

2. Write the two words that are made up of *ever* and another word.

3. Circle the compound word you wrote for **2** in which a letter was dropped when the two words were combined.

4. Write the compound word that is made up of three smaller words.

B. Change one word in each of these compounds to make a Unit word. Write each word only once.

5. everything

6. horseshoe

7. anyhow

8. weekday

9. yourself

10. bareback

11. windstorm

12. airmail

13. undercover

14. storybook

C. Read each sentence below. Write the Unit word that can take the place of the underlined word or words in the sentence.

15. Charlie walked on the grass <u>without shoes</u>.

16. Our baseball field is <u>a short distance away</u>.

17. Cheryl painted the <u>cabinet</u> white.

18. We spent last <u>Saturday and Sunday</u> at the beach.

19. A <u>sudden, heavy rainfall</u> ruined our picnic.

20. It was cloudy, but we went to the beach <u>in spite of it</u>.

Spelling and Language · Adverbs

Adverbs are words that tell *when*, *where*, or *how* things happen.

> *When?* anymore
> *Where?* everywhere, nearby, underwater

Finish these sentences with the adverbs given above. Use each word only once.

1. My best friend lives ____ .

2. I don't need this book ____ .

3. Mindy searched ____ for her gloves.

4. Noel swam ____ for several yards.

Writing on Your Own

Write a poem that tells a story about what one child did on a summer day. Be sure you have a beginning, a middle, and an ending to the story in your poem. Be sure the poem rhymes. You will probably need about ten lines to tell a good story. Use at least one Unit word in each line, and include some adverbs as you write. Read your narrative poem to a young friend.

Proofreading

Read the story. There are six misspelled words. Three words need capital letters. Two sentences need periods.

1. Find each of the errors in the story.

> Last weakend, while tracy and I were exploring an old farm nirby, there was a sudden cloudbirst. We ran inside a windmil that had not been used for years. It was dark inside. luckily we had a flashlite. We were startled by soft, crying sounds. We searched evrywhere, but couldn't find a thing As we turned to leave, we stumbled upon our neighbor's dog. We looked around some more. behind some rusty farm tools we found four newborn pups

2. Write the six misspelled words correctly. Then write the three words that should begin with capital letters.

3. Write the two sentences that need periods.

100

Spelling on Your Own

UNIT WORDS

Write each Unit word. Then write the two or three words that make up each compound word. When you have finished, use the small words to form four more compound words. For example, *under* (from *underwater*) and *foot* (from *barefoot*) *make underfoot.*

MASTERY WORDS

Change one word in each compound to make a Mastery word.

1. grandfather   **2.** football   **3.** bathroom

4. herself   **5.** firefly

Finish the paragraph with Mastery words.

One morning Reggie decided to surprise his __6__ . First he picked up his clothes from the __7__ floor and hung them up. Then he put away his __8__ glove and bat. He quietly crept downstairs. He built a fire in the __9__ . Then he cooked __10__ . Reggie was proud of __11__ . The day was off to a good start.

BONUS WORDS

1. Change the last word in *headline* to make a Bonus word.

2. Write the two words that have the sound /ōō/.

3. Write the three words that begin with clusters.

4. *HQ* and *tpk* are the abbreviations for two of the Bonus words. Write the two words.

5. Rewrite the sentence. Correct the four misspelled words. Then finish the story.

Thoughout the night, my roomate and I hid in the wearhouse hoping to evesdrop on the thieves' evil plot.

Review

Follow these steps when you are unsure how to spell a word.

- **Say** the word. Recall when you have heard the word used. Think about what it means.
- **Look** at the word. Find any prefixes, suffixes, or other word parts you know. Think about other words that are related in meaning and spelling. Try to picture the word in your mind.
- **Spell** the word to yourself. Think about the way each sound is spelled. Notice any unusual spelling.
- **Write** the word while looking at it. Check the way you have formed your letters. If you have not written the word clearly or correctly, write it again.
- **Check** your learning. Cover the word and write it. If you did not spell the word correctly, practice these steps until the word becomes your own.

UNIT 19

quarter
warmth
argue
toward
garden
award
carpet
tardy
warning
guard

UNIT 19 Follow the directions using words from Unit 19.

1. Write the two words that begin with /wôr/.

2. Write the two words with /ôr/ in their second syllable.

3. Write the five words with /är/ in the first syllable.

Finish these sentences.

4. He is shorter than Laura by a ____ of an inch.

5. We could not find seats at the show because we were ____ .

6. They began to ____ about the jar of glue.

7. Our dog loves to sleep on that old ____ .

UNIT 20

turkey
herd
thirsty
purchase
worst
curve
curb
nerve
worm
refer

UNIT 20 Follow the directions using words from Unit 20.

8. Write the two pairs of words in which the first three letters are the same in each pair.

9. Write the three words that have /ûr/ spelled *er*.

Finish these sentences. Circle the letters that spell /ûr/. Use the words from Unit 20.

10. A _____ is a large bird.

11. If you are _____ , get a drink of water.

12. Here is a quarter to _____ a newspaper.

UNIT 21 Follow the directions using words from Unit 21.

13. Write the four words that spell /ər/ with *or*.

14. Write the two words that begin with consonant clusters.

Write these misspelled words correctly.

15. celler   **16.** collor

17. poler   **18.** saucar

UNIT 22 Follow the directions using words from Unit 22.

Write the words that end with these letters. Circle the letters that spell /ən/.

19. ain (two words)

20. on

Write the words that end with these letters.

21. al (three words)

22. le (two words)

UNIT 21
clever
cellar
humor
tailor
collar
mayor
saucer
speaker
polar
inventor

UNIT 22
pupil
apron
hospital
whistle
certain
ankle
pedal
label
medal
captain

WORDS IN TIME

The word *hospital* comes from the Latin word *hospitale*, which means "an inn, or a place where travelers can find rest and food." What does *hospital* mean today? How did the meaning change over the years? The original meaning of "inn" survives in the English word for "friendly treatment," *hospitality*.

Write the word that fits best in each blank. Circle the letters that spell /əl/. Use the words from Unit 22.

23. a _____ in a classroom

24. an _____ on a leg

25. a _____ on a general's chest

26. a _____ on a jar

UNIT 23

UNIT 23 Change one word in each of these compound words to make a Unit 23 word.

27. whereby

28. anyway

29. forever

30. themselves

Mixed up in each sentence are two parts of a word from Unit 23. Underline the two parts. Then write the two parts as one word.

31. I hate to stand in line in the cold air.

32. I saw a light flash in the window of the old house.

33. Crusoe used a board for his table and a shell for his cup.

34. Jessie's job will end after this week.

35. Noah gave Dan a book with a note inside.

36. Match words in the left box with words in the right box to form compound words from Unit 23. Then write the words.

under	line
our	ever
air	end
cup	board
when	selves
week	water

UNIT 23

flashlight
wherever
cupboard
ourselves
notebook
weekend
airline
whenever
anymore
underwater

Spelling and Reading
Story Conversation

Read the following story beginning. Notice how the writer makes the conversation in the story sound realistic.

"Listen, Ashley. There's that odd whistle again," said my older cousin Brian, who was staying with us over the holiday weekend. "Are you certain we're here by ourselves?"

"Dad is in the garden," I said, "and I don't hear any whistle."

"Don't argue," Brian told me. "It sounded like it was coming from the cellar." He walked toward an old cupboard near the cellar door. "There's a flashlight in here. Come on."

"Come on? You always assume I'll just go along whenever you say!"

"I know you. If they ever award a medal for curiosity, you'll get the gold." Brian eased open the cellar door. "Now, do you want to stand guard here at the top? Or do you want to lead the way?"

"I'll stay here at the top. It's dark down there. Listen, I know your sense of humor. If this is a joke, it's one of the worst."

Then, suddenly, coming out of that black cellar, I heard the strange whistle.

Write the answers to the questions.

1. What sound do Brian and Ashley talk about in this conversation?
2. What does Brian say when Ashley says she doesn't hear any whistle?
3. Why does Brian get the flashlight from the old cupboard?
4. What might Ashley say after she hears the strange whistle?

Underline the review words in your answers. Check to see that you spelled the words correctly.

Spelling and Writing
Story Conversation

Think and Discuss

In a **conversation,** the writer gives the characters exact words. These words are written between quotation marks. A new paragraph begins each time the speaker changes. Look back at the story beginning on page 105. Who are the speakers in this conversation?

Writers use conversation to show what happens in a story. What do you learn about what is happening from the conversation on page 105? In the story beginning, the writer also builds a feeling of suspense and mystery. How do Brian's words in the first paragraph add to this feeling? How do Ashley's words in the sixth paragraph add to the feeling of suspense and mystery?

Writers also use conversation to show what their characters are feeling and to make a story seem realistic. Reread what Ashley says in the sixth paragraph. How does she seem to be feeling? In what way does Brian seem to feel differently? What words does the writer have Brian and Ashley say that make the story seem realistic?

Apply

Finish the story of Brian and Ashley for your classmates to enjoy. Use **conversation** to show what happens. Follow the writing guidelines on the next page.

106

Prewriting

Decide what Brian and Ashley find in the cellar. Think about the events they might go through in finding it.

- Make a three-column chart.
- In the middle column, write the events of the story in order. Start after Ashley hears the whistle.
- On the left, note what Brian might say at each point in the story.
- On the right, note what Ashley might say at each point.

 THESAURUS For help finding vivid words, turn to page 205.

Composing

Use your prewriting chart to write the first draft of your story conversation.

- Write what Brian and Ashley say as they go down to the cellar.
- Use statements, questions, exclamations, and commands.
- Build suspense and show how the characters are feeling.
- Look back at the notes on your prewriting chart. Would you like to add any conversation to your first draft?

Revising

Read your conversation and show it to a classmate. Follow these guidelines to improve your work. Use the editing and proofreading marks on this page to show corrections.

Editing

- Make sure your conversation helps tell the story of what Ashley and Brian find in the cellar.
- Make sure your conversation sounds realistic.

Proofreading

- Check your spelling and correct any mistakes.
- Check your capitalization and punctuation.

Copy your conversation onto a clean sheet of paper. Write carefully and neatly.

 WRITER'S GUIDE For help in punctuation, turn to pages 281–283.

Publishing

Have a classmate pretend to be one of the characters in your conversation. Read aloud the conversation with your classmate to the rest of the class.

Editing and Proofreading Marks

≡	capitalize
⊙	make a period
∧	add something
⸝	add a comma
⸌⸍	add quotation marks
⸜	take something away
◯	spell correctly
¶	indent the paragraph
/	make a lowercase letter
∼tr	transpose

25 Synonyms and Antonyms

The Unit Words

The list of Unit words contains five pairs of synonyms and five pairs of antonyms.

Synonyms are words that have the same or nearly the same meaning. *Sorrow* and *sadness* are synonyms.

Antonyms are words that have opposite meanings. *Victory* and *defeat* are antonyms. If you replace *victory* with *defeat* in the sentence below, the meaning of the sentence changes completely.

The game ended in a *victory* for our school.

REMEMBER THIS

There are five syllables in the word *ac ci den tal ly,* but people often pronounce only four. Be sure you write the syllable *tal* when you spell *accidentally.*

108

Spelling Practice

A. Follow the directions using the Unit words.

1. Write the five pairs of synonyms.

2. Write the five pairs of antonyms.

B. The underlined word in each pair of sentences does not fit the meaning of the sentences. Replace that word with a Unit word that has the correct meaning.

3. The game ended in a <u>victory</u> for our school. Our team lost by 36 points.

4. I often sleepwalk during the night. One time, I <u>purposely</u> knocked over my lamp.

5. The tornado nearly ruined our house. Now we have to <u>damage</u> it.

6. Denise was having trouble learning her piano lesson. So she decided to <u>decrease</u> her practice time.

7. The soldiers were losing the battle and were ordered to <u>attack</u>.

C. Each word below is an antonym for a pair of synonyms. Write synonyms that are Unit words.

8. happiness   **9.** alert   **10.** tiny

Spelling and Language · Adjectives

UNIT WORDS

victory
defeat
sadness
sorrow
drowsy
sleepy
increase
decrease
troublesome
annoying
damage
repair
enormous
vast
rely
depend
attack
retreat
accidentally
purposely

Adjectives are words that describe nouns.

extra food   a *crunchy* cracker   a *clumsy* person

Read each of these sentences. Find the adjective. Then write the adjective and the noun it describes.

1. Vast areas in Alaska are covered with ice.
2. There are enormous snowdrifts.
3. The troublesome dogs want to play in the snow.
4. The drowsy cat does not like the cold.

Writing on Your Own

Pretend you are a coach writing a short speech. You want to tell young people about an after-school sports program. Choose three sports and explain how they are alike. Use as many Unit words as you can. Choose vivid adjectives.

 WRITER'S GUIDE   For a sample comparison paragraph, turn to page 269.

Using the Dictionary to Spell and Write

When you write, you sometimes need to know how to spell different forms of a word. In the dictionary, a run-on entry word appears in boldface at the end of the main entry. A **run-on entry word** is the entry word with a suffix such as *-ly* or *-ness*. Each run-on entry word is followed by a part-of-speech abbreviation. Read the entry for *clumsy*.

> **clum·sy** /klum′zē/ *adj.* **clum·si·er, clum·si·est**
> Not graceful; awkward: The *clumsy* man tripped over his own feet. **—clum′si·ly** *adv.* **—clum′si·ness** *n.*

Look up these words in the **Spelling Dictionary**. Find the run-on entries. Write the run-on entry words and their part-of-speech abbreviations.

1. accidental   **2.** enormous   **3.** drowsy   **4.** sleepy

Spelling on Your Own

Write a question that includes the word *victory*. Then write an answer to that question using the word *defeat*. Here's an example: "Is this a *victory* party? No, we are trying to cheer ourselves up after our *defeat*." Write questions and answers using each pair of synonyms and antonyms.

MASTERY WORDS

afraid
scared
above
below
price
cost

Write the Mastery word that has each of these long vowel sounds. Next to each word, write its synonym or antonym.

1. /ā/　　**2.** /ī/　　**3.** /ō/

Read each sentence. Then write the Mastery word that is a synonym or antonym for the underlined word.

4. The price of the airplane ticket was $95.
5. I am not scared of flying.
6. From the airplane, the cars above seem very tiny.

Write a sentence using each of these adjectives.

7. afraid　　　　　　**8.** scared

BONUS WORDS

temporary
permanent
confessed
admitted
exterior
interior
rarely
frequently

Follow the directions using the Bonus words.

1. Write the three pairs of words that are antonyms.
2. Write the two words that are synonyms.
3. The Latin root *exter* means "being on the outside." Use the Bonus word with this root in a sentence.

Complete these analogies with Bonus words.

4. *Enormous* is to *vast* as *admitted* is to ____ .
5. *Temporary* is to *permanent* as *rarely* is to ____ .
6. *Outside* is to *exterior* as *inside* is to ____ .
7. *Permit* is to *permitted* as *admit* is to ____ .

26 Social Studies Words

UNIT WORDS

1. explorer
2. republic
3. justice
4. pioneer
5. freedom
6. liberty
7. tariff
8. political
9. statehood
10. constitution
11. capitol
12. government
13. treaty
14. president
15. amendment
16. continent
17. election
18. congress
19. colony
20. frontier

The Unit Words

For more than 200 years, members of Congress have used the words in this unit in their speeches and documents.

Some Unit words, such as *liberty* and *justice,* come from Latin. Latin was the language of the Roman Empire.

Read the Latin words and their meanings below. Can you find the Unit words that come from these Latin words?

libertas	"freedom"
jus	"right or law"
gubernare	"to steer or govern"
congressus	"meeting"
constituere	"to set up or establish"
res publica	"public interest"
praesidere	"to sit in front of or in authority over"

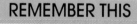

REMEMBER THIS

There's a d<u>o</u>me on the *capitol.* Be sure to write o in *capitol* when you mean the building in which a legislature meets. The homophone for *capitol* is *capital.* Write *capital* with an *a* when you mean the city in which a government is located.

Spelling Practice

A. Follow the directions using Unit words.

1. Write the two words that end with double consonant letters.

2. Write the two words that end with the final sounds in *cashier*.

3. Write the word that is the homophone for *capital*.

B. Write the Unit words that have these base words.

4. explore   5. politic   6. free   7. just

C. Add the suffix *-ion* or *-ment* to each base word to make a Unit word.

8. amend   9. constitute   10. elect   11. govern

D. Add the missing letters to each word. Write Unit words.

12. _ _ _ _ _ nent   13. _ _ _ _ _ lic

14. _ _ _ _ _ _ _ cal   15. _ _ _ _ _ hood

E. Write the Unit word that is a synonym for each word.

16. chief official   17. freedom   18. settlement

19. assembly   20. agreement   21. tax

22. wilderness   23. settler

F. Finish the paragraph using Unit words.

More than 200 years ago, our __24__ was written. It states that a __25__ is to be the head of our government. It also explains that to choose this chief of state, we must hold an __26__ every four years.

Spelling and Language · Capitalization

UNIT WORDS

explorer
republic
justice
pioneer
freedom
liberty
tariff
political
statehood
constitution
capitol
government
treaty
president
amendment
continent
election
congress
colony
frontier

You use capital letters when you write proper nouns. Proper nouns are the names of particular people, places, organizations, government bodies, and documents.

President John F. Kennedy   House of Representatives

Rewrite the underlined proper nouns correctly on a separate sheet of paper.

On April 30, 1789, **(1)** president george washington became America's first leader under the **(2)** constitution. Shortly afterward, he approved plans for the **(3)** united states capitol. In 1800, **(4)** congress met in the Capitol for the first time.

Writing on Your Own

Pretend that a pen pal from another country has asked you to explain how one part of the United States government works. Write a paragraph that could be used for a short research report on the subject. First you may want to check the facts in a history book or an encyclopedia. Try to use the following Unit words: *republic, constitution, government, congress, president,* and *election.*

Proofreading

Read Laura's social studies report. She misspelled six words and forgot four capital letters. Two sentences need periods.

1. Find each of the errors in the report.

America's fronteer was pushed farther west in 1803. Prezident Thomas Jefferson paid $15 million to france for the Louisiana Territory. No one really knew how big the territory was. Lewis and clark were sent to explore the land. The explawrers returned two years later to report on its size and beauty A new movement west began. Pionears made the dangerous journey across the contanint by wagon train. despite the hardships, more and more people moved west to settle on the free land When enough people had settled in a certain area, they applied to the United States congress for stathood.

2. Write the six misspelled words correctly. Then write the four words that should begin with capital letters.

3. Write the two sentences that need periods.

Spelling on Your Own

UNIT WORDS

Make up a history quiz. Write questions, using one or more Unit words in each question. Use all the Unit words. The questions should be about historical events and people. For example: "What was the first English *colony* in North America?" Use your social studies book if you need help. Then exchange quizzes with a classmate. Each of you will write the answers to the other's questions.

MASTERY WORDS

Write the Mastery words that have these meanings.

state
world
family
country
county
village

1. nation
2. the earth
3. small town
4. part of a state
5. part of a nation
6. parents and children

Put the Mastery words in order using this scale. Begin with the word that suggests the smallest number of people. End with the word that suggests the greatest number of people.

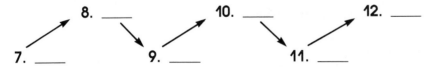

8. ___   10. ___   12. ___

7. ___   9. ___   11. ___

BONUS WORDS

Write the Bonus word for each definition. Use the **Spelling Dictionary** if you need help.

society
agricultural
industrial
economy
commerce
production
manufacturing
irrigation

1. having to do with farming
2. trade
3. making things by hand or machine
4. supplying land with water from ditches
5. the management of money and resources

Follow the directions using Bonus words.

6. Write the word that is related to *social*.
7. Write the four words with four syllables each.
8. Add the suffix *-ion* to *product* and *irrigate*. Then use each word in a sentence.

115

27 Prefixes

UNIT WORDS

1. disappear
2. disobey
3. disagree
4. dislike
5. dissatisfy
6. dishonest
7. refuel
8. repaint
9. rewrite
10. rebuild
11. reheat
12. rewind
13. unpleasant
14. uncover
15. unselfish
16. unbutton
17. unload
18. unlock
19. incorrect
20. incomplete

appear   dis appear

The Unit Words

Each Unit word has a prefix. A **prefix** is a word part that is added to the beginning of a word to change its meaning. Adding *dis-* to *appear* makes a new word that means the opposite of *appear*.

The meanings of the prefixes *dis-, re-, un-,* and *in-* are shown below. Read the chart to help you understand the meanings of the Unit words.

PREFIX	MEANING	EXAMPLE
dis-	"the opposite of"	disappear
re-	"again"	rewrite
un-	"not"	unpleasant
	"the opposite of"	uncover
in-	"not"	incomplete

Spelling Practice

A. Add a prefix to form an antonym for each of these adjectives.

1. honest   **2.** selfish   **3.** pleasant

4. complete   **5.** correct

B. Add a prefix that means "the opposite of" to each of these verbs.

6. agree   **7.** satisfy   **8.** like

9. button   **10.** obey   **11.** cover

C. Finish the sentences with words that have the prefix *re-*.

12. Everyone arrived late. I had to ____ the soup.

13. Let's ____ the room. I don't like the color.

14. After I proofread my story, I had to ____ it.

15. The storm destroyed our barn. We had to ____ it.

16. The plane was low on fuel, so it stopped in Bangor to ____

D. Complete this chart. Add prefixes to base words. You will make some Unit words and some new words. Write the words that go in the chart.

	re-	un-
appear		
load		
wind		
lock		

E. Write the word that can replace the underlined word to make the sentence mean the opposite.

17. My cat is <u>like</u> any other cat.

18. She <u>likes</u> all kinds of fish.

Spelling and Language · Irregular Verbs

UNIT WORDS

disappear
disobey
disagree
dislike
dissatisfy
dishonest
refuel
repaint
rewrite
rebuild
reheat
rewind
unpleasant
uncover
unselfish
unbutton
unload
unlock
incorrect
incomplete

You do not add *ed* to some verbs to form the past. Certain verbs form the past in some other way. These are called **irregular verbs.**

Read the sentences. Write the correct verb forms.

1. My mother (rewrite, rewrote) _____ my list of chores.
2. First I (rebuild, rebuilt) _____ the woodpile in the yard.
3. Then I (kneel, knelt) _____ down and scrubbed the porch stairs.
4. Finally I had to (wring, wrung) _____ out the wet rags.

Writing on Your Own

Pretend that you have bought a kit for building a birdhouse. When you open the kit, you find there are no directions, and pieces are missing. Write a letter to the company telling what is wrong and asking for your money back. Use as many Unit words as you can.

 WRITER'S GUIDE For a sample business letter, turn to page 272.

Using the Dictionary to Spell and Write

When you are learning to spell a word, it is important to know how to pronounce the word. Many words have more than one accented syllable. The dictionary uses two marks to show accent: the primary accent mark (′) and the secondary accent mark (′). The **primary accent mark** shows which syllable is said with the most force. The **secondary accent mark** shows which syllable is said with some force.

Read this sentence to yourself: "I understood what Mr. Underwood said." The word *understood* and the name *Underwood* have the same vowel sounds, but their accent patterns are different. In *understood* the last syllable is said with the most force. The first syllable has a secondary accent: /un′dər·stŏŏd′/. The opposite is true for *Underwood*. Here the first syllable is said with the most force. The last syllable has a secondary accent: /un′dər·wŏŏd′/.

Write the word for each pronunciation. Draw one line under the syllable with the primary accent. Draw two lines under the syllable with the secondary accent.

1. /dis′ə·pir′/
2. /dis′ə·grē′/
3. /dis′ə·bā′/
4. /in′kəm·plēt′/

Spelling on Your Own

UNIT WORDS

Make a list of all the Unit words that are verbs. Make another list of the words that are adjectives. Then write five sentences. Use one adjective and one verb from your lists in each sentence. Here's an example: "Chris had to *rewrite* his *incomplete* report."

MASTERY WORDS

unkind
unlucky
retold
unlike
refill
unhappy

Write the Mastery words that have these meanings.

1. not like
2. not lucky
3. not happy
4. not kind
5. told again
6. fill again

Follow the directions using the Mastery words.

7. Write the word that is the past form of *retell*.

8. Write the two words that have double consonant letters.

Finish the sentences with Mastery words.

9. His bicycle is ____ any I've ever seen.

10. We ____ the adventures we had on our trip.

11. She asked me to ____ her glass with milk.

12. I don't want to be mean or ____ to my sister.

13. The ____ girl lost her lunch money.

BONUS WORDS

impatient
inaccurate
reconsider
disconnect
discourage
reunite
unbelievable
uncomfortable

1. Rewrite this sentence to make it mean the opposite. Replace the underlined words. "<u>Connect</u> the hose <u>to</u> the faucet."
2. Add *ed* to *discourage* and use the word in a sentence.
3. Write the four Bonus words with prefixes that mean "not."
4. Write the two words with the prefix that adds the meaning "again."
5. Write the word related to *belief*.
6. Use all the Bonus words in four sentences.

28 Suffixes

UNIT WORDS

1. graceful
2. hopeless
3. powerful
4. painless
5. helpless
6. sleepless
7. meaningful
8. truthful
9. useless
10. doubtful
11. harmless
12. peaceful
13. fearful
14. healthful
15. speechless
16. endless
17. thoughtful
18. breathless
19. worthless
20. forceful

The Unit Words

Each word in this unit has a suffix. A **suffix** is a word part that is added to the end of a word. The two suffixes in this unit are *-ful* and *-less*. You can add these suffixes to many different nouns to form adjectives.

grace + ful = graceful
fear + ful = fearful

The suffixes *-ful* and *-less* have opposite meanings. The meaning of *-ful* is "full of." The meaning of *-less* is "without." When you add the two suffixes to the same word, you make a pair of antonyms, or words that have opposite meanings. *Graceful* and *graceless* are antonyms. Can you name the antonyms for *hopeless* and *fearful*?

Spelling Practice

A. Write each word with the suffix that means "full of."

1. peace   **2.** meaning   **3.** truth

4. thought   **5.** force   **6.** grace

B. Write each word with the suffix that means "without."

7. breath   **8.** worth   **9.** use

10. help   **11.** speech   **12.** end

C. Write the Unit words that have these meanings.

13. full of power   **14.** without hope   **15.** without pain

16. without sleep   **17.** full of health   **18.** without harm

D. Write a Unit word with the suffix *-ful* that is a synonym for each word.

19. quiet   **20.** frightened   **21.** honest   **22.** uncertain

E. Add the suffix *-ful* or *-less* to the words in ( ) to finish the story.

    I had spent many months building a remote control model airplane and now I was ready to enter my plane in the Owens Airfield Youth Day contest. I was nervous as I watched my model plane take off. It soared in the air, but I was (doubt) __23__ that my (power) __24__ airplane could land safely. My friends were also (fear) __25__ about the final moment. We were (speech) __26__ as we watched my plane near the tiny grass runway at Owens Airfield. But my plane glided to a (grace) __27__ landing without a disaster. The flight was a success and I won the contest! It was a really (meaning) __28__ day for me.

Spelling and Language · Antonyms

Antonyms are words that have opposite meanings. Sometimes you can make a pair of antonyms by adding the suffixes *-ful* and *-less* to the same word. *Harmless* and *harmful* are antonyms.

Add *-ful* and *-less* to each word. Write antonyms.

1. power   **2.** meaning

3. pain   **4.** fear

Replace each underlined word with its antonym. Write Unit words.

5. This broken clock is <u>useful</u>.

6. That <u>graceless</u> skater just won a medal.

Writing on Your Own

Imagine that you and two friends are at the beach. One friend likes everything about the day, and the other complains about everything. Write a paragraph that includes a conversation between your friends. Have one complain and the other answer with something good. Use as many Unit words and their antonyms as you can.

Proofreading

Read the announcement posted on the school bulletin board. There are six misspelled words. Three words need capital letters.

1. Find each of the errors in the announcement.

Join the Salisbury School Physical Fitness Program

We will set up a daily program of exercise for you. We will talk about the value of a good diet. You will learn which foods are healthfull. after a month you will see the results. You will no longer be brethles after a run around the track. you will have developed more powetul muscles and become more gracefull.

If you are doubtfull of the benefits of the program, see Mr. lee in Room 210. He promises that the exercises will be paneless.

---

2. Write the six misspelled words correctly. Then write the three words that should begin with capital letters.

UNIT WORDS

graceful
hopeless
powerful
painless
helpless
sleepless
meaningful
truthful
useless
doubtful
harmless
peaceful
fearful
healthful
speechless
endless
thoughtful
breathless
worthless
forceful

Spelling on Your Own

UNIT WORDS

Each Unit word is an adjective. Remember that adjectives describe nouns. Write each adjective together with a noun. Look at the examples.

<u>helpless</u> baby   <u>endless</u> day

MASTERY WORDS

Add the suffix -ful or -less to each base word. Write the Mastery words.

1. cheer   **2.** taste   **3.** help
4. colorful   **5.** fear   **6.** thank

helpful
tasteless
cheerful
colorful
fearless
thankful

Finish the sentences with the Mastery words. Use each word once.

7. Frank was ____ for his sister's help.
8. My ____ coach showed me how to improve my pitching.
9. My teacher was in a ____ mood today.
10. The banana bread was ____ because I forgot to add the honey.
11. The ____ firefighter entered the burning house.
12. Everyone noticed his ____ shirt.

BONUS WORDS

Write the Bonus word that can describe each of these nouns. Use each word once.

1. mystery   **2.** hobo   **3.** fish   **4.** driver

respectful
reckless
suspenseful
heartless
boneless
faithful
grateful
penniless

Write the Bonus word that is the antonym for each of these words. Then use each word in a sentence.

5. cautious   **6.** bony   **7.** kind   **8.** wealthy

Write the Bonus word that is the synonym for each of these words.

9. thankful   **10.** courteous   **11.** poor   **12.** loyal

123

29 Noun Suffixes

UNIT WORDS

1. addition
2. agreement
3. amusement
4. business
5. confusion
6. darkness
7. department
8. discussion
9. education
10. expression
11. fairness
12. likeness
13. punishment
14. refreshment
15. requirement
16. settlement
17. sickness
18. suggestion
19. tardiness
20. weakness

add + ition

The Unit Words

The words in this unit have three different suffixes: *-ion, -ness,* and *-ment.* You can add these suffixes to words to form nouns.

suggest + -ion = suggestion
dark + -ness = darkness
agree + -ment = agreement

The spelling changes when you add *-ion* and *-ness* to some words.

● Sometimes you must drop the letter *e*.
educate + -ion = education

● Sometimes you must change *y* to *i*.
tardy + -ness = tardiness

☐ In *addition*, you add *-ition*.
add + -ition = addition

REMEMBER THIS

You spell /j/ with *d* in *education*. Keep this sentence in mind when you write the word.
Ed, U must remember to begin *education* with *edu*.

Spelling Practice

A. Follow the directions using Unit words.

1. Write the word that is the antonym for *reward*.

2. Write six more words that have the suffix *-ment*.

3. Write the word that has the suffix *-ition*.

B. Add the suffix *-ness* to each of these words.

4. like   **5.** tardy   **6.** fair

7. weak   **8.** sick   **9.** busy

C. Add the suffix *-ion* to each of these words.

10. confuse   **11.** educate

12. express   **13.** suggest

D. Add the suffix *-ment*, *-ion*, or *-ness* to the underlined word in the first sentence. Write the word to finish the second sentence.

14. The room is <u>dark</u>. The ____ scares me.

15. I <u>suggest</u> we have a party. That's a great ____.

16. She became <u>sick</u> overnight. Her ____ kept her home in bed.

17. Glenda is often <u>tardy</u>. Her teacher has talked to her about her ____.

18. Let's <u>discuss</u> your problem. We can have our ____ tonight.

19. We seldom <u>agree</u>. But we made an ____ to work out our differences.

20. "The law must <u>punish</u> you for not paying your parking tickets," said the judge. "Your ____ will be a $30 fine."

21. His ankles are <u>weak</u>. This ____ kept him from trying out for the track team.

Spelling and Language · Word Families

addition
agreement
amusement
business
confusion
darkness
department
discussion
education
expression
fairness
likeness
punishment
refreshment
requirement
settlement
sickness
suggestion
tardiness
weakness

A **word family** is a group of words that has the same base word. *Fair* is the base word of *fairly, unfair,* and *fairness.* The four words belong to the same word family.

Each of the words below is part of a word family. Write the Unit word that is related to each word.

1. unsettled
2. expressive
3. educator
4. addend
5. amusing
6. darkly

Writing on Your Own

Pretend that you are on a committee to help improve your city or town. Write a letter to the mayor. Explain what you would like to do to make your community a better place to live. Use as many Unit words as you can.

 WRITER'S GUIDE For a sample business letter, turn to page 272.

Using the Dictionary to Spell and Write

When you write, use a dictionary to help you find definitions of both words and idioms. An **idiom** is a group of words that has a meaning different from the meanings of the individual words. For example, *monkey business* is an idiom that means "silly actions" or "foolish tricks." Its meaning is not related to a monkey or a business.

Look up each of these words in the **Spelling Dictionary.** Read the idiom and its definition at the end of the entry. Then replace the underlined word or words in each sentence with the correct idiom.

goodness business addition

1. Emma ate two hot dogs <u>besides</u> a hamburger at the barbecue.
2. We saw a <u>real</u> alligator in the Everglades National Park.
3. We always promise to study hard, but this time we <u>are serious.</u>

SPELLING DICTIONARY Remember to use your **Spelling Dictionary** when you write.

Spelling on Your Own

Write each Unit word. Then divide the word into its base word and suffix. For example, divide *expression* into *express* + *ion*. Next, choose seven Unit words. Write a sentence using the base word. Then write a related sentence using the Unit word. For example, "I can *add* very well. You don't have to check my *addition*."

MASTERY WORDS

kindness
payment
softness
happiness
enjoyment
goodness

Add the suffix *-ness* or *-ment* to each of these words. Write the Mastery words.

1. soft
2. happy
3. good
4. enjoy
5. pay
6. kind

Answer each question with a Mastery word.

7. Did you pay this month's rent? I made the ____ yesterday.

8. Could you tell if Kim was happy? Kim's ____ showed on his face.

9. Did you enjoy the holidays? I had three days of ____ .

10. Is the dough soft enough to work with? The ____ of the dough makes it easy to knead.

BONUS WORDS

examination
readiness
superstition
forgiveness
tournament
encouragement
subscription
judgment

1. Write the Bonus word in which *y* is changed to *i* before *-ness* is added.
2. Write the two words with four syllables each.
3. Add *-tion* to *subscribe*. Write the word.
4. Write the Bonus word in which *e* is dropped before *-ment* is added.
5. Write the word that is a synonym for *pardon*.
6. Write the word that means "a sports match."
7. Find two words related to *examination* in a dictionary. Use all three words in a sentence.

Review

Follow these steps when you are unsure how to spell a word.

- **Say** the word. Recall when you have heard the word used. Think about what it means.
- **Look** at the word. Find any prefixes, suffixes, or other word parts you know. Think about other words that are related in meaning and spelling. Try to picture the word in your mind.
- **Spell** the word to yourself. Think about the way each sound is spelled. Notice any unusual spelling.
- **Write** the word while looking at it. Check the way you have formed your letters. If you have not written the word clearly or correctly, write it again.
- **Check** your learning. Cover the word and write it. If you did not spell the word correctly, practice these steps until the word becomes your own.

UNIT 25

repair
drowsy
attack
sorrow
depend
victory
sleepy
annoying
enormous
accidentally

UNIT 25 Follow the directions using words from Unit 25.

Write the word that is a synonym for the underlined word in each sentence.

1. Naomi remembered the day with sadness.
2. By midnight Gilberto felt tired.
3. That troublesome dog is in the garden again!
4. They rely on Megan to help win the game.
5. The Sahara Desert is huge.

Finish each sentence with an antonym for the word in (   ).

6. Our team's (defeat) _____ made us practice even more.
7. When he raises the flag, (retreat) _____ at once.
8. The baby was (awake) _____ all day.
9. Jason (purposely) _____ dropped the tray.
10. Did Amanda (damage) _____ the clock?

UNIT 26

government
president
continent
liberty
election
explorer
pioneer
freedom
congress
amendment

UNIT 26 Follow the directions using words from Unit 26.

11. Write the words that have these base words.

govern   elect

12. Write the two words that are synonyms. Use the words from Unit 26.

Write the word that best fits each description. Use words from Unit 26.

13. a chief official: a ____

14. a group of leaders who makes laws: a ____

15. one of the first to try something: a ____

16. someone who travels to discover a place: an ____

17. a law added to the Constitution: an ____

18. a land mass larger than a country: a ____

UNIT 27   Follow the directions using words from Unit 27.

In each sentence, write a word that can take the place of the underlined words.

19. Did they all state different opinions about what to do?

20. These figures are not right.

21. I have to copy over these sentences.

22. This report is not finished.

23. Please take the cloth off the table.

24. Joyce is not thoughtless of others.

25. Jamie can make this coin go out of sight.

26. Use the key to open this box.

27. The day was not very good because it was cold.

28. We have to stop to get gas once more.

29. Write the two words that begin with a prefix that means "again."

UNIT 28   Follow the directions using words from Unit 28.

30. Write the two words that are synonyms.

Write the words that are antonyms for these words.

31. certain

32. unthinking

UNIT 27
uncover
disagree
incorrect
rewrite
disappear
refuel
unpleasant
unselfish
unlock
incomplete

UNIT 28
breathless
harmless
thoughtful
powerful
peaceful
meaningful
truthful
useless
doubtful
worthless

Write the words that have these meanings. Use the words from Unit 28.

33. full of calm

34. full of strength

35. full of meaning

36. full of honesty

37. Write the four words that have a suffix meaning "without."

UNIT 29 Follow the directions using words from Unit 29.

Change the verbs below into nouns.

38. educate

39. add

40. require

41. suggest

42. Write two words that suggest the state of being ill.

Complete this paragraph.

Jennifer and Joshua decided to start a __43__ selling sporting goods. Jennifer's __44__ to Joshua was that she be in charge of the special __45__ selling camping gear. They put their __46__ in writing. They did not want any __47__ later over who was to do what.

48. Write the word from Unit 29 that changed *y* to *i* when a suffix was added.

49. Write two words from Unit 29 in which the base word lost the letter *e* when a suffix was added.

UNIT 29

suggestion
sickness
business
requirement
agreement
addition
confusion
department
education
weakness

WORDS IN TIME

The word *business* is the noun form of *busy*. At one time, *business* meant "the state of being active, occupied, or busy." By the nineteenth century, *business* came to mean "a person's occupation, trade, or profession" and "commerical transactions in general." People then found it necessary to create a new word, *busyness*. Why do you think this new word was needed?

Spelling and Reading
A News Story

Read the following news story from a school newspaper. Notice details in the story that answer the questions *who, what, when,* and *where*.

ELECTIONS MOVED TO JANUARY

The December 17 student-body election has been changed to January 6. The student-body president, Felicia Garcia, said the agreement to do so was reached at Tuesday's student-council meeting. The council acted on a suggestion made by the Department of Education.

The Department of Education sent the same notice to all the schools. They suggested putting off all activities that depend on large numbers of students. They stated that about 40 percent of the students have been absent this month due to sickness. Because the reports are still incomplete, the actual numbers may be even higher.

"A December election would be worthless," said President Garcia. "It is doubtful that the government leaders chosen now would really represent the students."

Some people disagree with President Garcia. "It is very annoying," said Lee Preston. "My best friend is running for president. We know he would have a victory next week. This will decrease his chances, and it may increase Felicia's chances of being reelected. I think the council is too powerful. It should not be able to rewrite our election rules so easily."

Write the answers to the questions.

1. What decision did the writer tell about in this news story?
2. Who suggested that the students postpone activities such as the elections?
3. Why do you think Lee Preston would like the elections to be held as originally scheduled?
4. Why did the writer include the quotation in the last paragraph?

Underline the review words in your answers. Check to see that you spelled the words correctly.

Spelling and Writing
A News Story

Words to Help You Write

victory
enormous
government
president
election
disagree
incorrect
unselfish
thoughtful
powerful
meaningful
suggestion
agreement
education

Think and Discuss

A **news story** is a clear, accurate report about a real event. The writer of a news story is called a reporter. Every news story begins with a title, or **headline.** A good headline tells exactly what the news story is about. Look at the news story on page 131. What is the headline? What do you learn about the news story from the headline?

The first paragraph of a news story is called the **lead paragraph.** Here the writer gives the most important facts about the event. The lead paragraph answers the questions *who, what, when,* and *where.* In the news story about the elections, what main event does the reporter tell about? Who is involved in this event? When and where did the event take place?

After the lead paragraph, the reporter adds details about the subject. The paragraphs after the lead paragraph are called the **body** of the news story. Reread the second paragraph of the news story on page 131. What question does the reporter answer in this paragraph? What details in the paragraph help give this answer? Reread the last two paragraphs. What information is given in these paragraphs? Why did the reporter include this information?

Apply

Write a **news story** for a school newspaper about an event in your school or community. Write about an event that has just happened or is still happening. Follow the writing guidelines on the next page.

Prewriting

Choose an event to write about.

- Talk to people involved in the event. Take notes about what they tell you.
- Organize your notes. Make a chart with *who, what, when,* and *where* listed down the left-hand side. On the right-hand side, jot down facts that help answer each question.

Composing

Use your notes to write the first draft of your news story.

- Write the lead paragraph. Answer the questions *who, what, when,* and *where.*
- Write the body of your news story. Add interesting details about the information in the lead paragraph. Include quotations from people involved in the event.
- Write an exciting headline for your news story.
- Look back over your prewriting notes. Do you want to add any details to your news story?

Revising

Read your news story and show it to a classmate. Follow these guidelines to improve your work. Use the editing and proofreading marks on this page to show corrections.

 WRITER'S GUIDE   For help revising your news story, use the checklist on page 265.

Editing

- Make sure all your facts are correct.
- Make sure your lead paragraph tells *who, what, when,* and *where.*
- Make sure you included interesting details about the subject.
- Make sure your headline is interesting and tells what the story is about.

Proofreading

- Check your spelling and correct any mistakes.
- Check your capitalization and punctuation.

Copy your news story onto a clean sheet of paper. Write carefully and neatly.

Publishing

Share your news story with your classmates. Then create a class newspaper to share with another class in your school.

Editing and Proofreading Marks

≡	capitalize
⊙	make a period
∧	add something
⋏	add a comma
⌄⌄	add quotation marks
⌐	take something away
◯	spell correctly
⌙	indent the paragraph
/	make a lowercase letter
∼ tr	transpose

---

31 Word Families

UNIT WORDS

1. entrance
2. enter
3. entry
4. leadership
5. mislead
6. leader
7. careful
8. careless
9. carefree
10. discount
11. counter
12. countless
13. account
14. remove
15. movement
16. mover
17. movable
18. handy
19. handle
20. handicraft

The Unit Words

Each of the Unit words belongs to one of six different word families. A **word family** is a group of words that has the same base word.

Look at the words below. Name the base word of each word. Name the prefix or suffix that has been added to each base word. Then find the other Unit words that have the same base word.

careful	leader	entrance
discount	movable	handy

Spelling Practice

A. Follow the directions using the Unit words.

1. Write the four words that have the base word *count*.

2. Write the three words that have the base word *care*.

3. Write the three words that have the base word *lead*.

B. Finish the sentences with *enter* and its two related words.

4. The music fans crowded around the stage door _____.

5. The fans tried to gain _____ to the theater.

6. But the sign on the stage door read, "Do not _____."

C. Write a word from the *move* family for each definition.

7. able to be moved

8. the act of moving

9. one who moves things

10. take off or take away

D. Finish the sentences with words that have the base word *hand*.

11. Making patchwork quilts is a _____.

12. Debbie can easily _____ the most difficult designs.

13. She is _____ with a needle.

E. Read each of these analogies and see how the first two words are related. Then complete the analogy with a Unit word.

14. *Use* is to *misuse* as *lead* is to _____.

15. *Value* is to *valuable* as *move* is to _____.

16. *Thoughtful* is to *thoughtless* as *careful* is to _____.

17. *Friend* is to *friendship* as *leader* is to _____.

Spelling and Language ·
Nouns, Verbs, and Adjectives

- A **noun** names a person, place, or thing.

- A **verb** describes action or being.

- An **adjective** describes a noun.

adj.   n.   v.

Only a *careful mover handles* my furniture.

Complete each sentence with a Unit word. The base word is given. The abbreviation shows if the word is a noun, a verb, or an adjective.

1. move   We rearranged the (adj.) ____ desks.
2. move   I must (v.) ____ the wallpaper before I paint.
3. count   Joyce opened a bank (n.) ____ with $1000.
4. hand   Ken could not (v.) ____ the hot pot.

Writing on Your Own

Write a book report about a book you read recently and enjoyed. When you tell about the characters, use colorful describing words. Use as many Unit words as you can.

Proofreading

Read Paco's list of things to do. He misspelled six words and forgot two capital letters.

1. Find each of the errors in the list.

> *Things to Remember*
> - *Send in the entry blank for the go-cart race.*
> - *Screw the brass handel onto the dresser drawer.*
> - *Help Dad bolt the movible chairs to the boat deck.*
> - *See the band leider on friday for tryouts.*
> - *Rewrite my social studies report. be carefull to spell the names of presidents correctly.*
> - *Deposit the club members' dues in our bank acount.*

2. Write the six misspelled words correctly. Then write the two words that should begin with capital letters.

136

Spelling on Your Own

UNIT WORDS

Complete the chart. Write the Unit words that have each of these vowel sounds in the base word. Then write a paragraph using one group of related words.

leader
mislead
leadership

/a/ snag	/e/ extra	/ē/ creak	/ou/ doubt	/o͞o/ proof	/âr/ their

MASTERY WORDS

Follow the directions using the Mastery Words.

1. Write the two words that have the base word *run*.

2. Write the two words that contain the word *side*.

3. Write the two words that have the base word *joy*.

Finish each sentence with two Mastery words. Both words should belong to the same word family.

4. Phil dropped his book ____ me on the ____ .

5. The ____ watched a ____ of the film of the race.

6. When Kelly heard the ____ news, she knew she would ____ her day.

rerun
runner
joyful
enjoy
sidewalk
beside

BONUS WORDS

Write the Bonus word for each pronunciation. Then write the word that is related to each.

1. /mā′jər/   2. /mus′əl/   3. /his′tə·rē/   4. /sīn/

Follow the directions using the Bonus words.

5. Write the words that have the base words *sign* and *history*. Then use a dictionary to find words that are related to each.
6. Write the two words that have "silent" letters. Then write the two words in which those same letters are pronounced.
7. Use *major*, *historical*, and *muscular* in sentences.

major
majority
history
historical
muscle
muscular
sign
signature

137

32 Syllable Patterns

UNIT WORDS

1. *hunger*
2. *reptile*
3. *sample*
4. *tangle*
5. *whisper*
6. *swallow*
7. *fable*
8. *jungle*
9. *silver*
10. *grumble*
11. *target*
12. *single*
13. *candle*
14. *blanket*
15. *lantern*
16. *tender*
17. *stable*
18. *sprinkle*
19. *husband*
20. *vegetable*

The Unit Words

The "syllabulator" is a word-making machine. To make a word you must punch two buttons. Then the word will appear on the screen. The first syllable of a word — *rep* — is already on the screen. Suppose you could punch the button for *tile*. Which word would you make?

Each syllable has one vowel sound. Most of the Unit words have two syllables.

Some of the Unit words have two consonant letters between two vowel letters. You divide these words into syllables between the two consonants.

hunger   hun·ger

The rest of the Unit words end with a consonant letter before *le*. You divide these words before the consonant.

sample   sam·ple

REMEMBER THIS

Whether you say /vej'ə·tə·bəl/ or /vej'tə·bəl/, be sure you write the second *e*.

veg·e·ta·ble

Spelling Practice

A. Add one of the syllables in boldface to one of the numbered syllables. Write the words.

dle	tern	der	ket	band	tile	ple	ver	low	ger

1. hun   **2.** blan

3. lan   **4.** swal

5. ten   **6.** can

7. hus   **8.** rep

9. sam   **10.** sil

B. Follow the directions using the Unit words.

11. Write the four words that end with the syllable *ble*.

12. Write the three words that end with the syllable *gle*.

13. Write the word that rhymes with *wrinkle*.

C. How much do you know about dogs? Finish each statement with one or more Unit words. The first syllable is given in ( ) to help you. Then tell if you think each statement is true (**T**) or false (**F**).

14. If dogs could pick their own diet, they would rarely eat a (sin) ____ common (veg) ____.

15. Only extreme (hun) ____ causes dogs to gulp their food.

16. Dogs have keen hearing and can pick up even the softest (whis) ____.

17. If you see a dog standing with body and tail stiff, you may be the (tar) ____ of its unfriendliness.

18. Puppies should not play with small objects because they might (swal) ____ them.

Spelling and Language · Adding *ed* and *ing*

UNIT WORDS

hunger
reptile
sample
tangle
whisper
swallow
fable
jungle
silver
grumble
target
single
candle
blanket
lantern
tender
stable
sprinkle
husband
vegetable

Verbs with *ed* added tell about the past. Verbs with *ing* added can be used with the forms of *be*. Remember to drop the final *e* in a word before you add *ed* or *ing*.

Add *ed* or *ing* to the words in ( ). Complete the sentences with Unit words.

1. The wind (tangle) _____ her long hair.
2. He is (sprinkle) _____ cinnamon on the pancake.
3. I am (sample) _____ your clam chowder.
4. Abigail was (single) _____ out for an award.

Writing on Your Own

Imagine that you are a famous writer about to begin a new book. This one is an adventure about two people lost in a steamy rain forest. Write the first two paragraphs of the story. Introduce the characters and tell something about the problems they face. Use at least ten of the Unit words in the paragraph.

Using the Dictionary to Spell and Write

Sometimes words that are spelled and pronounced the same way are really different words with completely different meanings. When you check the spelling or meaning of such words in the dictionary, you will find a separate entry for each meaning. There is a number after each entry word.

sta·ble[1] /stā′bəl/ *adj.* **sta·bler, sta·blest** Not easily moved or shaken; firm.	**sta·ble**[2] /stā′bəl/ *n.* A building for housing and feeding horses.

Write *stable*[1] or *stable*[2] to show which word is used in each sentence.

1. The tornado destroyed our <u>stable</u>.
2. I had to tighten the loose legs on the table to make it <u>stable</u>.

Look up *swallow*[1] and *swallow*[2] in the **Spelling Dictionary.** Read the definitions. Then write *swallow*[1] or *swallow*[2] to show which word is used in each of these sentences.

3. It is hard to <u>swallow</u> when I have a sore throat.
4. I watched a <u>swallow</u> in flight.

Spelling on Your Own

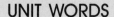

UNIT WORDS

The first syllable of each Unit word is written below in code. To decode a syllable, look at each letter. Then write the letter that comes before it in the alphabet. When you have finished decoding the first syllable, add the second syllable to make a Unit word. For one word, you will need to add three syllables. Here's an example: sfq = rep + tile = reptile.

1. kvo	**2.** ufo	**3.** mbo	**4.** gb	**5.** tjo	**6.** tub
7. wfh	**8.** txbm	**9.** sfq	**10.** hsvn	**11.** dbo	**12.** cmbo
13. ivo	**14.** tqsjo	**15.** tjm	**16.** ubs	**17.** tbn	**18.** ivt
19. xijt	**20.** ubo				

MASTERY WORDS

Add the second syllables and write Mastery words.

1. pur   **2.** fin   **3.** num

4. win   **5.** cat   **6.** mid

Write the Mastery word that . . .

7. names a color.   **8.** names a part of the body.

9. tells how many.   **10.** means the same as *center*.

11. names animals that move in herds.

12. names something you can open and close.

> window
> cattle
> purple
> number
> finger
> middle

BONUS WORDS

Write the Bonus words that are synonyms for these words.

1. glitter   **2.** shake   **3.** huge   **4.** university

5. suitcases   **6.** trip   **7.** bewilder   **8.** vote

Follow the directions using the Bonus words.

9. Write the five words that have double consonant letters. Draw a line between the two syllables of each word.

10. Write the three words that begin with consonant clusters.

11. Write a story with the title "The Case of the Missing Luggage." Use as many Bonus words as you can in your story.

> mammoth
> college
> luggage
> ballot
> baffle
> tremble
> stumble
> sparkle

33 Syllable Patterns

UNIT WORDS

1. robot
2. credit
3. model
4. comet
5. frozen
6. limit
7. profit
8. nation
9. basin
10. private
11. product
12. total
13. basic
14. rigid
15. dragon
16. final
17. chosen
18. petal
19. pirate
20. neither

neither

I am an <u>elmod</u> <u>botro</u>. I'll be an <u>itcred</u> to your house.

Wow-Bow

The Unit Words

There is a short in Botro the Robot's system. Botro and his dog reverse the syllables in every two-syllable word. Can you say the three underlined words correctly?

Each of the Unit words has two syllables. The first syllable in each word is accented. Here are some rules to follow when you divide words into syllables.

● If there is a long vowel sound in the first syllable, divide the word before the middle consonant sound.

robot   ro·bot

● If there is a short vowel sound in the first syllable, divide the word after the middle consonant sound.

dragon   drag·on

REMEMBER THIS

The word *neither* can be pronounced two ways: /nē′thər/ or /nī′thər/. To help you spell the word, remember that the first pronunciation has long *e*. The second has long *i*. Write *e* and *i* together in *neither*.

142

Spelling Practice

A. These first syllables have long vowel sounds. Add the second syllables to spell Unit words.

1. na   **2.** nei   **3.** ba (two words)

B. These first syllables have short vowel sounds. Add the second syllables to spell Unit words.

4. prod   **5.** com

6. drag   **7.** prof

C. Write the Unit words that have these long vowel sounds in the first syllables. Then draw a line between the syllables in each word.

8. /ō/ (four words)

9. /ī/ (three words)

D. Write the Unit words that have these short vowel sounds in the first syllables. Then draw a line between the syllables in each word.

10. /e/ (two words)

11. /i/ (two words)

E. Write the words that end with these sounds.

12. /əl/ (four words)

13. /ən/ (five words)

F. Write the words that begin with the same sounds as these words.

14. baker   **15.** profit   **16.** pilot

17. river   **18.** rodeo   **19.** copy

143

Spelling and Language · Adverbs

UNIT WORDS

robot
credit
model
comet
frozen
limit
profit
nation
basin
private
product
total
basic
rigid
dragon
final
chosen
petal
pirate
neither

Adverbs are words that tell *when, where,* or *how* things happen. Adverbs that tell *how* usually end in *-ly*.

drives carefully   waited breathlessly

Add *-ly* to the words in boldface. Write the words.

private **1.** Mr. Ashike spoke to him ____ after school.
total   **2.** I am ____ exhausted from running.
final   **3.** We ____ decided to take a vacation.
rigid   **4.** Robots walk ____ .

Writing on Your Own

Draw a picture of a robot. Then write a paragraph that tells exactly how the robot looks and works. Use at least five of the Unit words and several vivid adverbs. Give the paragraph to a friend and ask him or her to make a drawing of the robot you described. When your friend is finished, compare the drawings. How well did your description help your friend "see" the robot?

Proofreading

Read Flora's report on robots. She misspelled six words and forgot three capital letters. Two sentences need periods.

1. Find each of the errors in the report.

> A robat may be a perfectly pleasant thing to have around the house Klatu, a modal robot that does basik household tasks, may soon be on sale to the public. klatu has a rigad frame and movable arms. Instead of legs, it has spoked wheels that can climb stairs Klatu can scrub, sweep, make beds, serve meals, and greet guests. there is no limet to what a robot can do. But it only can do those tasks that it has been programmed to do. wouldn't it be wonderful to have your own privat robot?

2. Write the six misspelled words correctly. Then write the three words that should begin with capital letters.

3. Write the two sentences that need periods.

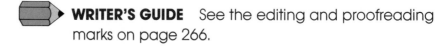 **WRITER'S GUIDE** See the editing and proofreading marks on page 266.

Spelling on Your Own

Use all the Unit words to make a word search puzzle. You can write the words across or down. Fill in the empty spaces with other letters. When you finish your puzzle, let someone else solve it.

MASTERY WORDS

Write the Mastery words that have these vowel sounds in the first syllables. Draw a line between the syllables.

1. /ī/ (two words)   **2.** /ā/

3. /a/ (two words)   **4.** /i/

Finish these sentences with Mastery words. The first syllable is given in ( ) to help you.

5. The (pi) _____ said we would be landing in an hour.

6. This would be our first (vis) _____ to Rexon.

7. The pilot handed us each a slip of (pa) _____ .

8. It read, "Do not touch the plants with purple flowers. The (mag) _____ leaves will make your fingers stiff."

9. "Do not touch any of the (spi) _____ webs. Your fingers will be forever glued to them."

paper
visit
salad
spider
pilot
magic

BONUS WORDS

Follow the directions using the Bonus words.

1. Write the three words that have /ē/ or /ī/ in the first syllable. Draw a line between the syllables.

2. Write the four words that have short vowel sounds and accented first syllables. Draw a line between the syllables.

3. Write the word that has an accented second syllable.

Write the Bonus word that is related to each word. Use one pair of words in a sentence.

4. legendary   **5.** perilous   **6.** silence   **7.** logical

guitar
silent
logic
legend
peril
virus
legal
gravel

34 Three-Syllable Words

UNIT WORDS

1. elephant
2. pajamas
3. electric
4. manager
5. wonderful
6. chocolate
7. artistic
8. remember
9. handkerchief
10. emperor
11. exercise
12. envelope
13. dangerous
14. area
15. serious
16. terrible
17. medium
18. enemy
19. melody
20. favorite

ELETELEPHONY

Once there was an elephant,
Who tried to use the telephant —
No! no! I mean an elephone
Who tried to use the telephone —
(Dear me! I am not certain quite
That even now I've got it right.)

Howe'er it was, he got his trunk
Entangled in the telephunk;
The more he tried to get it free,
The louder buzzed the telephee —
(I fear I'd better drop the song
Of elephop and telephong!)

LAURA E. RICHARDS

The Unit Words

Each of the Unit words has three syllables. Each syllable has one vowel sound. Say *elephant,* and listen for the three syllables: *el e phant.*

When you say a word, pronounce each syllable carefully. Make sure that you say each vowel sound. This will help you spell the word correctly.

You can hear the syllables more clearly in some words than in others. Say these words to yourself. Do you say all three syllables? When you spell these words, be sure to write each syllable.

chocolate   favorite

Spelling Practice

A. The middle syllables of some Unit words are given below. Add the first and last syllables and write the words.

1. ker   **2.** per   **3.** lec   **4.** ve

B. Write *1, 2,* or *3* to show which syllable is accented. Then write the whole word. Check your answers in the **Spelling Dictionary.**

5. ter·ri·ble   **6.** ex·er·cise   **7.** mel·o·dy

8. ar·e·a   **9.** me·di·um   **10.** pa·ja·mas

C. Write the Unit words that are antonyms for these words.

11. awful   **12.** safe   **13.** friend

14. forget   **15.** joking   **16.** terrific

D. Write the Unit words that have these base words.

17. manage   **18.** artist   **19.** danger   **20.** favor

E. Finish these sentences with Unit words.

21. In 1879, Thomas Alva Edison invented the first practical ____ light bulb. His ____ invention continued to burn for 45 hours.

22. The gummed ____ was first used in 1844.

23. In 1882, the London Zoo sold Jumbo, the largest ____ ever seen in captivity, to circus owner P.T. Barnum.

24. In 1906, a ____ earthquake struck the city of San Francisco.

25. In 1877, Euphemia Allen, a 16-year-old British girl, composed the little ____ known as "Chopsticks." So far as we know, she never wrote another piece of music. This piano piece is still a ____ among children.

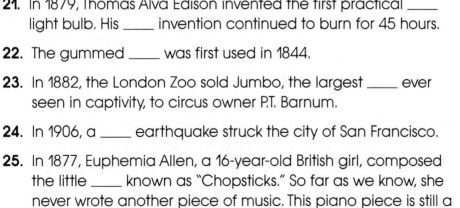

Spelling and Language · Using Plural Nouns

You add *s* to most nouns to make them plural. For nouns that end with a consonant and *y,* you change *y* to *i* and add *es.*

emperor   emperors   colony   colonies

Finish the sentences with the plurals of Unit words.

1. Today most of us use tissues instead of ____ .
2. The store ____ attended a sales meeting.
3. Baby ____ weigh about 200 pounds.
4. Don helped us put all the letters into ____ .
5. I can play all my favorite ____ on my recorder.

Writing on Your Own

Imagine that you have a pet dog that you like very much. For a gift, someone gives you a tiny electric toy dog. Write a paragraph that explains the *differences* between the live dog and the toy. Use as many of the Unit words as you can. Use as many plurals as possible.

Using the Dictionary to Spell and Write

When you write, the dictionary can help you divide a word correctly at the end of a line. First find the word you need to divide in the dictionary. Look at the way it is separated into syllables. Then end your line with as many syllables as you have room for. Do not leave just one letter of a word at the end of a line, and do not start the next line with just the last letter of the word. When you have decided how to divide the word, make a hyphen (-) after the last syllable on the line. Write the rest of the word on the next line.

Read the sentences. Look up in the **Spelling Dictionary** the words that were divided at the end of a line. Check to see if they have been divided correctly. Then write the words that were divided incorrectly. Insert hyphens at the syllable breaks.

1. Sgt. Parker volunteered to go on a dangerous mission.
2. Karen remembered to pack her red pajamas and bathrobe.
3. Swimming and skating are Nick's favorite sports.

Spelling on Your Own

UNIT WORDS

Decide if each Unit word is a noun, an adjective, or a verb. Then write the Unit word in the correct column. You will write some of the Unit words in more than one column. When you have finished the chart, use each adjective in a sentence.

Nouns	Verbs	Adjectives

MASTERY WORDS

idea
governor
yesterday
carnival
suddenly
beautiful

The first and last syllables of the Mastery words are given below. Add the middle syllables and write the words.

1. i·____·a   **2.** beau·____·ful   **3.** gov·____·nor

4. car·____·val   **5.** sud·____·ly   **6.** yes·____·day

Write the Mastery words for these meanings.

7. a festival   **8.** pretty   **9.** quickly

10. the day before today   **11.** the leader of a state

BONUS WORDS

convention
performance
marvelous
sensible
dismissal
numerous
attitude
familiar

1. Write the four words that are adjectives.

2. Write the four words that are nouns.

3. Add *-ly* to *sensible* and *marvelous*. Remember to drop the *le* in *sensible*. Then use the adverbs you formed in sentences.

4. Match each Bonus word that is an adjective to a Bonus word that is a noun. Then use each pair in a sentence. Here's an example: "That was a *marvelous performance*."

35 Language Arts Words

UNIT WORDS

1. noun
2. pronoun
3. adjective
4. verb
5. adverb
6. statement
7. subject
8. predicate
9. vocabulary
10. homophone
11. syllable
12. singular
13. plural
14. outline
15. paragraph
16. quotation
17. fiction
18. nonfiction
19. biography
20. dictionary

The Unit Words

All the Unit words are used in the study of grammar, composition, and literature. Understanding the meanings of these words can help you become more skillful in using language.

Some Unit words are used in the study of grammar.

> pronoun   adjective   noun   verb
> adverb   singular   plural
> subject   predicate   statement

Some Unit words are used in the study of composition.

> outline   paragraph   quotation   homophone
> syllable   vocabulary   dictionary

Other Unit words are used in the study of literature.

> fiction   nonfiction   biography

Spelling Practice

A. Follow the directions using the Unit words.

1. Write the three words that have /f/ spelled with *ph*.

2. Write the four words that have the sound /sh/ spelled with *ti*.

3. Write the five words that name the parts of speech.

4. Write the two words that name the parts of a sentence.

B. Finish these sentences. Use Unit words.

4. The two main parts of a sentence are the ____ and the ____ .

5. *Mouse* is a ____ word, and *mice* is its ____ form.

6. Words of only one ____ make up my baby sister's ____ .

7. Making an ____ first will help you write your report.

8. Is this sentence a question? This sentence is a ____ .

C. Write the word below that describes each numbered word or item.

homophones paragraph adjective noun quotation verb

9 — Our cat Webster has a peculiar habit. — 10
Sometimes he sits on the stairs and stares at the
wall. Webster often cries out or suddenly jumps as — 11
if he's seen something on the wall. But nothing is
ever there. Our veterinarian told us that Webster is — 12
showing how imaginative he is in his play. "A cat
sees a wall as a blank screen," she said. "A tiny — 13
speck of dust on the wall can become a moth or
bird for a cat to grab." She suggested we play — 14
shadow games with our "wall-cat." Shining a
flashlight on the wall will give enjoyment to some
cats for hours.

Spelling and Language · Word Study

UNIT WORDS

noun
pronoun
adjective
verb
adverb
statement
subject
predicate
vocabulary
homophone
syllable
singular
plural
outline
paragraph
quotation
fiction
nonfiction
biography
dictionary

Some of the Unit words come from Latin and Greek. Study these Latin prefixes and words.

PREFIXES		WORDS	
non-	"not"	*fictio*	"the act of making"
ad-	"near"	*nomen*	"name"
pro-	"substituting for"	*verbum*	"a word"

Write the Unit word that comes from each of these Latin words. Then add a prefix to form another Unit word.

1. fiction   **2.** verbum

Writing on Your Own

Imagine that you are the manager of a bookstore. You have an idea about how to sell more books to young people. Write a report to the owner of the store telling your idea and giving three reasons to support your opinion. Use the Unit words *fiction, nonfiction, biography, dictionary.*

 WRITER'S GUIDE For a sample opinion paragraph, turn to page 269.

Proofreading

Read the list of language arts words and their meanings that Juan wrote in his notebook. He misspelled nine words and forgot two capital letters.

1. Find each of the errors in the list.

- *An ajective describes a noun.*
- *An advirb tells when, where, or how things happen.*
- *a noun names a person, place, or thing.*
- *The predakit of a sentence tells something about the subject.*
- *A pronound takes the place of a noun.*
- *A qoutation gives the exact words said by a person.*
- *the subjeck tells who or what the sentence is about.*
- *A silable is a word part that has only one vowel sound.*
- *A virb describes action or being.*

2. Write the misspelled words correctly.

Spelling on Your Own

UNIT WORDS

Write the Unit words in alphabetical order. Then, next to each word, write the number of syllables you hear when you say the word.

MASTERY WORDS

reading
misspell
sentence
writing
plot
stories

Write the Mastery words that have these base words.

1. spell   **2.** write   **3.** read   **4.** story

Finish the conversation with Mastery words.

Jay: I just finished __5__ one of your stories. The __6__ of the story was filled with action. Your first __7__ really caught my interest. "The strange object whirled above me, then sped away."

Lucy: I'm glad you like it. One of my favorite pastimes is __8__ adventure __9__ .

Finish the riddle with a Mastery word.

10. What is needed for a successful garden or a successful book? A good ____ .

BONUS WORDS

literature
accent
publish
dialogue
suffix
autobiography
journal
phrase

Write the Bonus words that have these meanings. Then use each word in a sentence.

1. all written works   **2.** a small word group   **3.** to print and sell
4. ending of a word   **5.** diary of thoughts   **6.** to say with force

Follow the directions using the Bonus words.

7. Write the word that has a prefix added to a Unit word.

8. The Greek word *logos* means "speech." Write the Bonus word that comes from this word.

9. Write a dialogue that might take place in a library. Use at least three Bonus words.

36 Review

Follow these steps when you are unsure how to spell a word.

- **Say** the word. Recall when you have heard the word used. Think about what it means.
- **Look** at the word. Find any prefixes, suffixes, or other word parts you know. Think about other words that are related in meaning and spelling. Try to picture the word in your mind.
- **Spell** the word to yourself. Think about the way each sound is spelled. Notice any unusual spelling.
- **Write** the word while looking at it. Check the way you have formed your letters. If you have not written the word clearly or correctly, write it again.
- **Check** your learning. Cover the word and write it. If you did not spell the word correctly, practice these steps until the word becomes your own.

UNIT 31

mislead
discount
remove
handle
entrance
enter
leader
careful
account
movable

UNIT 31 Follow the directions using words from Unit 31.

1. Write the words that have the base word *move.*

Write the words that have these base words.

2. hand   3. care

4. Write the two words from the same word family that begin with the letter *e.*

UNIT 32

single
sprinkle
swallow
silver
blanket
hunger
sample
whisper
tender
vegetable

Finish each sentence with a word from the *lead* or *count* word family.

5. Let's play follow the _____ all the way to the bank.

6. I want to put money in my savings _____ .

7. I will use my savings to buy things at _____ prices.

8. No one can _____ me into spending my money foolishly.

UNIT 32 Follow the directions using words from Unit 32.

Write a word that rhymes with these words. Then draw a line between the syllables in each word.

9. follow   10. wrinkle   11. example   12. jingle

13. Write the four words that have /r/. Use words from Unit 32.

Finish these sentences using words from Unit 32.

14. I found the last ____ in the garden.

15. Then snow began to ____ around me.

16. The next day a ____ of snow covered the garden.

17. It sparkled like ____ in the sunshine.

UNIT 33   Follow the directions using words from Unit 33.

18. Write the words that have short vowel sounds in the first syllable. Then draw a line between the syllables in each word.

19. Write the words that have /ō/ in the first syllable. Then draw a line between the syllables in each word.

Finish these sentences.

20. This is the ____ week the movie will play.

21. ____ Bao nor Marco wants to see the movie.

22. It will be shown in a ____ room.

23. It's a film about our great ____ .

UNIT 34   Follow the directions using words from Unit 34.

Write each word below. Then write 1, 2, or 3 next to the word to show which syllable is accented.

24. e-lec-tric

25. en-ve-lope

26. fa-vor-ite

27. re-mem-ber

28. choc-o-late

29. ar-e-a

UNIT 33
nation
product
model
neither
private
frozen
total
final
chosen
petal

UNIT 34
electric
remember
favorite
chocolate
exercise
wonderful
envelope
dangerous
serious
area

WORDS IN TIME

The word *remember* comes from the Latin word *rememorari*, which combines *re*, "again," with *memor*, "mindful." To *remember* something is to bring it back to mind, or *memory*. To *memorize* something is to put it in your mind.

Write the words that are synonyms for these words using words from Unit 34.

30. not playful   **31.** terrific

32. workout   **33.** not safe

34. place   **35.** call to mind

UNIT 35 Follow the directions using words from Unit 35.

36. Write the words that have /sh/.

37. Write the words that have /f/ spelled *ph*.

38. Write the four words that have to do with the study of grammar.

UNIT 35

biography
dictionary
paragraph
syllable
fiction
noun
vocabulary
singular
plural
verb

Write either singular or plural to describe each underlined word in the sentences below.

39. Carole has two new <u>kittens</u>.

40. She lets them play with a <u>piece</u> of yarn.

41. Then she gives them a big <u>bowl</u> of milk.

42. Soon the kittens curl up in their <u>beds</u> to take a nap.

Write a word from Unit 35 that goes with each definition.

43. a story about imaginary people or events

44. a book of words and their meanings

45. a group of letters with one vowel sound

46. a word that names a person, place, or thing

47. a group of sentences that develops an idea

48. the words people know and use

49. a story of someone's life

50. a word that shows action

Spelling and Reading
Directions

Read the following directions. Notice the order in which the directions are given.

Stevenson House
DIRECTIONS FOR CONDUCTING TOURS

1. Meet your group at the main entrance to the house.
2. Welcome your group. Tell them that this house was the home of one of the world's favorite writers of fiction. Read them the short biography of Robert Louis Stevenson. Explain that Stevenson wrote some wonderful stories in this house, even though he spent a total of only three months here. Also, mention that Stevenson had serious health problems when he was living here.
3. Before you enter, ask people not to handle anything in the house. Ask parents to keep a careful eye on young children.
4. Remember to tell the group not to go into any area marked "private." Explain that these places are off limits because they are under repair and may be dangerous.
5. Remind everybody that neither food nor drink may be taken inside.
6. Have the members of your group form a single line to enter.
7. Take your group first to the room where Stevenson wrote. Point out the sample page of writing, the desk, the lantern, and the old dictionary. Explain that Stevenson wrote an account of his trip across the ocean at this desk.

Write the answers to the questions.

1. In these directions, where does the writer say the guides should meet their groups?
2. What places must the tour group stay out of?
3. Which step of the directions was written to prevent damage to the house?
4. If you were leading this tour, which step of the directions would you most enjoy following? Why?

Underline the review words in your answers. Check to see that you spelled the words correctly.

157

Spelling and Writing
Directions

Robert Louis Stevenson House

Words to Help You Write

mislead
enter
entrance
careful
single
neither
total
final
remember
favorite
biography
dictionary

Think and Discuss

Directions are the steps you follow to make or do something. For example, you may follow directions to take an exam, bake a cake, or get across town. Sometimes the directions you follow are written instead of spoken. Why might written directions be more useful than spoken ones?

Written directions usually have a title. The title tells you what the directions are for. Reread the title above the directions on page 157. What do these directions tell you how to do?

In any set of directions, the order of steps is important. Look at the first step of the directions on page 157. Why is this step written first? Reread steps 5, 6, and 7. Why must step 7 come after step 5?

Notice that the directions on page 157 are brief and to the point. Suppose step 5 had been written this way: "Look around to see if anyone has brought a sandwich or some orange juice or anything like that. After all, food and drink could really make a mess." Why would this not be a good way to state step 5?

Apply

Write **directions** that tell how to get from your house to your school. Imagine that you are writing the directions for a new neighbor who will be a student at your school. Follow the writing guidelines on the next page.

Prewriting

Think about the way you go to school. Picture each step in your mind.

- On a sheet of paper, draw a map of the way to school.
- Draw a square to show where your house is and a triangle to mark your school.
- Draw a line to show the streets you walk down to get from your house to the school.
- If you take a bus, draw two maps. Show the way from your house to the bus stop on one map. On the other map show the way from the bus stop to the school.
- Label your house, your school, and all the streets on your maps.

Composing

Use your maps to help you write your directions.

- Write each step of your directions in the correct order.
- Make the steps clear and easy to understand.
- Give your directions a title that tells what they are for.
- Compare your directions to your prewriting maps. Have you left out any steps?

Revising

Read your directions and show them to a classmate. Follow these guidelines to improve your work. Use the editing and proofreading marks on this page to show corrections.

 WRITER'S GUIDE For help revising your work, see the checklist on page 265.

Editing

- Make sure your directions give all the steps to follow clearly and in the correct order.

Proofreading

- Check your spelling and correct any mistakes.
- Check your capitalization and punctuation.

Copy your directions neatly onto a clean sheet of paper.

Publishing

Give your directions to a friend or a new student. Ask that person to see how clear they are.

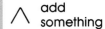

Editing and Proofreading Marks

≡	capitalize
⊙	make a period
∧	add something
⋀	add a comma
ⱽⱽ	add quotation marks
ˍ◦	take something away
◯	spell correctly
⊓	indent the paragraph
/	make a lowercase letter
∿ tr	transpose

SPELLING DICTIONARY

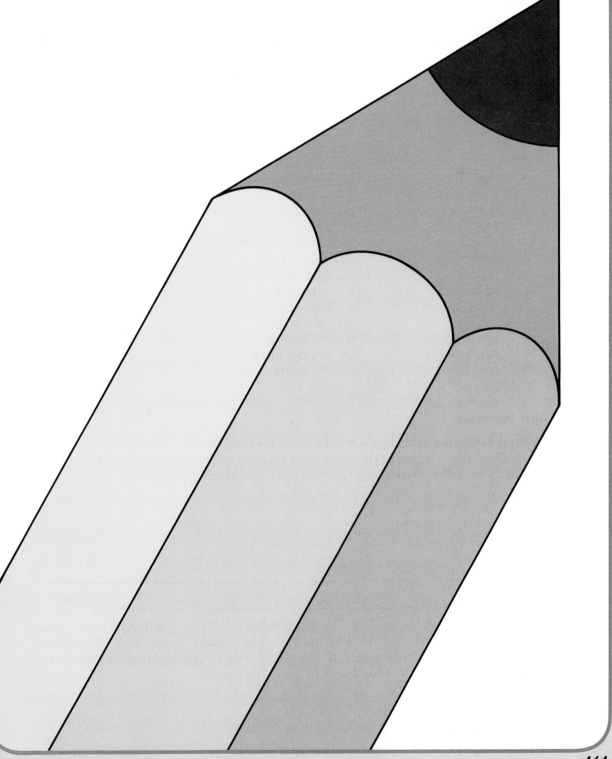

PRONUNCIATION KEY

Remember these things when you read pronunciations:

- When you see parentheses around a sound, it means that the sound is not always pronounced. /at′ə·t(y)o͞od/
- This mark ′ comes after the syllable you say with the most force. This lighter mark ′ comes after the syllable you say with a little less force. /han′dē·kraft′/

/a/	act, cat	/m/	mother, room	/u/	up, come
/ā/	ate, rain	/n/	new, can	/û/	early, hurt
/â/	care, bear	/ng/	sing, hang	/yo͞o/	mule, few
/ä/	car, father	/o/	on, stop	/v/	very, five
/b/	bed, rub	/ō/	over, go	/w/	will
/ch/	chair, watch	/ô/	or, saw	/y/	yes
/d/	duck, red	/oi/	oil, toy	/z/	zoo, buzz
/e/	egg, hen	/ou/	out, cow	/zh/	treasure
/ē/	even, see	/o͞o/	food, too	/ə/	The schwa
/f/	fish, off	/o͝o/	book, pull		is the sound
/g/	go, big	/p/	pig, hop		these letters
/h/	hat, hit	/r/	ran, car		stand for:
/i/	if, sit	/s/	see, miss		a in ago
/ī/	ice, time	/sh/	show, wish		e in listen
/j/	jump, bridge	/t/	take, feet		i in giraffe
/k/	cat, look	/th/	thing, tooth		o in pilot
/l/	lost, ball	/t͟h/	that, weather		u in circus

Word Histories

A word history explains how a word and its meaning have developed. A word history usually gives the meaning of the older word that the modern English word comes from. This sign ► in a dictionary entry tells you that a word history follows.

---

abandon	above

A

a·ban·don /ə·ban′dən/ *v.* **1** To give up completely: to *abandon* a plan. **2** To desert or leave behind: to *abandon* ship.

a·bove /ə·buv′/ **1** *adv.* At a higher place: The clouds *above* look threatening. **2** *prep.* Over: Jim hung his award *above* the couch.

accent

ac·cent /*n.* ak′sent, *v.* ak′sent *or* ak·sent′/ **1** *n.* The stress or force given to some words or syllables in speech. **2** *v.* To say with force: *Accent* the first syllable. **3** *n.* A mark showing where the stress is located in a word, often (′) for a strong stress and (′) for a weaker one.

ac·ci·den·tal /ak′sə·den′təl/ *adj.* Happening unexpectedly: Spilling my glass of milk was *accidental.*—**ac′ci·den′tal·ly** *adv.*

ac·cord·ing /ə·kôr′ding/ *prep.* With *to.* **1** As stated by or in: *According to* Pat, they had already left. **2** In agreement with: *according to* the law.

ac·count /ə·kount′/ *n.* **1** An explanation or description: We gave them a full *account* of our trip. **2** A record of money owed, paid out, or received.

ache /āk/ *v.* **ached, ach·ing,** *n.* **1** *v.* To suffer with a dull, steady pain. **2** *n.* A dull, steady pain.

a·cre /ā′kər/ *n.* A unit for measuring area, equal to 43,560 square feet.

ac·tion /ak′shən/ *n.* The act of doing something: The doctor's quick *action* saved the man's life.

ad·di·tion /ə·dish′ən/ *n.* **1** The act or process of adding: *addition* of fractions. **2** Something added: They built an *addition* onto the house.—**in addition to** Besides.

ad·dress /ə·dres′/ **1** *n.* The writing on an envelope or package that tells where and to whom it is to go. **2** *v.* To write an address on a letter or package.

ad·jec·tive /aj′ik·tiv/ *n.* A word that describes a noun.

ad·mit /ad·mit′/ *v.* **ad·mit·ted, ad·mit·ting 1** To permit to enter or join. **2** To confess: The criminal *admitted* his guilt.

ally

ad·verb /ad′vûrb/ *n.* A word that tells when, where, or how things happen.

ad·vice /ad·vīs′/ *n.* A suggestion made or an opinion given: The coach's *advice* helped me to improve my batting.

ad·vise /ad·vīz′/ *v.* **ad·vised, ad·vis·ing 1** To make suggestions; to give advice: I *advised* her to save money. **2** To inform: *Advise* the staff of the new plan.

a·fraid /ə·frād′/ *adj.* Scared.

a·gainst /ə·genst′/ *prep.* **1** Next to; upon: *against* the wall. **2** Not in favor of: *against* an idea.

age /āj/ *n., v.* **aged, ag·ing 1** *n.* The time someone or something has lived. **2** *v.* To grow old. **3** *n.* A period of time in history: the *age* of computers.

a·gent /ā′jənt/ *n.* A person or group that has the power to act for another: The actor's *agent* got him a one-million-dollar film contract.

a·gree·ment /ə·grē′mənt/ *n.* **1** The result of both sides' agreeing: We were in *agreement* on which movie to see. **2** A contract or treaty.

ag·ri·cul·tur·al /ag′rə·kul′chər·əl/ *adj.* Of or having to do with agriculture or farming.

air·line /âr′līn′/ *n.* A company that transports people and cargo by air: I fly with that *airline* because of their low rates.

al·ley /al′ē/ *n.* **1** The narrow space between or behind buildings. **2** A lane for bowling.

al·low /ə·lou′/ *v.* To permit.

al·ly /al′ī *or* ə·lī′/ *v.* **al·lied, al·ly·ing,** *n.,* *pl.* **al·lies 1** *v.* To join together for a cause or purpose: The United States *allied* itself with England during World War II. **2** *n.* A person or country joined with another for a purpose; a friend: The *allies* made an agreement.

Abbreviations

n. = noun;   *pron.* = pronoun;   *v.* = verb;   *adj.* = adjective;   *adv.* = adverb;   *prep.* = preposition;   *conj.* = conjunction

amendment

a·mend·ment /ə·mend′mənt/ *n.* A change or addition: the first ten *amendments* to the Constitution.

a·mount /ə·mount′/ **1** *v.* To add up; to total: Your bill *amounts* to $10. **2** *n.* Quantity; total.

a·muse·ment /ə·myoōz′mənt/ *n.* **1** The state of being entertained or amused: The seal balanced balls on its nose for our *amusement*. **2** Something that entertains: Listening to music is Gino's favorite *amusement*.

an·chor /ang′kər/ **1** *n.* A heavy object attached to a boat by a rope and cast overboard to hold the boat in place. **2** *v.* To keep in place with an anchor: They decided to *anchor* the boat.

an·cient /ān′shənt/ *adj.* **1** Having to do with times long past. **2** Very old.

an·kle /ang′kəl/ *n.* The part of the body that joins the foot and the leg.

an·noy /ə·noi′/ *v.* To bother.

an·noy·ing /ə·noi′ing/ *adj.* Troublesome; irritating: an *annoying* habit.

an·y·more /en′ē·môr′/ *adv.* At the present time; now: I don't jog *anymore*.

a·part·ment /ə·pärt′mənt/ *n.* A room or set of rooms that make up a dwelling.

ap·ple /ap′əl/ *n.* A round fruit with a thin red, yellow, or green skin: Carla enjoyed having a juicy *apple* as a snack.

ap·ply /ə·plī′/ *v.* **ap·plied, ap·ply·ing** **1** To put on: to *apply* a coat of wax. **2** To put to a particular use: She *applied* her artistic talent to decorating my house. **3** To make a request: to *apply* for membership.

ap·point /ə·point′/ *v.* To choose someone for a job: The President *appointed* new people to his cabinet.

a·pron /ā′prən/ *n.* A garment worn over clothes to protect them. ▶*Apron* comes from the Middle French word *naperon*, "a small cloth."

arch·er·y /är′chər·ē/ *n.* The art or sport of shooting with a bow and arrow.

attitude

ar·e·a /âr′ē·ə/ *n.* **1** Region; section of land: the Chicago *area*. **2** The size of a surface: the *area* of a square.

ar·gue /är′gyoō/ *v.* **ar·gued, ar·gu·ing** **1** To disagree. **2** To give reasons for or against: to *argue* for a tax cut.

ar·gu·ment /är′gyə·mənt/ *n.* **1** The act of arguing; quarrel. **2** The reason or reasons for or against something: an *argument* for a larger sports budget.

a·rise /ə·rīz′/ *v.* **a·rose, a·ris·en** /ə·riz′ən/, **a·ris·ing** To get up; to rise: to *arise* from bed.

ar·mor /är′mər/ *n.* A metal covering to protect the body during fighting.

ar·range /ə·rānj′/ *v.* **ar·ranged, ar·rang·ing** **1** To put things in a particular order: to *arrange* the desks. **2** To plan: to *arrange* to meet a friend.

ar·rive /ə·rīv′/ *v.* **ar·rived, ar·riv·ing** **1** To get to a place. **2** To come.

ar·tis·tic /är·tis′tik/ *adj.* **1** Having to do with art or artists: an *artistic* person. **2** Showing skill and good design: an *artistic* job of decorating.

a·shamed /ə·shāmd′/ *adj.* Feeling shame; not proud.

a·sleep /ə·slēp′/ *adj.* **1** Not awake. **2** Numb: My foot fell *asleep*.

as·sem·bly /ə·sem′blē/ *n., pl.* **as·sem·blies** **1** A gathering of people for a specific purpose. **2** A putting together of parts: the *assembly* of a rocket. **3** Part of the legislature in most states.

as·sure /ə·shoŏr′/ *v.* **as·sured, as·sur·ing** To convince or promise: I *assure* you I'll be home on time.

at·tack /ə·tak′/ **1** *v.* To begin fighting, as in a battle; to hurt. **2** *n.* The act of attacking: The *attack* took us by surprise. **3** *n.* An unexpected illness: a heart *attack*.

at·ti·tude /at′ə·t(y)oōd/ *n.* A way of feeling or looking at things: He has a good *attitude* toward school.

| author | between |

au·thor /ô′thər/ *n.* A person who writes original stories, books, etc.

au·to·bi·og·ra·phy /ô′tə·bī·og′rə·fē/ *n., pl.* **au·to·bi·og·ra·phies** The story of a person's life written by that person.

a·void /ə·void′/ *v.* To keep away from; to dodge: I try to *avoid* fights.

a·ward /ə·wôrd′/ **1** *n.* A prize. **2** *v.* To give a prize.

B

baf·fle /baf′əl/ *v.* **baf·fled, baf·fling** To confuse completely; to bewilder.

bag·gage /bag′ij/ *n.* Suitcases and trunks used for traveling; luggage.

bak·er·y /bāk′(ə·)rē/ *n., pl.* **bak·er·ies** A place where breads are baked and sold.

bal·let /bal′ā′ *or* ba·lā′/ **1** A graceful form of dance. **2** A group that performs this form of dance.

bal·lot /bal′ət/ *n.* **1** A piece of paper on which a voter records his or her choice. **2** The total number of votes in an election.

bam·boo /bam·boo′/ *n.* A tall grass with hollow woody stems.

bar·ber /bär′bər/ *n.* A person who cuts hair.

bare·foot /bâr′foot′/ *adj., adv.* Without shoes or socks.

bar·gain /bär′gən/ **1** *n.* An agreement made about a trade or payment. **2** *n.*

Something sold at a lower price than usual; a good buy. **3** *v.* To try to get a better price.

bark¹ /bärk/ **1** *n.* The sound a dog makes. **2** *v.* To make a sound like a dog.

bark² /bärk/ *n.* The outside covering of a tree.

bar·rel /bar′əl/ *n.* A round container that is flat at the top and bottom.

base·ball /bās′bôl′/ *n.* **1** A small, hard ball. **2** A team game played by hitting such a ball with a bat.

ba·sic /bā′sik/ *adj.* Forming the basis or most important part: The *basic* tools for home repairs are hammers, screwdrivers, pliers, and saws.

ba·sin /bā′sən/ *n.* **1** A wide bowl used to hold liquids. **2** A sink.

bat·ter·y /bat′ər·ē/ *n., pl.* **bat·ter·ies** An electric cell that produces current.

ba·zaar /bə·zär′/ *n.* A fair to raise money for a certain purpose.

beau·ti·ful /byoo′tə·fəl/ *adj.* Lovely; pretty; full of beauty.

bed·room /bed′room′/ *n.* A room for sleeping.

be·have /bi·hāv′/ *v.* **be·haved, be·hav·ing** **1** To act. **2** To act properly.

be·low /bi·lō′/ **1** *adv.* At a lower place: From the roof, I watched the parade *below.* **2** *prep.* Lower than or under in place or amount: I swam *below* the surface of the water.

bend /bend/ *v.* **bent, bend·ing** **1** To make something curve: I *bent* the nail. **2** To stoop or bow.

be·side /bi·sīd′/ *prep.* Next to: My clock radio is *beside* my bed.

be·tween /bi·twēn′/ *prep.* In the space dividing two things: Sometimes, I snack *between* meals.

---

act, āte, câre, ärt;   egg, ēven;   if, īce;   on, ōver, ôr;   book, food;   up, tûrn;
ə = a in *ago,* e in *listen,* i in *giraffe,* o in *pilot,* u in *circus;*   yoo = u in *music;*   oil;   out;
chair; sing; shop; thank; that; zh in *treasure.*

bicycle

bi·cy·cle /bī′sik·əl/ *n.* A vehicle with two wheels, pedals, and handlebars.

bi·og·ra·phy /bī·og′rə·fē/ *n., pl.* **bi·og·ra·phies** An account of a person's life.

bis·cuit /bis′kit/ *n.* A bread baked in small cakes.

bite /bīt/ *v.* **bit, bit·ten** *or* **bit, bit·ing,** *n.* **1** *v.* To cut with the teeth. **2** *n.* The act of biting. **3** *n.* A wound or sting gotten by biting.

blan·ket /blang′kit/ **1** *n.* A large piece of soft cloth usually used to cover a person while sleeping. **2** *n.* Anything that covers like a blanket: a *blanket* of snow. **3** *v.* To cover completely: Dust *blanketed* the furniture.

blast /blast/ **1** *n.* A loud noise: the *blast* of a horn. **2** *v.* To make a loud noise: The music was *blasting*. **3** *n.* An explosion. **4** *v.* To blow up with explosives.

blend /blend/ **1** *v.* To mix. **2** *n.* A mixture.

block /blok/ **1** *n.* A solid piece of wood, stone, etc., with six flat sides. **2** *n.* An area surrounded by four streets. **3** *n.* One side of such an area. **4** *n.* Something that stands in the way. **5** *v.* To be in the way of: The new building *blocks* our view.

blun·der /blun′dər/ **1** *n.* A stupid mistake. **2** *v.* To make a blunder.

blur /blûr/ *v.* **blurred, blur·ring,** *n.* **1** *v.* To smudge; to make messy or unclear. **2** *n.* A fuzzy or unclear image: Until I focused the camera, everything was a *blur*.

bone·less /bōn′lis/ *adj.* Without bones.

book·let /book′lit/ *n.* A small, soft-cover book.

boost /boost/ **1** *v.* To push up or forward: Luis *boosted* his friend over the fence. **2** *n.* A lift.

bot·tle /bot′əl/ *n.* A narrow jar with a small opening at the top.

burden

bounce /bouns/ *v.* **bounced, bounc·ing** **1** To hit and spring back: I *bounced* up and down on my bed. **2** To cause to bounce: to *bounce* a ball.

braid /brād/ **1** *v.* To weave three or more strands together. **2** *n.* Anything woven like this: a *braid* of hair.

break·fast /brek′fəst/ *n.* The first meal of the day.

breath·less /breth′lis/ *adj.* Out of breath; holding breath because of fear or excitement.

bring /bring/ *v.* **brought, bring·ing** To carry to or carry along.

bris·tle /bris′əl/ *n.* Anything made with stiff hairs: brush *bristles*.

broil /broil/ *v.* To cook food near a source of heat: to *broil* a steak.

broom /broom/ *n.* A brush with a long handle, usually used for sweeping.

bud·dy /bud′ē/ *n., pl.* **bud·dies** A close friend.

bump /bump/ **1** *v.* To knock against: I *bumped* into the table. **2** *n.* A swelling caused by bumping. **3** *n.* An uneven part: a *bump* in the road.

bunch /bunch/ *n.* A number of things of the same kind, growing or placed together: *bunches* of bananas.

bur·den /bûr′dən/ **1** *n.* Something carried; a load. **2** *n.* Something hard to

burglar

carry or handle: Working after school was a *burden*.   **3** *v.* To trouble: I try not to *burden* you with my problems. ►*Burden* comes from the Old English word *byrthen*, "to carry."

bur·glar /bûr′glər/ *n.* A person who breaks into a building to steal.

busi·ness /biz′nis/   **1** *n.* A job, profession, or trade.   **2** *n.* A place where things are produced or sold: a clothing *business*. **3** *adj.* Relating to business: a *business* suit.—**mean business** To be serious.

bus·y /biz′ē/ *adj.* **bus·i·er, bus·i·est** **1** Doing things: We're *busy* making the costumes for the show.   **2** Full of things to do: a *busy* afternoon.   **3** In use: Your telephone is usually *busy*.

but·ter /but′ər/   **1** *n.* A yellow spread made from cream.   **2** *v.* To spread butter on.

C

camp /kamp/   **1** *n.* A group of tents or cabins used for vacations.   **2** *v.* To stay outdoors in a tent or trailer.

can·dle /kan′dəl/ *n.* A stick of wax with a wick, or string, for burning.

cane /kān/ *n.*   **1** A stick people use to help them walk.   **2** The woody stem of a plant.   **3** Sugar cane.

ca·noe /kə·nōō′/ *n., v.* **ca·noed, ca·noe·ing**   **1** *n.* A small, narrow, lightweight boat moved by paddling. **2** *v.* To paddle or go in a canoe.

cap·i·tol /kap′ə·təl/ *n.* The building in which a state or national legislature meets to make the laws.

cap·tain /kap′tən/ *n.*   **1** A high officer in the armed forces.   **2** A person in command; a leader.   ► *Captain* comes from the Latin word *caput*, "head."

cap·ture /kap′chər/ *v.* **cap·tured, cap·tur·ing,** *n.*   **1** *v.* To catch; to take

cellar

prisoner.   **2** *n.* The act of catching: the *capture* of a robber.

card /kärd/ *n.*   **1** A piece of stiff paper with writing on it: a birthday *card*. **2** A card used for playing a game.

care·free /kâr′frē′/ *adj.* Without worries; happy: a *carefree* day.

care·ful /kâr′fəl/ *adj.* Cautious; taking or done with care: a *careful* driver.

care·less /kâr′lis/ *adj.* Reckless; done without care or effort: Todd handed in *careless* work.

car·ni·val /kär′nə·vəl/ *n.* A fair or festival with rides and games: They loved riding the Ferris wheel at the *carnival*.

car·pet /kär′pit/   **1** *n.* A floor covering; rug.   **2** *v.* To cover with a carpet.

car·ry /kar′ē/ *v.* **car·ried, car·ry·ing** To take from one place to another.

car·ton /kär′tən/ *n.* A cardboard box or container: a *carton* of milk.

cart·wheel /kärt′(h)wēl′ / *n.* A sideways handspring.

carve /kärv/ *v.* **carved, carv·ing**   **1** To shape wood, marble, etc., by cutting: She *carved* an animal from wood.   **2** To cut meat into serving pieces: She *carved* the roast into thin slices.

cash·ier /ka·shir′/ *n.* A person who handles money, as in a shop or bank: The *cashier* gave me $7.60 change.

cas·tle /kas′əl/ *n.* A large stone building, usually surrounded by a moat.

catch /kach/ *v.* **caught, catch·ing,** *n.* **1** *v.* To get hold of: to *catch* a ball.   **2** *v.* To trap: to *catch* a butterfly in a net. **3** *v.* To find: to *catch* a thief.   **4** *v.* To get an illness: I *caught* a cold.   **5** *n.* The act of catching.

cat·tle /kat′əl/ *n., pl.* **cat·tle** Cows, bulls, and steers.

cel·lar /sel′ər/ *n.* An underground room beneath a building; basement.

---

act, āte, câre, ärt;   egg, ēven;   if, īce;   on, ōver, ôr;   book, food;   up, tûrn;
ə = a in *ago*, e in *listen*, i in *giraffe*, o in *pilot*, u in *circus*;   yōō = u in *music*;   oil;   out;
chair;   sing;   shop;   thank;   that;   zh in *treasure*.

cereal

ce·re·al /sir′ē·əl/ *n.* **1** Grain that can be eaten. **2** A food made from grain.

cer·tain /sûr′tən/ *adj.* **1** Entirely sure. **2** Not just any: I only drink a *certain* brand of juice.

chal·lenge /chal′ənj/ *v.* **chal·lenged, chal·leng·ing,** *n.* **1** *v.* To ask for a contest or fight; to dare. **2** *n.* A dare: They accepted our team's *challenge.*

change /chānj/ *v.* **changed, chang·ing,** *n.* **1** *v.* To make or become different. **2** *v.* To replace one thing with another. **3** *n.* The money returned when a person gives more than is owed. **4** *n.* Coins.

char·ac·ter /kar′ik·tər/ *n.* **1** All of the individual ways of thinking, feeling, and acting that make people what they are: Angie is a person of good *character.* **2** A person in a story.

char·i·ty /char′ə·tē/ *n., pl.* **char·i·ties** **1** Good will and love toward others. **2** Kindness in judging people's faults. **3** The giving of help to the poor, sick, or helpless. **4** An organization or fund for helping those in need.

charm /chärm/ **1** *n.* The ability to delight. **2** *v.* To delight or please: The host *charmed* his guests. **3** *n.* A word, object, or action believed to have magical powers: a good luck *charm.*

check·ers /chek′ərz/ *n., pl.* A game of skill played on a checkerboard by two players. The object is to capture the other player's pieces.

cheer·ful /chir′fəl/ *adj.* Happy; full of cheer.

chem·i·cal /kem′i·kəl/ **1** *adj.* Having to do with chemistry. **2** *n.* A substance

clamp

made or used in a laboratory: Most medicines are made of *chemicals.*

chest /chest/ *n.* **1** The front part of the body between the neck and the stomach. **2** A box with a lid to hold or store things.

chew /chōō/ *v.* To grind up with the teeth.—**chew out** To scold roughly.

chim·ney /chim′nē/ *n.* A brick, metal, or stone structure that carries away smoke from fireplaces and furnaces.

choc·o·late /chôk′(ə·)lit *or* chok′(ə·)lit/ **1** *n.* Roasted and ground cacao nuts. **2** *n.* A drink or candy made from this. **3** *adj.* Made or flavored with this: *chocolate* milk.

choke /chōk/ *v.* **choked, chok·ing** **1** To stop someone's breathing by squeezing the throat. **2** To have or cause difficulty in breathing because something is stuck in the throat.

choose /chōōz/ *v.* **chose, cho·sen, choos·ing** **1** To pick out. **2** To decide to do something.

chose /chōz/ *v.* Past tense of *choose.*

church /chûrch/ *n.* A building where Christian people worship.

cir·cuit /sûr′kit/ *n.* **1** A route that returns to where it began: The race cars made a *circuit* of the track. **2** The various wires, outlets, and switches in an electrical system.

cit·i·zen /sit′ə·zən/ *n.* A person who is a native of a particular country or becomes a member of a country by passing a special test.

civ·il /siv′əl/ *adj.* **1** Having to do with being a citizen: *civil* rights. **2** Having to do with legal matters that do not involve a crime: Divorce cases are handled in a *civil* court. **3** Within a country or nation: a *civil* war. **4** Polite: a *civil* answer.

clamp /klamp/ **1** *n.* A tool used to hold things together. **2** *v.* To hold in place as with a clamp.

class	comic

class /klas/ *n.* **1** A group of students who are taught together. **2** People or things alike in some way: Reptiles are one *class* of animals.

clev·er /klev′ər/ *adj.* **1** Showing skill: a *clever* idea. **2** Very smart; bright: A chimpanzee is a *clever* animal.

climb /klīm/ **1** *v.* To go up. **2** *v.* To go down, over, or into. **3** *n.* The act of climbing.

clos·et /kloz′it/ *n.* A small room where things are stored on hangers or shelves.

cloud·burst /kloud′bûrst′/ *n.* A sudden, heavy rainfall.

club /klub/ *n.* **1** A heavy stick. **2** A stick used to hit a ball: a golf *club*. **3** A group of people who join together: a drama *club*.

clum·sy /klum′zē/ *adj.* **clum·si·er, clum·si·est** Not graceful; awkward. —**clum′si·ly** *adv.*—**clum′si·ness** *n.*

coal /kōl/ *n.* **1** A black mineral made mostly of carbon, used as fuel. **2** A hot, glowing piece of coal or wood.

coast /kōst/ **1** *n.* Land by or near the ocean. **2** *v.* To roll or slide down a slope without the use of force.

coast·al /kōs′təl/ *adj.* Of or along a coast: *coastal* waters.

coax /kōks/ *v.* To persuade gently and sweetly.

co·coa /kō′kō/ *n.* **1** Chocolate powder made from cacao beans. **2** A hot drink made with this powder.

code /kōd/ *n., v.* **cod·ed, cod·ing** **1** *n.* A set of letters, words, or symbols, used in sending messages. **2** *v.* To put a message into code.

coin /koin/ *n.* A piece of metal stamped by a government for use as money.

col·lapse /kə·laps′/ *v.* **col·lapsed, col·laps·ing,** *n.* **1** *v.* To fall in or apart. **2** *v.* To fail: The business *collapsed*.

3 *v.* To become weak; to break down: to *collapse* from the heat. **4** *n.* The act of collapsing: the *collapse* of a roof.

col·lar /kol′ər/ *n.* **1** A fold of cloth that goes around your neck: The dress has a white *collar*. **2** A band put on an animal's neck.

col·lect /kə·lekt′/ *v.* **1** To gather together: to *collect* rocks. **2** To bring together for study or as a hobby: to *collect* stamps. **3** To ask or receive payments: to *collect* dues.

col·lege /kol′ij/ *n.* A school of higher learning, usually entered after graduating from high school.

col·o·ny /kol′ə·nē/ *n., pl.* **col·o·nies** **1** A group of people who left their own country to settle somewhere else; a settlement. **2** A land that is ruled by another country.

col·or·ful /kul′ər·fəl/ *adj.* Full of colors: a *colorful* sunset.

com·et /kom′it/ *n.* A bright heavenly body, with a tail of gaseous elements, that moves in orbit around the sun.

com·ic /kom′ik/ **1** *adj.* Funny. **2** *n.* (*pl.*) A series of drawings that often tell a funny story.

---

act, āte, câre, ärt;   egg, ēven;   if, īce;   on, ōver, ôr;   bŏŏk, fōōd;   up, tûrn;
ə = a in *ago*, e in *listen*, i in *giraffe*, o in *pilot*, u in *circus*;   yōō = u in *music*;   oil;   out;
chair; sing; shop; thank; that; zh in *treasure*.

commerce

crack

com·merce /kom′ərs/ *n.* The exchange or buying and selling of goods, especially between nations; trade.

com·mit·tee /kə·mit′ē/ *n.* A group of people who volunteer or are chosen to do specific things.

com·plain /kəm·plān′/ *v.* **1** To find fault with; to grumble. **2** To report something wrong to a person in authority.

con·ceal /kən·sēl′/ *v.* **1** To put out of sight; to hide. **2** To keep secret.

con·cern /kən·sûrn′/ **1** *v.* To have to do with. **2** *n.* Anything that relates to one; affair; business. **3** *v.* To be interested in. **4** *v.* To worry. **5** *n.* A worry.

con·cert /kon′sûrt/ *n.* A musical performance or program.

con·fess /kən·fes′/ *v.* To admit (guilt, love, shame, etc.).

con·fine /kən·fīn′/ *v.* **con·fined, con·fin·ing** To keep from going out; to limit: She was *confined* to bed.

con·fu·sion /kən·fyoo′zhən/ *n.* A mixed-up or disordered state of mind or of things.

con·gress /kong′gris/ *n.* An assembly of people chosen or elected to make laws.

con·sti·tu·tion /kon′stə·t(y)oo′shən/ *n.* A document setting forth the basic laws by which a country or organization is governed.

con·sum·er /kən·soo′mər/ *n.* A person who uses goods and services.

con·ti·nent /kon′tə·nənt/ *n.* One of the major land areas of the earth; Europe, Asia, Africa, Australia, North America, South America, or Antarctica.

con·tin·ue /kən·tin′yoo/ *v.* **con·tin·ued, con·tin·u·ing** **1** To keep on. **2** To go on again after a pause or break.

con·ven·tion /kən·ven′shən/ *n.* A large meeting held for a specific purpose: a political *convention*.

cop·y /kop′ē/ *n., pl.* **cop·ies,** *v.* **cop·ied, cop·y·ing** **1** *n.* One thing that looks just like another. **2** *n.* One of many things made at one time: a *copy* of a magazine. **3** *v.* To make a copy: I *copied* over my report. **4** *v.* To imitate.

cost /kôst/ *n., v.* **cost, cost·ing** **1** *n.* The amount someone charges or pays for something. **2** *v.* To have as its price: The game *costs* $4.00.

couch /kouch/ *n.* A piece of furniture for sitting or sleeping; sofa.

coun·ter /koun′tər/ *n.* **1** A long table on which things, especially food or goods, are put. **2** A chip used for counting or keeping score.

count·less /kount′lis/ *adj.* Too many to be counted: I've had *countless* meals in the school cafeteria.

coun·try /kun′trē/ *n., pl.* **coun·tries** **1** A nation. **2** The land outside of cities and towns.

coun·ty /koun′tē/ *n., pl.* **coun·ties** An administrative area within a state.

cov·er /kuv′ər/ **1** *n.* Anything put over something else: a *cover* on the pot. **2** *v.* To be put over or to put something over: to *cover* with a blanket.

cow·ard /kou′ərd/ *n.* A fearful person; a person with no courage.

cow·er /kou′ər/ *v.* To crouch in fear: The cat *cowered* under the chair.

co·zy /kō′zē/ *adj.* **co·zi·er, co·zi·est** Warm and comfortable.

crack /krak/ **1** *n.* A narrow break: a *crack* in a glass. **2** *v.* To break or split apart: to *crack* ice.

crank

crank /krangk/ **1** *n.* A handle for turning that makes a machine work. **2** *v.* To turn using a crank. **3** *n.* A grouchy person.

crash /krash/ **1** *n.* A loud noise. **2** *n.* One thing hitting something else. **3** *v.* To hit, making a loud noise.

creak /krēk/ **1** *v.* To make a squeaking sound. **2** *n.* A sharp, squeaking sound.

cred·it /kred'it/ *n.* Payment over a number of months or years.

crew /krōō/ *n.* **1** A group of people who work on a ship. **2** Any group of people working together: a construction *crew.*

crook /krŏŏk/ *n.* A bend or curve.

crop /krop/ *n.* Something that is grown on a farm: a *crop* of potatoes.

cross /krôs/ **1** *n.* A mark made with two straight lines: +. **2** *v.* To go to the other side: *Cross* the street. **3** *v.* To draw a line through: *Cross* your *t's.* **4** *v.* To put or lay across: *Cross* your fingers. **5** *adj.* Angry.

crunch·y /krun'chē/ *adj.* **crunch·i·er, crunch·i·est** Crisp.

crust /krust/ *n.* **1** The outer part of bread. **2** The shell or cover of a pie.

crutch /kruch/ *n.* A support used to help an injured person walk.

cul·ture /kul'chər/ *n.* The way of life of a group of people.

cun·ning /kun'ing/ **1** *adj.* Clever or tricky. **2** *n.* Cleverness or slyness.

cup·board /kub'ərd/ *n.* A cabinet where dishes or food is kept.

curb /kûrb/ *n.* The raised edge of a street.

cur·tain /kûr'tən/ *n.* **1** Cloth hung at a window, door, or opening. **2** Cloth used to hide a stage from the audience.

curve /kûrv/ *n., v.* **curved, cur·ving** **1** *n.* A line that is part of a circle. **2** *n.* Something having the shape of a curve: a *curve* in the path. **3** *v.* To bend: The road *curves* to the left.

cus·tom·er /kus'təm·ər/ *n.* A buyer of goods or services.

decide

D

dai·ly /dā'lē/ *adj., adv.* Once a day: a *daily* task; I brush my hair *daily.*

dai·sy /dā'zē/ *n., pl.* **dai·sies** A flower with a round yellow center and white petals.

dam·age /dam'ij/ *n., v.* **dam·aged, dam·ag·ing** **1** *n.* Harm or injury. **2** *v.* To do or cause damage: The frost *damaged* the orange crop.

dance /dans/ *v.* **danced, danc·ing,** *n.* **1** *v.* To move in time to music. **2** *n.* A set of steps for dancing: a square *dance.* **3** *n.* A party where people dance.

dan·ger /dān'jər/ *n.* Something that can hurt or cause damage.

dan·ger·ous /dān'jər·əs/ *adj.* Not safe; able to cause harm.

dark·ness /därk'nis/ *n.* The condition of being dark or without light.

deaf /def/ *adj.* Not able to hear completely or in part.

deal·er /dē'lər/ *n.* **1** A person who buys and sells things. **2** A person who gives out playing cards in a game.

de·bate /di·bāt'/ *v.* **de·bat·ed, de·bat·ing,** *n.* **1** *v.* To give reasons for or against; to argue; to consider: We are *debating* about an after-school sports program. **2** *n.* The act of debating: a *debate* between candidates.

debt /det/ *n.* **1** Something that is owed by one person to another: a *debt* of $500. **2** The condition of owing: in *debt* to a bank.

de·cide /di·sīd'/ *v.* **de·cid·ed, de·cid·ing** To make up your mind.

---

act, āte, câre, ärt; egg, ēven; if, īce; on, ōver, ôr; bŏŏk, fōōd; up, tûrn;
ə = a in *ago,* e in *listen,* i in *giraffe,* o in *pilot,* u in *circus;* yōō = u in *music;* oil; out;
chair; si**ng**; **sh**op; **th**ank; **th**at; **zh** in *treasure.*

deck

deck /dek/ *n.* **1** The floor of a ship. **2** A pack of playing cards.

dec·o·rate /dek′ə·rāt/ *v.* **dec·o·rat·ed, dec·o·rat·ing** **1** To make something look beautiful; to trim: to *decorate* a Christmas tree. **2** To paint or add new furniture to (as a room or house).

de·crease /*v.* di·krēs′, *n.* dē′krēs *or* di·krēs′/ *v.* **de·creased, de·creas·ing,** *n.* **1** *v.* To make or become less: The cost of bread has *decreased*. **2** *n.* A reduction: a *decrease* in service.

de·feat /di·fēt′/ **1** *v.* To beat an enemy or opponent: Our baseball team has *defeated* every team in the league. **2** *n.* A victory: the Royals' *defeat* of the Tigers. **3** *n.* A loss: This was our first *defeat* after ten wins.

de·fend /di·fend′/ *v.* **1** To protect. **2** To give reasons in support of: to *defend* an opinion. **3** To act as a lawyer for an accused person.

de·lay /di·lā′/ **1** *v.* To make late: The bad weather *delayed* our flight for four hours. **2** *v.* To put off until later. **3** *n.* The act of delaying.

de·li·cious /di·lish′əs/ *adj.* Tasty.

dent /dent/ **1** *n.* A part of a hard surface that has been pushed in by a blow or by pressure: a *dent* in the car. **2** *v.* To make or get a dent.

de·ny /di·nī′/ *v.* **de·nied, de·ny·ing** To say that something is not true.

de·part·ment /di·pärt′mənt/ *n.* A separate part of a larger whole, as of a company, store, or college: the jewelry *department*.

de·pend /di·pend′/ *v.* To put trust in; to rely: to *depend* on a friend.

de·sire /di·zīr′/ *v.* **de·sired, de·sir·ing,** *n.* **1** *v.* To wish; to want. **2** *n.* A wish; a want.

desk /desk/ *n.* A table with drawers, used for writing or studying.

des·sert /di·zûrt′/ *n.* A sweet food that is served at the end of a meal.

disapprove

de·vour /di·vour′/ **1** *v.* To eat greedily: The pigeons *devoured* the bread crumbs. **2** To destroy: The fire *devoured* every store on the street.

di·a·logue /dī′ə·lôg′ *or* dī′ə·log′/ *n.* Conversation involving two or more speakers, as in a book or play.

di·a·ry /dī′(ə·)rē/ *n., pl.* **di·a·ries** **1** A record kept daily of what you do or think about. **2** A book for keeping such a record.

dic·tion·ar·y /dik′shən·er′ē/ *n., pl.* **dic·tion·ar·ies** A book of words and their meanings in alphabetical order.

dif·fi·cult /dif′ə·kult *or* dif′ə·kəlt/ *adj.* Hard to do or understand.

dim /dim/ *adj.* **dim·mer, dim·mest,** *v.* **dimmed, dim·ming** **1** *adj.* Not bright: a *dim* light. **2** *adj.* Not clearly seen: I see a *dim* outline of a cabin. **3** *v.* To make or grow dim.

din·ner /din′ər/ *n.* The main meal of the day; supper.

di·rec·tion /di·rek′shən *or* dī·rek′shən/ *n.* **1** *(usually pl.)* Instructions. **2** The line along which anything moves, faces, or lies: He gave me a ride because he was going in my *direction*.

dis·a·gree /dis′ə·grē′/ *v.* **dis·a·greed, dis·a·gree·ing** **1** To fail to agree: We *disagree* on the answer. **2** To argue.

dis·ap·pear /dis′ə·pir′/ *v.* To pass out of sight; to vanish: My brother *disappeared* in the crowd.

dis·ap·prove /dis′ə·proov′/ *v.* **dis·ap·proved, dis·ap·prov·ing** To think of something as bad or wrong.

disconnect

dis·con·nect /dis′kə·nekt′/ *v.* To break the connection between; to separate; to unplug: to *disconnect* the TV.

dis·count /dis′kount/ **1** *n.* An amount subtracted from the real cost: a twenty-percent *discount* on all books. **2** *v.* To subtract or reduce a part of the cost.

dis·cour·age /dis·kûr′ij/ *v.* **dis·cour·aged, dis·cour·ag·ing** To cause to lose courage, hope, or confidence.

dis·cus·sion /dis·kush′ən/ *n.* The act of talking over; an exchange of ideas.

dis·hon·est /dis·on′ist/ *adj.* Not honest, as someone who lies or cheats.

dis·like /dis·līk′/ *v.* **dis·liked, dis·lik·ing** To find unpleasant: I *dislike* sour fruit.

dis·may /dis·mā′/ **1** *n.* A feeling of alarm or disappointment: Drew watched the boat sink with *dismay*. **2** *v.* To fill with alarm or diappointment: She was *dismayed* to learn that she had lost.

dis·miss·al /dis·mis′əl/ *n.* **1** The act of sending away: We had an early *dismissal* because of snow. **2** The act of firing someone from a job.

dis·o·bey /dis′ə·bā′/ *v.* To be unwilling or fail to obey.

drain

dis·play /dis·plā′/ **1** *v.* To exhibit or show: to *display* artwork. **2** *n.* A show or exhibit for the public: Anna enjoyed looking at the colorful window *display*.

dis·sat·is·fy /dis·sat′is·fī/ *v.* **dis·sat·is·fied, dis·sat·is·fy·ing** To fail to satisfy; to leave discontented: We were *dissatisfied* with our photos.

dis·tance /dis′təns/ *n.* **1** The amount of space between two points: a *distance* of two miles. **2** A place far off: I can see an airplane in the *distance*.

diz·zy /diz′ē/ *adj.* **diz·zi·er, diz·zi·est** Having the feeling that your head is spinning and you're about to fall. —**diz′zi·ly** *adv.* —**diz′zi·ness** *n.*

don·key /dong′kē *or* dung′kē/ *n.* An animal like a horse but smaller, with longer ears and a shorter mane.

dou·ble /dub′əl/ *adj., v.* **dou·bled, dou·bling 1** *adj.* Twice as much; twice as large: a *double* ice cream cone. **2** *adj.* Having two parts: I cooked pudding in a *double* boiler. **3** *v.* To make twice as great: The coach *doubled* our practice time one week before the big game.

doubt /dout/ **1** *v.* To be unsure or uncertain: I *doubt* that he will come. **2** *n.* The condition of being unsure: The outcome was in *doubt*.

doubt·ful /dout′fəl/ *adj.* Having doubt; unsure.

draft /draft/ *n.* A flow of air: Close the window because I feel a *draft*.

drag·on /drag′ən/ *n.* A huge beast, in legend, with wings and claws, that often breathes fire.

drain /drān/ **1** *v.* To draw off a liquid slowly: We *drained* water from the pond. **2** *v.* To empty a liquid from something: to *drain* a sink. **3** *n.* A pipe that allows a liquid to be carried off.

---

act, āte, câre, ärt;   egg, ēven;   if, īce;   on, ōver, ôr;   bŏŏk, fōōd;   up, tûrn;
ə = a in *ago*, e in *listen*, i in *giraffe*, o in *pilot*, u in *circus*;   yōō = u in *music*;   oil;   out;
chair; sing; shop; thank; that; zh in *treasure*.

draw

draw /drô/ *v.* **drew, drawn, draw·ing** To make a picture with a pencil or crayon.

drew /drōō/ *v.* Past tense of *draw.*

drift /drift/ **1** *v.* To move or float along in water or air. **2** *n.* Snow or sand piled or heaped up by the wind.

driz·zle /driz′əl/ *v.* **driz·zled, driz·zling,** *n.* **1** *v.* To rain lightly but continuously. **2** *n.* A light, continuous rain; mist.

drop /drop/ *n., v.* **dropped, drop·ping 1** *n.* A tiny amount of liquid: a *drop* of water. **2** *v.* To fall or let fall. **3** *v.* To leave out: *Drop* the e in *taste* before you add ing.

drow·sy /drou′zē/ *adj.* **drow·si·er, drow·si·est** Sleepy: The long bus ride made me *drowsy.* —**drow′si·ly** *adv.* —**drow′si·ness** *n.*

dusk /dusk/ *n.* The time just before night falls; the opposite of *dawn.*

dust /dust/ **1** *n.* Tiny pieces of dirt. **2** *v.* To wipe away dust.

dwarf /dwôrf/ *n.* A person, animal, or plant much smaller than normal size.

dwell /dwel/ *v.* To live or make your home: Birds *dwell* in trees.

E

ea·sel /ē′zəl/ *n.* A three-legged frame with a narrow ledge, used to hold an artist's canvas.

eaves·drop /ēvz′drop′/ *v.* **eaves·dropped, eaves·drop·ping** To listen in on a conversation secretly.

e·con·o·my /i·kon′ə·mē/ *n., pl.* **e·con·o·mies 1** Use of money or other resources in a way that avoids waste. **2** The management of money and resources: Our new president promises to improve the nation's *economy.*

ed·i·tor /ed′i·tər/ *n.* **1** A person who edits or prepares stories and articles for publication. **2** A person who runs a newspaper or a magazine.

enjoyable

ed·u·ca·tion /ej′ōō·kā′shən/ *n.* **1** The act of learning or gaining knowledge. **2** The knowledge and skills gained from being educated.

e·lect /i·lekt′/ *v.* **1** To select for an office by voting: We *elect* a mayor every four years. **2** To decide.

e·lec·tion /i·lek′shən/ *n.* **1** The selection of a person for an office or an honor by voting. **2** A choice.

e·lec·tric /i·lek′trik/ *adj.* **1** Made of or having to do with electricity: an *electric* light. **2** Producing or transmitting electricity: an *electric* current. **3** Operated by electricity: an *electric* guitar.

el·e·phant /el′ə·fənt/ *n.* The largest of all land animals, having a very long snout, or trunk, and two ivory tusks.

else /els/ **1** *adj.* Other; besides: I won't eat anything *else.* **2** *adv.* Otherwise: Leave now, or *else* you'll be late.

em·bar·rass /im·bar′əs/ *v.* To make self-conscious or uncomfortable.

em·blem /em′bləm/ *n.* **1** A symbol that stands for an idea, belief, nation, etc.: The eagle is an *emblem* of the United States. **2** A badge with an emblem on it.

em·per·or /em′pər·ər/ *n.* The ruler of an empire.

em·ploy /im·ploi′/ *v.* To give work and pay to.

en·cour·age·ment /in·kûr′ij·mənt/ *n.* Something that gives confidence; the act of giving confidence.

end·less /end′lis/ *adj.* Having no end; lasting or going on without stopping: This road seems *endless.*

en·e·my /en′ə·mē/ *n., pl.* **en·e·mies 1** A person or country that tries to harm or fight another. **2** Anything that harms: Some insects are *enemies* of crops.

en·joy /in·joi′/ *v.* To take pleasure in: I *enjoy* playing checkers.

en·joy·a·ble /in·joi′ə·bəl/ *adj.* Pleasant; satisfying.

enjoyment

en·joy·ment /in·joi′mənt/ *n.* Pleasure; delight: We found *enjoyment* in caring for our neighbors' cats.

e·nor·mous /i·nôr′məs/ *adj.* Very large; huge; vast.—**e·nor′mous·ly** *adv.*

en·ter /en′tər/ *v.* **1** To come in or go into. **2** To join or participate.

en·tire /in·tīr′/ *adj.* In all its parts; whole: the *entire* class.

en·trance /en′trəns/ *n.* **1** A door or gate for entering. **2** The act of entering: a sudden *entrance*.

en·try /en′trē/ *n., pl.* **en·tries** **1** The place where a door or gate is located. **2** A word and its meaning in a dictionary. **3** A thing or person entered in a contest.

en·ve·lope /en′və·lōp *or* än′və·lōp/ *n.* A flat paper wrapper having a gummed flap, used to send a letter or card.

en·vy /en′vē/ *n., v.* **en·vied, en·vy·ing** **1** *n.* The desire to have what someone else has. **2** *v.* To feel envy toward.

e·qual /ē′kwəl/ **1** *adj.* The same in size, amount, or value. **2** *v.* To be or make equal: One pint *equals* two cups.

e·rode /i·rōd′/ *v.* **e·rod·ed, e·rod·ing** To wear away, especially soil or rock by water or wind.

explorer

e·ven /ē′vən/ **1** *adj.* Flat and smooth. **2** *adj.* Steady, regular: The plane flew at an *even* speed. **3** *adj.* On the same level: This picture is *even* with that one. **4** *adj.* Equal: *even* amounts. **5** *adv.* Still: I know an *even* better way of going. **6** *v.* To make or become level: *Even* out the cake batter in the pans. **7** *v.* To make equal: His home run *evened* the score.

eve·ry·where /ev′rē·(h)wâr′/ *adv.* In all places; all around: My clothes were scattered *everywhere*.

e·vil /ē′vəl/ **1** *adj.* Wicked; the opposite of *good: evil* thoughts. **2** *n.* Something that is evil; wickedness.

ex·am·i·na·tion /ig·zam′ə·nā′shən/ *n.* **1** Careful inspection: I went to the doctor for an *examination*. **2** A test.

ex·cept /ik·sept′/ *prep.* Leaving out; other than; but: I've tried every cereal *except* one.

ex·cite /ik·sīt′/ *v.* **ex·cit·ed, ex·cit·ing** To stir up feelings; to make active: Planning the trip *excited* us.

ex·er·cise /ek′sər·sīz/ *v.* **ex·er·cised, ex·er·cis·ing,** *n.* **1** *v.* To develop or train the body or mind by active or repeated movement or use: to *exercise* your legs. **2** *n.* Active movement of the body to strengthen it and keep it healthy. **3** *n.* (*usually pl.*) A series of movements done for or as a means of practice: piano *exercises*.

ex·haust /ig·zôst′/ **1** *v.* To make or become very tired. **2** *v.* To use up completely: to *exhaust* the supply of fuel. **3** *n.* The fumes or the gases that escape from an engine.

ex·pect /ik·spekt′/ *v.* To look forward to as likely to happen.

ex·plor·er /ik·splôr′ər/ *n.* A person who seeks to learn or discover something.

---

act, āte, câre, ärt;   egg, ēven;   if, īce;   on, ōver, ôr;   bŏŏk, fōōd;   up, tûrn;
ə = **a** in *ago*, **e** in *listen*, **i** in *giraffe*, **o** in *pilot*, **u** in *circus*;   yōō = **u** in *music*;   oil;   out;
ch**air**; si**ng**; **sh**op; **th**ank; **th**at; **zh** in *treasure*.

expression

ex·pres·sion /ik·spresh′ən/ *n.* **1** The act of putting ideas into words: an *expression* of my feelings. **2** A look on the face that shows what a person is feeling: a happy *expression*.

ex·tend /ik·stend′/ *v.* **1** To stretch out. **2** To increase in time or space: The bank *extended* its hours.

ex·te·ri·or /ik·stir′ē·ər/ **1** *n.* The outside: the *exterior* of the house. **2** *adj.* On or for the outside: the *exterior* surface.

ex·tra /ek′strə/ **1** *adj.* Additional: an *extra* key. **2** *n.* A person, thing, or charge in addition to what is needed or expected.

eye /ī/ *n., v.* **eyed, eye·ing 1** *n.* A part of the body by which humans and animals see. **2** *v.* To look at carefully. **3** *n.* Something that is like an eye in some way: The *eye* of a needle. **4** *n.* The center: the *eye* of the storm.

F

fa·ble /fā′bəl/ *n.* **1** A tale that teaches a lesson, especially one with animals that behave like people. **2** A made-up story; a lie.

fail /fāl/ *v.* **1** To be unsuccessful. **2** To neglect; to omit or forget to do something: Don't *fail* to pick me up at three o'clock. **3** To get a test grade that is below passing.

fair·ness /fâr′nis/ *n.* The quality of not favoring one group or person over another; the condition of being fair or just.

faith·ful /fāth′fəl/ *adj.* Loyal; true: She has always been a *faithful* friend.

fa·mil·iar /fə·mil′yər/ *adj.* **1** Well acquainted: I'm *familiar* with Spanish customs. **2** Often seen, heard, or experienced: a *familiar* joke.

fam·i·ly /fam′(ə)·lē/ *n., pl.* **fam·i·lies 1** Parents and their children. **2** Animals or plants that are related in some way: Donkeys and mules are part of the horse *family*.

flame

farm /färm/ **1** *n.* Land where crops are grown or animals are raised. **2** *v.* To have and run a farm.

fash·ion /fash′ən/ *n.* **1** A style of dress popular at a particular time. **2** Way; manner: Sidney organized his records in his own *fashion*.

fas·ten /fas′ən/ *v.* **1** To close. **2** To attach.

fa·vor /fā′vər/ *n.* A kind act.

fa·vor·ite /fā′vər·it *or* fāv′rit/ **1** *n.* A person or thing that is liked best. **2** *adj.* Best loved or liked

fear·ful /fir′fəl/ *adj.* Frightened; full of fear: I am *fearful* of spiders.

fear·less /fir′lis/ *adj.* Brave; without fear: the *fearless* alligator.

fern /fûrn/ *n.* A plant with featherlike leaves and no flowers or seeds.

fic·tion /fik′shən/ *n.* Any story about imaginary people and events.

fi·nal /fī′nəl/ *adj.* **1** Last: *final* exams. **2** Not to be changed: The results of the election are *final*.

fin·ger /fing′gər/ *n.* One of the five end parts that make up the hand.

fire·place /fīr′plās′/ *n.* A place where a fire is built.

flag /flag/ *n., v.* **flagged, flag·ging 1** *n.* A piece of cloth with special colors and designs on it, used as a symbol of a country or organization. **2** *v.* To stop by signaling: He *flagged* down a police car.

flame /flām/ *n., v.* **flamed, flam·ing 1** *n.* The colored, burning gas that rises from a fire giving off light or heat: the *flame* of a candle. **2** *v.* To rise in

flames; to blaze: The campfire is *flaming.* **3** *n. (pl.)* The condition of burning: The old house is in *flames.*

flash·light /flash′līt′/ *n.* A small electric light that runs on batteries.

flew /flōō/ *v.* Past tense of *fly*[1].

flirt /flûrt/ **1** *v.* To act in a playful, loving way to capture someone's interest. **2** *n.* A person who flirts.

flock /flok/ **1** *n.* A large group of animals or birds. **2** *n.* A large crowd of people. **3** *v.* To move in a large group: to *flock* around a speaker.

floun·der[1] /floun′dər/ *v.* To struggle or move about clumsily: The car *floundered* through the snowdrifts.

floun·der[2] /floun′dər/ *n.* A flatfish used as food.

flur·ry /flûr′ē/ *n., pl.* **flur·ries** A light, brief snowfall, often with wind.

fly[1] /flī/ *v.* **flew, flown, fly·ing** **1** To go through the air: The moths *flew* toward the bright light. **2** To wave in the air: We *flew* the flag on Memorial Day. **3** To cause to float in the air: I am *flying* my kite. **4** To go by plane.

fly[2] /flī/ *n., pl.* **flies** An insect with two wings that flies.

fo·li·age /fō′lē·ij *or* fō′lij/ *n.* The leaves of a tree or plant.

force /fôrs/ *n., v.* **forced, forc·ing** **1** *n.* Power; strength. **2** *v.* To break open; to take by strength. **3** *v.* To make someone do something. **4** *n.* A group of people who do a particular job: a police *force.*

force·ful /fôrs′fəl/ *adj.* Strong; energetic: a *forceful* manager.

fore·warn /fôr·wôrn′/ *v.* To warn in advance: The announcer *forewarned* us of the approaching storm.

for·give·ness /fər·giv′nis/ *n.* Pardon; the act of forgiving.

for·tune /fôr′chən/ *n.* **1** What is going to happen to a person. **2** Luck or chance. **3** A large amount of money; wealth.

foul /foul/ **1** *adj.* Very dirty; smelly. **2** *adj.* Evil: a *foul* act. **3** *adj.* Stormy: *foul* weather. **4** *adj.* Not fair; against the rules: a *foul* play. **5** *n.* In baseball, a ball that is hit outside a certain area.

foun·tain /foun′tən/ *n.* Something that shoots water into the air.

fowl /foul/ *n., pl.* **fowl** *or* **fowls** **1** A bird, such as a chicken, duck, or turkey, used as food. **2** Any bird.

free·dom /frē′dəm/ *n.* The state of being free; liberty.

fre·quent /frē′kwənt/ *adj.* Often. **—fre′quent·ly** *adv.*

fringe /frinj/ *n., v.* **fringed, fring·ing** **1** *n.* A decorative border made of threads or cords. **2** *n.* Any edge or border: the *fringe* of town. **3** *v.* To trim or border: I *fringed* the cuffs with lace.

fron·tier /frun·tir′/ *n.* **1** The border between two countries. **2** A settled area that borders on an unsettled area.

fro·zen /frō′zən/ **1** *v.* Past participle of *freeze.* **2** *adj.* Turned into or covered with ice. **3** *adj.* Very cold.

fur·ni·ture /fûr′nə·chər/ *n.* The large, movable objects in a home or office.

---

act, āte, câre, ärt;   egg, ēven;   if, īce;   on, ōver, ôr;   bŏŏk, fōōd;   up, tûrn;
ə = a in *ago,* e in *listen,* i in *giraffe,* o in *pilot,* u in *circus;*   yōō = u in *music;*   oil;   out;
chair; si**ng**; **sh**op; **th**ank; **th**at; **zh** in *treasure.*

further

fur·ther /fûr′thər/ *adv.* To a more distant point: Akiko had to read *further* to gather more information.

fu·ture /fyōō′chər/ **1** *n.* The time to come. **2** *adj.* Having to do with the future: *future* plans.

G

gar·den /gär′dən/ **1** *n.* A small plot of land where flowers and vegetables are grown. **2** *v.* To work in a garden.

gel·a·tin /jel′ə·tin/ *n.* A protein made from animal parts; a substance like jelly used in foods: orange *gelatin*.

gene /jēn/ *n.* In plants, animals, and people, a part of a cell that determines the characteristics the offspring will get from parents: a *gene* for blue eyes.

gen·er·al /jen′ər·əl/ **1** *adj.* Having to do with everyone. **2** *adj.* Not detailed. **3** *n.* A high officer in an army. *General* comes from the Latin word *genus,* "kind or class."

gen·tle /jen′təl/ *adj.* Kind and tender.

gin·ger /jin′jər/ *n.* A spice made from the root of a tropical plant.

glis·ten /glis′ən/ *v.* To sparkle or shine: Water will *glisten* in the sunlight.

gloom·y /glōō′mē/ *adj.* **gloom·i·er, gloom·i·est 1** Dull; dark. **2** Sad.

gnat /nat/ *n.* A small biting or stinging fly: The *gnat* bit the girl on the arm.

goal /gōl/ *n.* **1** The end of a race. **2** Aim: My *goal* is to become an engineer. **3** In games, a score and the place where it can be made.

good·ness /gŏod′nis/ *n.* The condition of being good: Your *goodness* will be rewarded.—**honest to goodness** Really.

gov·ern·ment /guv′ər(n)·mənt/ *n.* **1** The management of a country, state, city, etc. **2** The system of this management: a democratic *government.* **3** The officials in a government.

grumble

gov·er·nor /guv′ər·nər/ *n.* The chief elected official of a state.

grab /grab/ *v.* **grabbed, grab·bing** To take hold of suddenly: He *grabbed* my hand during the scary movie.

grace·ful /grās′fəl/ *adj.* Full of grace in movement; not clumsy: The ballet dancer makes many *graceful* moves as he glides across the stage.

gra·cious /grā′shəs/ *adj.* Courteous; polite: a *gracious* hostess.

gram·mar /gram′ər/ *n.* The study of words and sentences and their use in speaking and writing.

grand·moth·er /gran(d)′muth′ər/ *n.* Your father's or mother's mother.

grate·ful /grāt′fəl/ *adj.* Thankful; full of gratitude: a *grateful* child.

grave /grāv/ *adj.* **gra·ver, gra·vest** Very important; serious: a *grave* illness.

grav·el /grav′əl/ *n.* A mixture of small stones and pebbles.

graze /grāz/ *v.* **grazed, graz·ing** To eat grass growing in a meadow: The sheep are *grazing* on the hill.

grease /*n.* grēs, *v.* grēs *or* grēz/ *n., v.* **greased, greas·ing 1** *n.* Animal fat in a soft state. **2** *n.* Any thick, oily substance. **3** *v.* To oil; to apply grease.

greed·y /grē′dē/ *adj.* **greed·i·er, greed·i·est** Wanting more than you need.

greet·ing /grē′ting/ *n.* **1** The act of welcoming. **2** *(pl.)* A friendly message sent for a special reason.

gro·cer·y /grō′sər·ē *or* grōs′rē/ *n., pl.* **gro·cer·ies 1** A store that sells food and supplies for the home. **2** *(pl.)* Food and supplies sold in this store.

grove /grōv/ *n.* A group of trees.

growl /groul/ **1** *n.* A deep, angry sound. **2** *v.* To make such a sound; to snarl.

grudge /gruj/ *n.* A feeling of hatred or anger against someone.

grum·ble /grum′bəl/ *v.* **grum·bled, grum·bling 1** To complain in a mumbling way: The impatient man *grum-*

guard

bled. **2** *v.* To make a low, heavy sound: My empty stomach is *grumbling*.

guard /gärd/ **1** *v.* To watch over or protect: The officer *guarded* the prisoner. **2** *n.* A person who guards.

guard·i·an /gär′dē·ən/ *n.* A person assigned by a court of law to care for someone else, especially a child.

guess /ges/ **1** *n.* An idea you have without knowing for sure. **2** *v.* To make a guess. **3** *v.* To suppose: I *guess* he is right.

gui·tar /gi·tär′/ *n.* An instrument played by strumming or plucking its strings.

gust /gust/ *n.* A strong rush of wind.

H

ham·burg·er /ham′bûr′gər/ *n.* **1** Ground beef. **2** A cooked patty of ground beef, usually eaten on a bun.

hand·i·craft /han′dē·kraft′/ *n.* **1** Skill in working with the hands. **2** An art or job requiring skillful hands: Weaving cloth is a *handicraft*.

hand·ker·chief /hang′kər·chif/ *n.* A small piece of cloth used for cleaning or wiping or for decoration.

han·dle /han′dəl/ *v.* **han·dled, han·dling,** *n.* **1** *v.* To touch or hold with the hand. **2** *n.* The part of something made to be held by the hand: the *handle* of a pan. **3** *v.* To manage: I can *handle* all of these chores.

hand·y /han′dē/ *adj.* **hand·i·er, hand·i·est 1** Within easy reach: I keep a pad and pencil *handy*. **2** Skillful with the hands: Seth is *handy* with clay.

hap·pen /hap′ən/ *v.* **1** To take place: What *happened* at school? **2** To take place by chance: We *happened* to meet.

hesitate

hap·pi·ness /hap′ē·nis/ *n.* The feeling of gladness or joy.

hard·ly /härd′lē/ *adv.* Almost not at all; barely: My cat *hardly* ever scratches.

harm·less /härm′lis/ *adj.* Causing no injury: Garter snakes are *harmless*.

har·vest /här′vist/ **1** *n.* The gathering and bringing in of crops. **2** *v.* To gather and bring in a crop. **3** *n.* The amount produced in a season of growing.

haul /hôl/ *v.* **1** To pull or drag with force: The horses *hauled* the wagon. **2** To move a load, as in a truck.

head·quar·ters (HQ) /hed′kwôr′tərz/ *n., pl.* The place from which people direct an organization, such as a police force or a military unit.

health·ful /helth′fəl/ *adj.* Contributing to good health: a *healthful* diet.

heart·less /härt′lis/ *adj.* Cruel; without kindness.

help·ful /help′fəl/ *adj.* Useful; giving help: *helpful* advice.

help·less /help′lis/ *adj.* Unable to help oneself: A newborn baby is *helpless*.

herb /(h)ûrb/ *n.* The leaves and stems of certain plants, used to flavor food: She baked chicken with fresh *herbs*.

herd /hûrd/ **1** *n.* A group of animals all of one kind. **2** *v.* To take care of or keep together a herd.

hes·i·tate /hez′ə·tāt/ *v.* **hes·i·tat·ed, hes·i·tat·ing 1** To feel doubtful; to pause: Don't *hesitate* to come. **2** To be unwilling or undecided.

---

act, āte, câre, ärt;   egg, ēven;   if, īce;   on, ōver, ôr;   bŏŏk, fŏŏd;   up, tûrn;
ə = a in *ago,* e in *listen,* i in *giraffe,* o in *pilot,* u in *circus;*   yŏŏ = u in *music;*   oil;   out;
chair; sing; shop; thank; that; zh in *treasure.*

high·way /hī′wā′/ *n.* A main road.

him·self /him·self′/ *pron.* His own self: Billy cleans up by *himself.*

hin·der /hin′dər/ *v.* To interfere with; to block: The mine cave-in *hindered* my search for the treasure.

hinge /hinj/ *n.* A joint that allows something to move back and forth, usually on a door or lid.

his·tor·i·cal /his·tôr′ə·kəl/ *adj.* Of or having to do with the past or history.

his·to·ry /his′tə·rē/ *n., pl.* **his·to·ries** Past events or the study or record of them.

hom·o·phone /hom′ə·fōn/ *n.* A word that sounds like another but has a different spelling and meaning: *Ring* and *wring* are *homophones.*

hon·est /on′ist/ *adj.* Truthful; fair.

hon·or /on′ər/ **1** *n.* Great respect and admiration; recognition. **2** *v.* To show or give respect and recognition. **3** *n.* An act or sign of high regard: the *honor* of receiving an award.

hood /hood/ **1** A part attached to a coat, jacket, or sweatshirt that covers the head and back of the neck. **2** Anything that looks or functions like a hood: the *hood* of a car.

hope·less /hōp′lis/ *adj.* Not having or giving hope: a *hopeless* cause.

hor·ror /hôr′ər/ *n.* The feeling of dread or great fear.

horse·back /hôrs′bak′/ *adv.* On the back of a horse: to ride *horseback.*

hos·pi·tal /hos′pi·təl/ *n.* A place for the care of the sick and the injured.

hour /our/ *n.* **1** One of 24 parts of a day; 60 minutes. **2** A particular time. **3** *(pl.)* The time spent at work or school: business *hours.*

howl /houl/ **1** *v.* To make a long, loud cry. **2** *n.* The sound of howling.

hu·mor /(h)yoo′mər/ *n.* **1** Something spoken, done, or written that is funny. **2** The ability to see the amusing side of things.

hun·ger /hung′gər/ *n.* **1** Weakness caused by lack of food. **2** A desire or need for food.

hur·dle /hûr′dəl/ *n.* **1** A standing frame or fence over which horses and people jump: I jumped the highest *hurdle.* **2** A difficulty or problem to be conquered: Overcoming her fear of water was a big *hurdle* for Joan.

hus·band /huz′bənd/ *n.* A married man.

hy·dro·gen /hī′drə·jən/ *n.* A colorless, odorless gas that combines with oxygen to form water (H_2O).

I

i·de·a /ī·dē′ə/ *n.* **1** A thought or opinion. **2** A plan or purpose.

im·ag·i·na·tion /i·maj′ə·nā′shən/ *n.* **1** The ability or power to picture absent, unknown, or unreal things in the mind. **2** The ability to view things in new ways or to develop new ideas: the *imagination* of a sculptor.

imagine | **jogger**

im·ag·ine /i·maj′in/ *v.* **im·ag·ined, im·ag·in·ing** To have an idea or form a picture in your mind.

im·mense /i·mens′/ *adj.* Vast; enormous.

im·pa·tient /im·pā′shənt/ *adj.* Not willing to accept delay; not patient.

in·ac·cu·rate /in·ak′yər·it/ *adj.* Incorrect; not accurate.

in·com·plete /in′kəm·plēt′/ *adj.* Unfinished; not complete.

in·cor·rect /in′kə·rekt′/ *adj.* Wrong; not right or correct.

in·crease /*v.* in·krēs′, *n.* in′krēs/ *v.* **in·creased, in·creas·ing,** *n.* **1** *v.* To make or become greater or larger. **2** *n.* A growing or becoming greater or larger in size, quantity, etc.: an *increase* in price.

in·dus·tri·al /in·dus′trē·əl/ *adj.* Having to do with industry or manufacturing: *industrial* workers.

in·flate /in·flāt′/ *v.* **in·flat·ed, in·flat·ing 1** To fill up with air or gas. **2** To increase or expand a great deal: to *inflate* meat prices.

in·quire /in·kwīr′/ *v.* **in·quired, in·quir·ing** To ask a question in order to get information: She stopped at the hospital to *inquire* about my health.

in·sect /in′sekt/ *n.* A very small animal with six legs and often with wings.

in·stead /in·sted′/ *adv.* Rather than; in the place of: Eat fruit *instead* of candy.

in·te·ri·or /in·tir′ē·ər/ **1** *n.* The inside: the *interior* of a house. **2** *adj.* On or for the inside; inner: the *interior* wall.

in·ter·rupt /in′tə·rupt′/ *v.* **1** To cause someone to stop doing something. **2** To stop an action.

in·ven·tor /in·ven′tər/ *n.* A person who invents or develops something for the first time.

in·ves·ti·gate /in·ves′tə·gāt/ *v.*

in·ves·ti·ga·ted, in·ves·ti·gat·ing To search for facts.

ir·ri·ga·tion /ir′ə·gā′shən/ *n.* A system for providing land with water through pipes, ditches, or canals.

is·sue /ish′ōō/ *n., v.* **is·sued, is·su·ing 1** *n.* Something sent out regularly: an *issue* of a magazine. **2** *v.* To send or give out.

it·self /it·self′/ *pron.* Its own self: The goat stumbled and hurt *itself.*

J

jam[1] /jam/ *v.* **jammed, jam·ming,** *n.* **1** *v.* To press or squeeze things or people together into a small space. **2** *n.* A large number of people or things crowded together so that they can't move easily: a traffic *jam.*

jam[2] /jam/ *n.* Fruit boiled with sugar until thick: blueberry *jam.*

jazz /jaz/ **1** *n.* A type of music, started by blacks in the South, that has a strong rhythm with accented notes. **2** *adj.* Of or like jazz: a *jazz* band.

jest /jest/ **1** *n.* A statement or action intended to cause laughter; a joke. **2** *v.* To joke; to speak or act playfully.

jew·el /jōō′əl/ *n.* **1** A precious stone. **2** An ornament set with gems.

jew·el·ry /jōō′əl·rē/ *n.* Objects worn for decoration, such as necklaces, rings, etc.

jog·ger /jog′ər/ *n.* A person who jogs or runs regularly for exercise.

---

act, āte, câre, ärt;   egg, ēven;   if, īce;   on, ōver, ôr;   bŏŏk, fōod;   up, tûrn;
ə = a in *ago,* e in *listen,* i in *giraffe,* o in *pilot,* u in *circus;*   yōo = u in *music;*   oil;   out;
chair; sing; shop; thank; that; zh in *treasure.*

join

join /join/ *v.*　**1** To bring or come together; to connect.　**2** To become a member of a group.　**3** To meet or be with others.

joke /jōk/ *n., v.* **joked, jok·ing**　**1** *n.* Something that makes you laugh.　**2** *v.* To do or say something funny.

jour·nal /jûr′nəl/ *n.*　**1** A daily record or account of events or thoughts.　**2** A newspaper, magazine, or other periodical.

joy·ful /joi′fəl/ *adj.* Glad; full of joy: Holidays are *joyful* times.

judg·ment /juj′mənt/ *n.*　**1** A decision or serious opinion: The jury will pass *judgment* on the man.　**2** Good sense.

jug·gle /jug′əl/ *v.* **jug·gled, jug·gling** To keep a number of objects in motion in the air by tossing and catching.

juice /jōōs/ *n.* The liquid part of fruits, vegetables, or meat.

jun·gle /jung′gəl/ *n.* A thick tropical forest of trees, vines, and bushes, usually filled with wild animals.

jus·tice /jus′tis/ *n.*　**1** The quality of being just or fair, according to the law. **2** A judge, one of nine on the Supreme Court.

K

ken·nel /ken′əl/ *n.* A place where dogs are bred, sold, and housed.

kind·ness /kīnd′nis/ *n.* Being kind.

knap·sack /nap′sak′/ *n.* A cloth bag for supplies, worn strapped to one's back.

knead /nēd/ *v.* To mix and press dough with your hands.

kneel /nēl/ *v.* **knelt** *or* **kneeled, kneel·ing** To go down on your knees.

label

knife /nīf/ *n., pl.* **knives** A tool with a sharp edge for cutting.

knight /nīt/ *n.* In the Middle Ages, a soldier who pledged loyalty to his king or queen.

knob /nob/ *n.*　**1** A round handle to be turned or pulled.　**2** A rounded lump, as on a tree trunk.

knock /nok/　**1** *v.* To hit.　**2** *v.* To hit and make fall.　**3** *v.* To make a pounding noise: to *knock* on a door.　**4** *n.* A pounding noise.

knot /not/ *n., v.* **knot·ted, knot·ting**　**1** *n.* A fastening made by tying ropes or string.　**2** *v.* To tie in a knot.　**3** *n.* Anything twisted like a knot: The yarn is in *knots*.　**4** *n.* A lump on the trunk of a tree where a branch grows out.

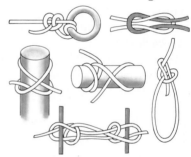

knot·ty /not′ē/ *adj.* **knot·ti·er, knot·ti·est** Full of knots: *knotty* hair, *knotty* pine.

know /nō/ *v.* **knew, known, know·ing**　**1** To be sure.　**2** To understand.　**3** To be familiar with.

knowl·edge /nol′ij/ *n.*　**1** The fact or condition of knowing or being aware: I had *knowledge* of the award.　**2** What a person knows.

known /nōn/ *v.* Past participle of *know.*

knuck·le /nuk′əl/ *n.* A joint of the finger.

L

la·bel /lā′bəl/　**1** *n.* A slip of paper or other material with information on it, fastened to clothing and other things.　**2** *v.* To attach a label to.

labor

la·bor /lā′bər/ **1** *n.* Hard work. **2** *v.* To work hard. **3** *n.* Workers in general.

lan·tern /lan′tərn/ *n.* An easily carried case, with transparent sides, used to hold and protect a light.

laugh /laf/ **1** *v.* To make sounds that show something is funny. **2** *n.* The sound of laughing.

lead·er /lē′dər/ *n.* A person who leads or directs.

lead·er·ship /lē′dər·ship′/ *n.* The ability to lead or guide.

league¹ /lēg/ *n.* A number of persons, groups, or countries united for some common purpose: a football *league.*

league² /lēg/ *n.* A unit for measuring length, equal to about three miles.

le·gal /lē′gəl/ *adj.* **1** Having to do with the law: a *legal* contract. **2** Allowed by or based on the law: The *legal* voting age is 18.

leg·end /lej′ənd/ *n.* **1** An old story of strange or remarkable happenings that may or may not have some basis in truth. **2** A key or guide accompanying a picture, map, graph, etc.

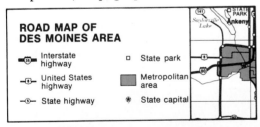

ROAD MAP OF DES MOINES AREA

- Interstate highway
- United States highway
- State highway
- □ State park
- Metropolitan area
- ✳ State capital

lib·er·ty /lib′ər·tē/ *n.* Freedom: We value our *liberty.*

li·cense /lī′səns/ *n., v.* **li·censed, li·cens·ing** **1** *n.* Legal permission to do, be, or own something: a *license* for driving. **2** *n.* A certificate, tag, or plate showing such permission: a dog *license.* **3** *v.* To issue a license: He is *licensed* to sell houses.

loyal

lie¹ /lī/ *v.* **lay, lain, ly·ing** **1** To rest in a flat position: I'm *lying* down for an hour. **2** To be located: Boston *lies* northeast of New York.

lie² /lī/ *n., v.* **lied, ly·ing** **1** *n.* A false statement. **2** *v.* To tell or write something that is false.

like·ness /līk′nis/ *n.* The condition of being alike: There is a real *likeness* between my father and me.

lim·it /lim′it/ **1** *n.* The final point beyond which something cannot go: The speed *limit* is 55 mph. **2** *n.* The largest quantity or amount allowed: There is a *limit* to the number of people that can board this bus. **3** *v.* To restrict; to set a limit to: to *limit* your spending.

line /līn/ *n.* **1** A straight mark. **2** A row: The desks are in a *line.*

liq·uid /lik′wid/ **1** *n.* Anything, such as water, that can be poured: a fluid. **2** *adj.* Able to be poured: *liquid* soap.

lit·er·a·ture /lit′·ər·ə·chər *or* lit′rə·chər/ *n.* Written works in general, including plays, poems, etc.

loaf /lōf/ *n., pl.* **loaves** **1** Bread baked in one piece. **2** Any food shaped like a loaf: meat *loaf.*

log·ic /loj′ik/ *n.* **1** The study of reasoning and proving. **2** A way of thinking through a problem.

lone·some /lōn′səm/ *adj.* Feeling lonely.

long /lông/ **1** *adj.* Not short: a *long* walk. **2** *adj.* Having a certain length: 8 feet *long.* **3** *adv.* For a long time: We didn't stay *long.*

loose /lōōs/ *adj.* **loos·er, loos·est** **1** Not tied. **2** Not tight. **3** Not firmly in place. **4** Free.—**turn loose** To give freedom to.

loud /loud/ *adj.* Not quiet; noisy: *Loud* music bothers her ears.

loy·al /loi′əl/ *adj.* True; faithful.

---

act, āte, câre, ärt;   egg, ēven;   if, īce;   on, ōver, ôr;   bŏŏk, fōōd;   up, tûrn;

ə = a in *ago,* e in *listen,* i in *giraffe,* o in *pilot,* u in *circus;*   yōō = u in *music;*   oil;   out;

chair; sing; shop; thank; that; zh in *treasure.*

loyalty

loy·al·ty /loi′əl·tē/ *n., pl.* **loy·al·ties** The condition of being loyal.

luck·y /luk′ē/ *adj.* **luck·i·er, luck·i·est** Having or bringing good luck.

lug·gage /lug′ij/ *n.* Suitcases and other baggage used in traveling.

lu·nar /lōō′nər/ *adj.* Of or having to do with the moon: *lunar* rocks.

M

mag·ic /maj′ik/ *n.* The art of pretending to do the impossible.

mag·ni·fy /mag′nə·fī/ *v.* **mag·ni·fied, mag·ni·fy·ing** 1 To make something look bigger than its real size. 2 To make something more important than it really is; to exaggerate: She often *magnifies* her problems.

mail /māl/ 1 *n.* Letters and packages handled by the post office. 2 *v.* To send a letter or package.

main·tain /mān·tān′/ *v.* 1 To continue or keep up; to keep: to *maintain* good work habits. 2 To support; to take care of: a fund to *maintain* the library. 3 To keep in good condition: to *maintain* city buses.

ma·jor /mā′jər/ *adj.* Important; greater or larger: a *major* part.

ma·jor·i·ty /mə·jôr′ə·tē/ *n., pl.* **ma·jor·i·ties** More than half the number.

mam·mal /mam′əl/ *n.* A warm-blooded animal having a backbone: A female *mammal* produces milk to feed her young.

mam·moth /mam′əth/ *adj.* Huge; enormous.

man·age /man′ij/ *v.* **man·aged, man·ag·ing** 1 To be in charge of. 2 To succeed in doing something. 3 To get by: We *manage* on very little money.

man·ag·er /man′ij·ər/ *n.* A person who manages a business or department: The *manager* will solve your problem.

medal

man·u·fac·ture /man′yə·fak′chər/ *v.* **man·u·fac·tured, man·u·fac·tur·ing,** *n.* 1 *v.* To make or produce things by hand or machine: His company *manufactures* stuffed animals. 2 *n.* The act or process of manufacturing.

ma·roon¹ /mə·rōōn′/ *v.* 1 To put ashore and leave on a barren island or coast. 2 To desert or leave helpless.

ma·roon² /mə·rōōn′/ *n., adj.* Dull, dark red.

mar·ry /mar′ē/ *v.* **mar·ried, mar·ry·ing** 1 To become husband and wife. 2 To join as husband and wife: The priest *married* five couples yesterday.

mar·vel·ous /mär′vəl·əs/ *adj.* 1 Causing wonder; amazing: a *marvelous* acrobat. 2 *informal* Very good; excellent.

may·or /mā′ər/ *n.* The chief elected official of a city.

mean·ing·ful /mē′ning·fəl/ *adj.* Full of meaning; important: Thanksgiving is a *meaningful* day for most Americans.

mea·sles /mē′zəlz/ *n., pl.* A disease that causes red spots on the skin.

meas·ure·ment /mezh′ər·mənt/ *n.* 1 The act of measuring. 2 The size, quantity, or amount found by measuring. 3 A system of measures.

me·chan·ic /mə·kan′ik/ *n.* A person whose work involves repairing machinery.

med·al /med′əl/ *n.* A small piece of metal, sometimes attached to a ribbon, with a picture or writing on it.

meddle

med·dle /med′əl/ v. **med·dled, med·dling** To interfere with something that is not your business.

me·di·um /mē′dē·əm/ adj. Between two conditions in amount, position, size, etc.; middle: I am of *medium* height.

mel·o·dy /mel′ə·dē/ n., pl. **mel·o·dies** A tune or song.

men·tion /men′shən/ v. To tell about; to refer to: Don't *mention* it to her.

mes·sage /mes′ij/ n. Information that is told or sent to another person.

mid·dle /mid′əl/ n. The center or halfway point.

milk /milk/ **1** n. A white liquid from cows. **2** n. Similar liquid produced by other female animals to feed their young. **3** v. To get milk from.

mis·chief /mis′chif/ n. **1** Behavior that can cause trouble or harm. **2** Pranks.

mis·lead /mis·lēd′/ v. **mis·led, mis·lead·ing 1** To lead in the wrong direction. **2** To cause someone to believe something that is not true.

mis·sile /mis′əl/ n. Something, especially a weapon, that is thrown or shot, as a bullet, stone, rocket, etc.

mis·spell /mis·spel′/ v. To spell a word incorrectly.

mod·el /mod′əl/ **1** n. A small-sized copy of something: a *model* of an airplane. **2** v. To form material into a model: to *model* clay. **3** n. A good person to copy; someone worth imitating. **4** adj. use: a *model* teacher. **5** n. A person who

murmur

poses for an artist or photographer. **6** v. To act as a model.

mon·arch /mon′ərk/ n. **1** A ruler, as a king or queen. **2** A large orange and black North American butterfly.

mort·gage /môr′gij/ n., v. **mort·gaged, mort·gag·ing 1** n. The contract that gives a bank the right to assume ownership of property if an owner fails to repay the loan used to buy that property. **2** v. To arrange a loan, using property as insurance: We *mortgaged* our home to buy a store.

mo·tion /mō′shən/ **1** n. Movement. **2** n. A signal; gesture. **3** v. To signal; to make a movement that shows meaning.

mo·tor /mō′tər/ **1** n. The engine that makes cars and other machines go. **2** adj. Run by a motor: a *motor* scooter.

mov·a·ble /mōō′və·bəl/ adj. Able to be moved: *movable* engine parts.

move /mōōv/ v. **moved, mov·ing 1** To go or make go from one place to another. **2** To change where you live. **3** To change position: to *move* your desk.

move·ment /mōōv′mənt/ n. The act of moving: the *movement* of waves.

mov·er /mōō′vər/ n. A company or person that moves things, especially furniture, from one place to another.

mov·ie /mōō′vē/ n. A film.

mur·mur /mûr′mər/ **1** n. A low, unclear sound. **2** v. To make such a sound: He *murmured* in his sleep.

---

act, āte, câre, ärt;　　egg, ēven;　　if, īce;　　on, ōver, ôr;　　book, food;　　up, tûrn;
ə = a in *ago*, e in *listen*, i in *giraffe*, o in *pilot*, u in *circus*;　　yōō = u in *music*;　　oil;　　out;
chair; sing; shop; thank; that; zh in *treasure*.

muscle

mus·cle /mus'əl/ *n.* One of the bundles of stringy tissue in the body that produce the body's movements by tightening and stretching.

mus·cu·lar /mus'kyə·lər/ *adj.* Having well-developed muscles.

my·self /mī·self'/ *pron.* My own self: I enjoy spending time by *myself*.

N

na·tion /nā'shən/ *n.* Country.

nat·u·ral·ly /nach'ər·əl·ē/ *adv.* **1** In a natural way: Talk *naturally*. **2** Having to do with nature: *naturally* wavy hair. **3** Certainly; of course.

na·ture /nā'chər/ *n.* The world except for those things made by people: She likes to photograph *nature*.

near·by /*adj.* nir'bī', *adv.* nir'bī'/ *adj., adv.* Close by; near: a *nearby* hospital. to play *nearby*.

neck /nek/ *n.* **1** The part of your body between your head and your shoulders. **2** The narrow part of a bottle.

neigh·bor·hood /nā'bər·hoŏd/ *n.* A small section of a city or town.

nei·ther /nē'thər *or* nī'thər/ **1** *adj., pron.* Not one or the other: *Neither* player hit a home run. *Neither* scored a run. **2** *conj.* Not either: I didn't want dessert; *neither* did my brother.

nerve /nûrv/ *n.* One of the many thread-like parts in the body that carry messages between the brain or spinal cord and all other parts of the body.

ner·vous /nûr'vəs/ *adj.* **1** Tense; uneasy. **2** Fearful.

nev·er·the·less /nev'ər·thə·les'/ *adv., conj.* In any event; however: The movie had started, but we bought tickets *nevertheless*. I hurt my arm; *nevertheless* I continued playing.

news·pa·per /n(y)ooz'pā'pər/ *n.* A publication, usually put out daily or weekly, containing news, editorials, advertisements, and other items.

nine·ty *or* **90** /nīn'tē/ *n., adj.* A number equal to ten nines.

non·fic·tion /non'fik'shən/ *n.* Any story about real people and events.

"Nonfiction: Biographies"

note·book /nōt'boŏk'/ *n.* A book with blank pages in which you can write.

no·tice /nō'tis/ *v.* **no·ticed, no·tic·ing** To see; to pay attention to.

noun /noun/ *n.* A word that names a person, place, or thing.

num·ber /num'bər/ **1** *n.* A unit in math. **2** *n.* An amount. **3** *v.* To give numbers to: to *number* the pages.

nu·mer·ous /n(y)oo'mə·rəs/ *adj.* A great number; very many: He received *numerous* cards for his birthday.

O

oc·cu·pa·tion /ok'yə·pā'shən/ *n.* Anything a person does, but especially what someone does for a living: My *occupation* is managing a store.

oc·cu·py /ok'yə·pī/ *v.* **oc·cu·pied, oc·cu·py·ing** **1** To take up or fill space or time. **2** To live in. **3** To keep busy.

occupy

occur

oc·cur /ə·kûr′/ v. **oc·curred, oc·curring**
1 To take place; to happen. **2** To come to mind.

of·fice /ôf′is/ n. **1** A place where business or work is done. **2** The people who work in an office. **3** An elected or appointed position.

of·fi·cial /ə·fish′əl/ **1** n. A person who holds an office or job and has certain duties or powers. **2** adj. Of or having to do with an office of authority.

oil /oil/ **1** n. A greasy liquid that will not mix with water. **2** v. To put oil on: to *oil* a baking pan.

op·er·a·tor /op′ə·rā′tər/ n. A person who runs or operates a machine.

op·pose /ə·pōz′/ v. **op·posed, op·pos·ing**
1 To work or fight against: to *oppose* a plan. **2** To be in contrast to: A leader must be strong as *opposed* to weak.

op·po·site /op′ə·zit/ **1** adj. Located on the other side: *opposite* sides of the gym. **2** adj. Entirely different: in *opposite* directions. **3** n. Something completely different: *Sweet* is the *opposite* of *sour*. **4** prep. Across from.

our·selves /our·selvz′/ pron. Us and no one else: We paid for it *ourselves*.

out·line /out′līn′/ n., v. **out·lined, out·lin·ing** **1** n. An organization of ideas that serves as a guide in writing a paragraph or report. **2** v. To make an outline.

o·ver·look /ō′vər·look′/ v. **1** To have a view from above. **2** To fail to see.

own·er /ō′nər/ n. The person who owns something.

oys·ter /ois′tər/ n. A shellfish used as food; some produce pearls.

P

pad·dle /pad′əl/ n., v. **pad·dled, pad·**

particular

dling **1** n. A short oar. **2** v. To use a paddle to move a boat. **3** v. To move your hands and feet in water.

paid /pād/ v. Past tense and past participle of *pay*.

pain·less /pān′lis/ adj. Without pain.

pa·ja·mas /pə·jä′məz/ n., pl. Clothes for sleeping.

pa·per /pā′pər/ **1** n. Material used for writing, printing, and wrapping things. **2** n. Paper with writing on it. **3** n. A newspaper. **4** adj. Made of paper.

par·a·graph /par′ə·graf′/ n. A group of sentences that develop an idea: Indent the first line of the *paragraph*.

par·cel /pär′səl/ n. Something wrapped; a package.

par·don /pär′dən/ **1** v. To forgive. **2** n. Forgiveness. **3** n. The legal order that frees someone from punishment.

par·ent /pâr′ənt/ n. A person's mother or father.

park /pärk/ **1** n. Land with trees, grass, and playgrounds. **2** v. To put a car, bicycle, etc., somewhere and leave it.

par·tial /pär′shəl/ adj. Not all; in part.

par·tic·u·lar /pər·tik′yə·lər/ adj. **1** Relating to a certain person, place, or thing: a *particular* park. **2** Unusual; special: This game is of *particular* importance. **3** Precise; hard to please: Yoko is very *particular* about the food she eats.

---

act, āte, câre, ärt;   egg, ēven;   if, īce;   on, ōver, ôr;   book, food;   up, tûrn;
ə = a in *ago*, e in *listen*, i in *giraffe*, o in *pilot*, u in *circus*;   yōō = u in *music*;   oil;   out;
chair; sing; shop; thank; that; zh in *treasure*.

pass | **plural**

pass /pas/ **1** *v.* To go by. **2** *n.* A permit allowing someone to do something: She was given a free *pass* to the movie theater. **3** *v.* To succeed: to *pass* a test. **4** *v.* To move from one person or place to another.

pas·ture /pas′chər/ *n.* A grassy field where cattle, sheep, or horses graze.

pa·tient /pā′shənt/ *adj.* **1** Able to wait or experience difficulties without complaining. **2** *adj.* Calm and understanding. **3** *n.* A person who is being treated for a sickness or an injury.

pay /pā/ *v.* **paid, pay·ing,** *n.* **1** *v.* To give money for something. **2** *n.* Money you get for working.

pay·ment /pā′mənt/ *n.* Money paid for something bought or done.

peace /pēs/ *n.* **1** A condition without war. **2** Calmness: *peace* and quiet.

peace·ful /pēs′fəl/ *adj.* Calm; quiet; full of peace: a *peaceful* vacation.

peach /pēch/ *n.* A round fruit with a fuzzy, yellowish-pink skin.

ped·al /ped′əl/ **1** *n.* A device pushed by the foot to control or operate something, as a bicycle. **2** *v.* To move or operate something by pushing down on this part. ► *Pedal* comes from the Latin root *pes,* "foot."

ped·dle /ped′əl/ *v.* **ped·dled, ped·dling** To travel around selling things: to *peddle* ice cream.

pen·ni·less /pen′i·lis/ *adj.* Very poor; without money: a *penniless* man.

peo·ple /pē′pəl/ *n.* Human beings.

per·form·ance /pər·fôr′məns/ *n.* **1** The act of performing or doing: The ranger rescued the family in the *performance* of his job. **2** A play, concert, or other kind of entertainment.

per·il /per′əl/ *n.* Danger; risk: The houses near the fire were in *peril.*

per·ma·nent /pûr′mən·ənt/ *adj.* Meant to last for a long time; not temporary.

per·mis·sion /pər·mish′ən/ *n.* Approval to do something.

pet·al /pet′əl/ *n.* One of the leaflike parts of a flower.

phrase /frāz/ *n., v.* **phrased, phras·ing** **1** *n.* In grammar, a sequence of two or more words, used as a single part of speech, that does not contain a subject and predicate: "In the sky" is a *phrase.* **2** *v.* To express in a particular way: The debater *phrased* the argument carefully.

pick·le /pik′əl/ *n.* A cucumber or other food soaked in salt water or vinegar.

pil·lar /pil′ər/ *n.* A column that supports a building.

pi·lot /pī′lət/ *n.* The person who steers or guides an airplane.

pi·o·neer /pī′ə·nir′/ *n.* A person who is the first to settle a new region.

pi·rate /pī′rit/ *n.* A person who attacks and robs ships at sea.

pit·y /pit′ē/ *n., v.* **pit·ied, pit·y·ing** **1** *n.* A feeling of sorrow or sympathy. **2** *v.* To feel sorry for.

plaid /plad/ **1** *n.* A cloth woven with bands of many colors, crossing each other in patterns. **2** *adj.* Having a pattern like that of plaid.

plot /plot/ *n., v.* **plot·ted, plot·ting** **1** *n.* A small piece of land. **2** *n.* A secret plan. **3** *v.* To plan in secret. **4** *n.* The events in a story.

plu·ral /plo͞or′əl/ **1** *adj.* Referring to more than one: a *plural* noun. **2** *n.* The form of a word to show more than one.

point

point /point/ *v.* **1** To show or indicate: The compass needle *points* north. **2** To aim or direct.

poi·son /poi′zən/ **1** *n.* A substance that can cause illness or death. **2** *v.* To give such a substance to.

po·lar /pō′lər/ *adj.* Having to do with the North or South Pole: *polar* bear.

pol·ish /pol′ish/ **1** *n.* Smoothness and shininess. **2** *n.* Wax or other substance rubbed on something to make it shiny. **3** *v.* To make shiny.

po·lit·i·cal /pə·lit′i·kəl/ *adj.* Having to do with government or politicians: *political* parties.

pon·der /pon′dər/ *v.* To think deeply about something.

porch /pôrch/ *n.* A covered entrance to a house or building.

pos·ses·sion /pə·zesh′ən/ *n.* **1** The fact of owning or having something: I have your missing keys in my *possession*. **2** Something owned: Our *possessions* were destroyed in the hurricane.

post·age /pōs′tij/ *n.* A charge for sending mail.

pow·der /pou′dər/ **1** *n.* Any solid substance pounded or ground into fine dustlike particles: baby *powder*. **2** *v.* To put powder on.

pow·er·ful /pou′ər·fəl/ *adj.* Strong; full of power: a *powerful* nation.

pred·i·cate /pred′i·kit/ *n.* A word or group of words that tell something about the subject.

pre·fer /pri·fûr′/ *v.* **pre·ferred, pre·fer·ring** To like better than.

pre·pare /pri·pâr′/ *v.* **pre·pared, pre·par·ing** To get ready; to make ready: We're *preparing* lunch.

pre·serve /pri·zûrv′/ *v.* **pre·served, pre·serv·ing,** *n.* **1** *v.* To protect or keep from danger: I waxed the wood table to

production

preserve the surface. **2** *v.* To prepare food so it can be kept without spoiling: They salted the fish to *preserve* it. **3** *v.* To keep from spoiling: My new refrigerator *preserves* food better than my old one. **4** *n.* An area set aside for the protection of plants and animals.

pres·i·dent /prez′ə·dent/ *n.* **1** A person selected to direct an organization, club, college, business, etc. **2** The chief official of a republic.

pres·sure /presh′ər/ *n.* The force made by one thing pressing against another.

prey /prā/ **1** *n.* An animal hunted for food. **2** *v.* To hunt animals for food.

price /prīs/ *n.* Cost.

prin·ci·pal /prin′sə·pəl/ **1** *adj.* Most important: the *principal* part in the play. **2** *n.* The head of a school.

prin·ci·ple /prin′sə·pəl/ *n.* **1** A truth, law, or rule: the *principle* of religious freedom. **2** Good standards of behavior: Our teacher is a woman of *principle*.

pri·vate /prī′vit/ *adj.* **1** Not meant to be shared with other people. **2** Not for public use.

prize /prīz/ *n.* Something won in a contest or game.

pro·ceed /prə·sēd′/ *v.* To go forward or go on, especially after a stop.

pro·duce /*v.* prə·d(y)o͞os′, *n.* prod′(y)o͞os or prō′d(y)o͞os/ *v.* **pro·duced, pro·duc·ing,** *n.* **1** *v.* To bring into being: Orchards *produce* fruit. **2** *n.* Farm products, as vegetables and fruits, grown for market. **3** *v.* To bring about; cause.

prod·uct /prod′əkt/ *n.* **1** A thing made or produced to be sold. **2** In math, the result gotten by multiplication.

pro·duc·tion /prə·duk′shən/ *n.* **1** The act or process of making or producing something. **2** The amount of goods or services produced.

---

act, āte, câre, ärt;　　egg, ēven;　　if, īce;　　on, ōver, ôr;　　bo͝ok, fo͞od;　　up, tûrn;
ə = a in *ago*, e in *listen*, i in *giraffe*, o in *pilot*, u in *circus*;　　yo͞o = u in *music*;　　oil;　　out;
chair; sing; shop; thank; that; zh in *treasure*.

189

profit

prof·it /prof′it/ **1** *n.* In business, the amount of money gained after subtracting all costs. **2** *v.* To gain; to benefit: He *profited* from his mistakes.

prom·ise /prom′is/ *n., v.* **prom·ised, prom·is·ing 1** *n.* A statement that someone will or will not do something. **2** *v.* To give a promise.

prompt /prompt/ *adj.* Right on time.

pro·noun /prō′noun/ *n.* A word that is used in place of a noun.

proof /prōof/ *n.* Facts that prove something is true or false.

proof·read /prōof′rēd′/ *v.* **proof·read, proof·read·ing** To read and correct errors in something written.

prop·er /prop′ər/ *adj.* Correct for a certain occasion or situation.

prove /prōov/ *v.* **proved, proved** *or* **prov·en, prov·ing** To show with facts that something is true or false.

pry /prī/ *v.* **pried, pry·ing** To force open with a wedge or lever.

pub·lish /pub′lish/ *v.* **1** To print and issue (as a book, magazine, or newspaper) for sale to the public. **2** To have one's work published: Our best-selling author *publishes* regularly. **3** To make known publicly.

pun·ish·ment /pun′ish·mənt/ *n.* **1** The act of giving a penalty for a wrong someone has done. **2** The penalty itself.

pu·pil[1] /pyōo′pəl/ *n.* The dark central part of the eye, which admits light to the back of the eyeball.

pu·pil[2] /pyōo′pəl/ *n.* A student.

pup·py /pup′ē/ *n., pl.* **pup·pies** A young dog.

pur·chase /pûr′chəs/ *v.* **pur·chased, pur·chas·ing,** *n.* **1** *v.* To buy. **2** *n.* Something bought.

pur·ple /pûr′pəl/ *n., adj.* A color that is a mixture of blue and red.

pur·pose·ly /pûr′pəs·lē/ *adv.* Happening or doing on purpose: Did you let out the dog *purposely*?

read

Q

quan·ti·ty /kwon′tə·tē/ *n., pl.* **quan·ti·ties** An amount.

quar·ter /kwôr′tər/ **1** *n.* One-fourth of a whole. **2** *v.* To divide into four parts. **3** *n.* A coin worth 25 cents.

quench /kwench/ *v.* To satisfy a thirst by drinking.

ques·tion /kwes′chən/ **1** *n.* Something you ask in order to find out. **2** *n.* A kind of sentence that ends with a question mark. **3** *v.* To ask questions.

quick /kwik/ *adj.* Done in a short time; fast: a *quick* trip to the store.

qui·et /kwī′ət/ **1** *adj.* Having or making little noise. **2** *adj.* Not busy; relaxed. **3** *v.* To make or become quiet.

quit /kwit/ *v.* **quit** *or* **quit·ted, quit·ting 1** To give up or stop doing something. **2** To give up a job: She *quit* her job because she was offered a better one.

quite /kwīt/ *adv.* **1** Completely: I am *quite* well. **2** Really: Simon's house is *quite* close to ours.

quo·ta·tion /kwō·tā′shən/ *n.* The exact words said by a person. You use quotation marks (" ... ") before and after a speaker's words.

R

range /rānj/ *n., v.* **ranged, rang·ing 1** *n.* The possibilities within certain limits: a wide *range* of colors. **2** *v.* To be found within known limits: to *range* in price. **3** *n.* A wide, grassy plain for roaming and grazing. **4** *n.* A stove.

rare /râr/ *adj.* **rar·er, rar·est** Not often seen or found; unusual.—**rare′ly.**

reach /rēch/ *v.* **1** To touch or get hold of. **2** To arrive at.

read /rēd/ *v.* **read** /red/, **read·ing 1** To get meaning from letters and words. **2** To say aloud something that is written: *Read* the list of ingredients to me and I'll place them on the table.

readiness

read·i·ness /red′ē·nis/ *n.* The condition of being ready or willing: Nina's swimming skill showed a *readiness* for the lifesaving course.

rea·son /rē′zən/ *n.* **1** Explanation; excuse. **2** Cause: Being thirsty is a good *reason* for drinking water.

re·build /rē·bild′/ *v.* **re·built, re·build·ing** To build again.

re·cent /rē′sənt/ *adj.* Not long past; having happened a little while ago.

re·cite /ri·sīt′/ *v.* **re·cit·ed, re·cit·ing** To repeat something memorized.

reck·less /rek′lis/ *adj.* Careless: *reckless* driving.

re·con·sid·er /rē′kən·sid′ər/ *v.* To consider again, possibly thinking of changing your mind.

re·fer /ri·fûr′/ *v.* **re·ferred, re·fer·ring** To turn to for information, help, or treatment: My doctor *referred* me to an eye specialist.

re·fill /rē·fil′/ *v.* To fill again.

re·fresh·ment /ri·fresh′mənt/ *n.* **1** The state of being refreshed. **2** *(pl.)* Food and drink.

re·fu·el /rē·fyoo′əl *or* rē·fyool′/ *v.* To fill again with fuel.

re·gard /ri·gärd′/ **1** *v.* To show thoughtfulness toward; to respect: I *regard* your feelings highly. **2** *n. (pl.)* Best wishes.

re·heat /rē·hēt′/ *v.* To heat again.

re·joice /ri·jois′/ *v.* **re·joiced, re·joic·ing** To be filled with joy: I *rejoiced* at her good fortune.

re·lay /*n.* rē′lā, *v.* ri·lā′ *or* rē′lā/ **1** *n.* A race in which each member of a team goes only a certain distance. **2** *v.* To pass along information: to *relay* a message.

re·ly /ri·lī′/ *v.* **re·lied, re·ly·ing** To put trust in; to depend: We can *rely* on George to keep our secret.

requirement

re·mem·ber /ri·mem′bər/ *v.* **1** To bring to mind again. **2** To keep in mind.

re·move /ri·moov′/ *v.* **re·moved, re·mov·ing** To take off or take away: She *removed* the paint from the table.

re·new /ri·n(y)oo′/ *v.* **1** To make like new: Rest *renewed* his health. **2** To get for another period of time; extend: to *renew* library books.

re·paint /rē·pānt′/ *v.* To paint again: to *repaint* with another color.

re·pair /ri·pâr′/ **1** *v.* To fix or mend. **2** *n. (pl.)* The act of repairing.

re·ply /ri·plī′/ *v.* **re·plied, re·ply·ing,** *n.* **1** *v.* To give an answer. **2** *n.* An answer.

rep·tile /rep′til *or* rep′tīl/ *n.* A cold-blooded animal that moves by hopping, crawling, or creeping, as a snake.

re·pub·lic /ri·pub′lik/ *n.* A type of government in which the power to make and carry out the laws is granted to elected officials: The United States is a *republic.*

re·quire·ment /ri·kwīr′mənt/ *n.* Something required or needed: What are the *requirements* for voting?

---

act, āte, câre, ärt;   egg, ēven;   if, īce;   on, ōver, ôr;   book, food;   up, tûrn;
ə = a in *ago,* e in *listen,* i in *giraffe,* o in *pilot,* u in *circus;*   yoo = u in *music;*   oil;   out;
chair; sing; shop; thank; that; zh in *treasure.*

rerun

re·run /rē'run' *or* rē'run'/ *v.* **re·ran, re·run, re·run·ning,** *n.* **1** *v.* To play or show a tape, TV program, or movie again. **2** *n.* A TV program or movie that is shown again: In the summer, most TV shows are *reruns.*

re·spect·ful /ri·spekt'fəl/ *adj.* Courteous; full of respect: My sister is *respectful* of my things.

re·spond /ri·spond'/ *v.* **1** To answer; to reply. **2** To react: Dad *responded* to the medicine.

rest[1] /rest/ **1** *v.* To sleep; to relax. **2** *n.* A break taken to get over being tired. **3** *n.* Something used for support.

rest[2] /rest/ *n.* The amount left over.

re·tell /rē·tel'/ *v.* **re·told, re·tell·ing** To tell again.

re·told /rē·tōld'/ *v.* Past tense and past participle of *retell.*

re·treat /ri·trēt'/ **1** *v.* To stop fighting, as in a battle; to go back; to withdraw. **2** *n.* The act of retreating: The soldiers' *retreat* signaled defeat.

re·u·nite /rē'yoo·nīt'/ *v.* **re·u·nit·ed, re·u·nit·ing** To get or cause to get together again: My friend and I were *re-united* after five years.

re·veal /ri·vēl'/ *v.* **1** To make known: to *reveal* a secret. **2** To make visible; to show: The curtain opened to *reveal* actors on a stage.

re·ward /ri·wôrd'/ **1** *n.* Money, praise, etc., given or received for working hard or doing something special. **2** *v.* To give a reward to or for.

re·wind /rē·wīnd'/ *v.* **re·wound, re·wind·ing** To wind again: I *rewound* the tape.

re·write /rē·rīt'/ *v.* **re·wrote, re·writ·ten, re·writ·ing** To write something over again.

rhythm /rith'əm/ *n.* **1** The repetition of a beat, sound, or accent in a regular pattern: the *rhythm* of drumbeats. **2** The pattern or arrangement of mu-sical sounds or of the syllables in po-etry: I tapped my foot in *rhythm* to the music.

rid·dle /rid'əl/ *n.* A tricky question or problem, usually having a funny an-swer.

rig·id /rij'id/ *adj.* Stiff; unbending: a *rigid* metal pole.

roast /rōst/ **1** *v.* To cook in an oven or over an open fire: We *roasted* two chick-ens for the picnic. **2** *adj.* Having been roasted: *roast* chicken.

ro·bot /rō'bot *or* rō'bət/ *n.* A machine that may look like a human being, built to do work in place of human beings.

rock·et /rok'it/ *n.* A machine that gets its power by burning fuel and oxygen, used to propel a missile or spacecraft.

room·mate /room'māt'/ *n.* A person who shares an apartment or house with an-other.

run·ner /run'ər/ *n.* A person who runs for exercise or in a race.

ru·ral /roor'əl/ *adj.* Having to do with the country rather than the city: *Rural* life is quieter than city life.

rus·tle /rus'əl/ *v.* **rus·tled, rus·tling,** *n.* **1** *v.* To make or cause to make the sound of things brushing against each other: The wind *rustled* the leaves. **2** *n.* The sound of things rubbing together: the *rustle* of paper.

rustle

| saddle | service |

S

sad·dle /sad′əl/ *n., v.* **sad·dled, sad·dling** **1** *n.* A padded seat, usually of leather, on a horse or bicycle. **2** *v.* To put a saddle on.

sad·ness /sad′nis/ *n.* The condition of being sad.

sal·ad /sal′əd/ *n.* Raw vegetables, such as lettuce, celery, or tomatoes, and sometimes chopped meat, fish, or eggs, served with a dressing.

sal·vage /sal′vij/ *v.* **sal·vaged, sal·vag·ing** To save from destruction: They were able to *salvage* the ship's log.

sam·ple /sam′pəl/ *n., v.* **sam·pled, sam·pling** **1** *n.* A part or an example of a larger thing: a *sample* of material. **2** *v.* To try, to take a taste.

san·dal /san′dəl/ *n.* A type of shoe consisting of a sole with straps to hold your foot in place.

sat·is·fy /sat′is·fī/ *v.* **sat·is·fied, sat·is·fy·ing** **1** To fill a need or desire completely: The meal *satisfied* my hunger. **2** To free from doubt; to convince: The suspect's story did not *satisfy* the police.

sau·cer /sô′sər/ *n.* **1** A round, almost flat dish, used to hold a cup. **2** Anything shaped like a saucer: a flying *saucer*.

scared /skârd/ *adj.* Afraid.

scarf /skärf/ *n., pl.* **scarves** /skärvz/ A square or long rectangular piece of silk, wool, cotton, etc., worn on the head or around the neck or shoulders.

sched·ule /skej′ool/ *n., v.* **sched·uled, sched·ul·ing** **1** *n.* A plan of the times when certain things are to be done or take place: a train *schedule*. **2** *v.* To establish a time order: I *scheduled* the class for 10 A.M.

scis·sors /siz′ərz/ *n., pl.* A cutting tool with two sharp blades that close together to cut.

scoop /skoop/ **1** *n.* A small measuring tool like a shovel. **2** *n.* The amount held by a scoop. **3** *v.* To take out or up with a scoop.

scowl /skoul/ **1** *v.* To frown; to look angry. **2** *n.* A frown; an angry look.

scrap /skrap/ *n.* A small piece of something: a *scrap* of food.

screen /skrēn/ *n.* **1** A door or window covering made of wire. **2** A surface on which movies or slides are shown.

scrub /skrub/ *v.* **scrubbed, scrub·bing** To clean by rubbing very hard.

sea·son /sē′zən/ *n.* **1** Spring, summer, autumn, or winter. **2** Some particular time of year: the football *season*.

se·lec·tion /si·lek′shən/ *n.* **1** The act of choosing; choice. **2** Something or someone chosen.

sense /sens/ *n., v.* **sensed, sens·ing** **1** *n.* Taste, smell, sight, hearing, or touch. **2** *n.* An awareness or understanding: a fine *sense* of humor. **3** *v.* To become aware of something: We *sensed* danger.

sen·si·ble /sen′sə·bəl/ *adj.* Having or showing good sense or judgment.

sen·tence /sen′təns/ *n.* A group of words that makes sense by itself.

ser·geant /sär′jənt/ *n.* A rank in the military or a police force.

se·ri·ous /sir′ē·əs/ *adj.* **1** Thoughtful; grave: a *serious* expression. **2** Very important: a *serious* matter.

serve /sûrv/ *v.* **served, serv·ing** **1** To perform a duty or function; to work: Our President may *serve* for two four-year terms. **2** To bring food; to wait on. **3** To put the ball in play, as in tennis.

ser·vice /sûr′vis/ *n., v.* **ser·viced, ser·vic·ing** **1** *n.* The act of serving: I received quick *service* in the shop. **2** *v.* To repair: to *service* a car.

---

act, āte, câre, ärt;　　egg, ēven;　　if, īce;　　on, ōver, ôr;　　book, food;　　up, tûrn;
ə = a in *ago*, e in *listen*, i in *giraffe*, o in *pilot*, u in *circus*;　　yoo = u in *music*;　　oil;　　out;
ch**air**; si**ng**; **sh**op; **th**ank; **th**at; **zh** in *treasure*.

settlement

set·tle·ment /set′əl·mənt/ *n.* **1** A place settled by a group of people; colony. **2** An agreement: a *settlement* of a labor dispute.

set·tler /set′lər/ *n.* A person who settles or makes a home in a new country or in a colony.

shack /shak/ *n.* A small building, usually one in bad condition; a hut.

sham·poo /sham·poo′/ **1** *n.* A soap used to wash hair. **2** *v.* To wash hair.

shelf /shelf/ *n., pl.* **shelves** /shelvz/ A thin piece of wood, glass, etc., attached to a wall or built into a piece of furniture, used to hold things.

shel·ter /shel′tər/ **1** *n.* Something that covers and protects from harm or bad weather, as a tent or house. **2** *n.* The condition of being sheltered: We found *shelter* before the storm broke. **3** *v.* To protect; to give shelter to.

shep·herd /shep′ərd/ *n.* A person who herds or takes care of sheep.

sher·bet /shûr′bit/ *n.* A frozen, usually fruit-flavored dessert, made with water and milk.

sher·iff /sher′if/ *n.* The chief law enforcement officer in a county.

shift /shift/ **1** *v.* To move from one position to another: He *shifted* his bookbag from one shoulder to the other. **2** *n.* A change in position or direction: a *shift* in the wind.

shin·y /shī′nē/ *adj.* **shin·i·er, shin·i·est** Bright; reflecting light.

shock /shok/ **1** *n.* An unexpected, violent shake or blow: the *shock* of an earthquake. **2** *n.* A sudden, violent, or upsetting event: My parrot's death was a great *shock*. **3** *v.* Cause to feel surprise, terror, or disgust: The bus accident *shocked* the community. **4** *n.* What the body feels when an electric current passes through it.

shook /shŏŏk/ *v.* Past tense of *shake*.

short /shôrt/ **1** *adj.* Not long. **2** *adj.*

silent

Not tall. **3** *adj.* Lacking a sufficient amount: You are a dime *short*. **4** *adv.* Suddenly: Rick stopped *short*. **5** *n.* *(pl.)* Pants that stop above the knees.

shout /shout/ **1** *n.* A sudden loud yell. **2** *v.* To make a sudden loud yell. **3** *v.* To talk loudly.

show·er /shou′ər/ **1** *n.* A short rainfall. **2** *v.* To rain. **3** *n.* A bath taken standing up with water coming from an overhead nozzle.

shrill /shril/ *adj.* Having a high, sharp sound: Some birds make *shrill* sounds.

shrink /shringk/ *v.* **shrank** *or* **shrunk, shrunk** *or* **shrunk·en, shrink·ing** To get or cause to get smaller.

shrub /shrub/ *n.* A low, treelike plant with many branches; a bush.

shrunk /shrungk/ *v.* A past tense and past participle of *shrink*.

shy /shī/ *adj.* Quiet; not at ease with strangers.

sick·ness /sik′nis/ *n.* **1** The condition of being sick or ill. **2** A certain disease or illness.

side·walk /sīd′wôk′/ *n.* A paved footpath along the side of a street.

sign /sīn/ **1** *n.* A symbol, object, expression, or motion that has a meaning or stands for something: The *sign* for multiplication is ×. **2** *n.* A board with writing that gives information or a warning. **3** *v.* To write your name in your own handwriting.

sig·na·ture /sig′nə·chər/ *n.* A person's name written by that person.

si·lent /sī′lənt/ *adj.* **1** Making no noise; soundless. **2** Remaining quiet; not speaking.

silver

sil·ver /sil′vər/ **1** *n*. A grayish-white metal. **2** *adj*. Made of or containing silver: *silver* jewelry. **3** *adj*. Having the color of silver.

sin·cere·ly /sin·sir′lē/ *adv*. **1** Honestly; really. **2** Truly, often used with *yours:* The letter closed with "*Sincerely* yours, Liza."

sin·gle /sing′gəl/ *adj., v.* **sin·gled, sin·gling** **1** *adj*. One by itself; used by one: a *single* bed. **2** *v*. To choose one out of a group: Celia was *singled* out for an honor. **3** *adj*. Not married.

sin·gu·lar /sing′gyə·lər/ **1** *adj*. Referring to only one: a *singular* noun. **2** *n*. The form of a word to show only one: *Tax* is the *singular* of *taxes*.

sketch /skech/ **1** *n*. A quick, rough, or unfinished drawing. **2** *v*. To make a rough drawing: I decided to *sketch* the landscape quickly and paint it later when I arrived home.

ski /skē/ *n., v.* **skied, skiing**, *adj.* **1** *n*. One of a pair of long runners fastened to the soles of boots for gliding over snow. **2** *v*. To move on skis. **3** *adj*. Having to do with skiing: *ski* boots.

skin /skin/ *n., v.* **skinned, skin·ning** **1** *n*. The outside covering of people, animals, fruits, etc. **2** *v*. To scrape off skin: to *skin* a knee.

skirt /skûrt/ *n*. A piece of clothing that hangs from the waist.

slant /slant/ **1** *v*. To slope: The floors *slant* in our old house. **2** *n*. A slanting line, direction, or surface: The roof has a sharp *slant*.

sleep·less /slēp′lis/ *adj*. Not able to sleep; without sleep: I spent a *sleepless* night worrying about the opening game.

sleep·y /slē′pē/ *adj*. **sleep·i·er, sleep·i·est** Tired enough to go to sleep; drowsy. —**sleep′i·ly** *adv*.—**sleep′i·ness** *n*.

society

slo·gan /slō′gən/ *n*. An expression or motto used in advertising or campaigning: "Buy one, get one free" is an example of a *slogan*. ► *Slogan* comes from the Gaelic word *sluagh-ghairm,* "a battle cry."

smash /smash/ *v*. **1** To break into pieces. **2** To hit with great force.

smooth /smo͞oth/ **1** *adj*. Without rough spots or lumps. **2** *v*. To make something smooth.—**smooth over** To make something seem more pleasant; to try to excuse.—**smooth sailing** Progress made without difficulty; a situation without problems.

smudge /smuj/ *v*. **smudged, smudg·ing**, *n*. **1** *v*. To blur, smear, or soil. **2** *n*. A dirty mark or spot.

snag /snag/ *v*. **snagged, snag·ging** To tear or catch on something sharp.

snail /snāl/ *n*. A slow-moving animal with a shell on its back.

snake /snāk/ *n*. A crawling reptile with a long, thin body and no legs.

snap /snap/ *v*. **snapped, snap·ping**, *n*. **1** *v*. To close or lock into place with a click. **2** *n*. A fastener or catch. **3** *v*. To try to bite: The dog *snapped* at me. **4** *v*. To break suddenly.

soak /sōk/ *v*. **1** To keep something in a liquid until it is completely wet. **2** To get very wet. **3** To absorb: *Soak* up the spilled milk with a towel.

so·cial /sō′shəl/ *adj*. **1** Living or liking to live with others. **2** Friendly toward other people. **3** Having to do with friendliness and companionship: a *social* event.

so·ci·e·ty /sə·sī′ə·tē/ *n., pl.* **so·ci·e·ties** **1** A group of people that depend on one another in many ways and have certain customs in common. **2** An organization.

---

act, āte, câre, ärt; egg, ēven; if, īce; on, ōver, ôr; bo͝ok, fo͞od; up, tûrn;
ə=a in *ago,* e in *listen,* i in *giraffe,* o in *pilot,* u in *circus;* yo͞o=u in *music;* oil; out;
chair; sing; shop; thank; that; zh in *treasure.*

softness

soft·ness /sôft′nis/ *n.* The condition of being gentle or not hard.

soil¹ /soil/ *n.* Ground; earth.

soil² /soil/ *v.* To make or become dirty.

sol·id /sol′id/ **1** *n.* Anything that is not a liquid or a gas: Most metals are *solids.* **2** *adj.* Not hollow; being of one material all the way through: a *solid* wooden door.

sor·row /sor′ō/ *n.* Great sadness or grief: He expressed deep *sorrow* when he heard that my grandfather had died.

sound /sound/ **1** *n.* Anything that can be heard. **2** *v.* To make a sound. **3** *v.* To seem: That *sounds* like a good idea.

space /spās/ *n.* **1** The unlimited area that holds the universe: The comet hurled through *space.* **2** A limited area; the area between two things or inside something: There is *space* for one more desk in our room.

space·craft /spās′kraft′/ *n.* A vehicle that can travel in outer space.

spade /spād/ *n.* A tool used for digging that looks like a shovel.

spar·kle /spär′kəl/ *v.* **spar·kled, spar·kling** To shine or glitter as if giving off sparks of light: The water *sparkled* in the bright sun.

speak·er /spē′kər/ *n.* A person who speaks or gives a speech.

spe·cial /spesh′əl/ *adj.* **1** Out of the ordinary: a *special* day. **2** For a particular purpose: a *special* dress.

speech·less /spēch′lis/ *adj.* Not speaking or unable to speak.

spi·der /spī′dər/ *n.* An insect that has eight legs and spins a web.

squirrel

splash /splash/ **1** *v.* To throw or scatter water or mud. **2** *n.* The act or sound of splashing: a big *splash.*

splint /splint/ *n.* A piece of wood or metal used to hold a broken bone in place.

spoil /spoil/ *v.* **spoiled** *or* **spoilt, spoil·ing** **1** To ruin. **2** To become bad: The butter *spoiled* in the hot sun. **3** To give someone everything he or she wants.

sponge /spunj/ *n., v.* **sponged, spong·ing** **1** *n.* A simple water animal whose dried skeleton is used for washing, cleaning, etc. **2** *n.* Any spongelike material that absorbs liquids. **3** *v.* To wipe or clean with a sponge.

sprin·kle /spring′kəl/ *v.* **sprin·kled, sprin·kling,** *n.* **1** *v.* To scatter in drops or bits, as of water or sugar. **2** *v.* To rain lightly. **3** *n.* A light rain. **4** *n.* A small quantity.

square /skwâr/ *n.* **1** A shape having four equal sides and four right angles (□). **2** *adj.* Having the shape of a square.

squeeze /skwēz/ *v.* **squeezed, squeez·ing** **1** To press hard on or together. **2** To push out by pressure: to *squeeze* oranges. **3** To force or push: We *squeezed* onto the crowded bus.

squir·rel /skwûr′əl/ *n.* A small furry animal with sharp teeth and a long bushy tail.

| stable | stream |

sta·ble¹ /stā′bəl/ *adj.* **sta·bler, sta·blest**
1 Not easily moved or shaken; firm.
2 Long-lasting or permanent.

sta·ble² /stā′bəl/ *n., v.* **sta·bled, sta·bling** **1** *n.* A building for housing and feeding horses. **2** *v.* To put or shelter in a stable.

stamp /stamp/ **1** *n.* A small piece of paper with glue on the back, used for mailing letters and packages. **2** *n.* A tool that makes a mark: a rubber *stamp*. **3** *v.* To put your foot down hard.

stand /stand/ *v.* **stood, stand·ing** **1** To take or keep an upright position: I *stood* up and walked away. **2** To put up with: He can't *stand* loud music.

starve /stärv/ *v.* **starved, starv·ing**
1 To suffer or die from lack of food.
2 To feel extremely hungry.

state /stāt/ *n.* An area within a country: Ohio is a *state*.

state·hood /stāt′hood/ *n.* The condition of being a state: Hawaii applied for *statehood* in 1959.

state·ment /stāt′mənt/ *n.* A sentence that tells something. It ends with a period.

sta·tion /stā′shən/ **1** *n.* A place, as a building or headquarters, occupied and used by a group working together: a fire *station*. **2** *n.* A place, and usually a building, where trains or buses stop and where passengers get on or off.

sta·tion·ar·y /stā′shən·er′ē/ *adj.* Staying or keeping in one place; not moving or movable.

sta·tion·er·y /stā′shən·er′ē/ *n.* Materials used in writing, especially letter paper and envelopes.

stay /stā/ **1** *v.* To remain. **2** *n.* A visit: a short *stay*.

steel /stēl/ **1** *n.* A hard metal that contains iron and carbon. **2** Made of steel: a *steel* tool.

step /step/ *n., v.* **stepped, step·ping**
1 *n.* A movement made by lifting your foot and putting it down in another place. **2** *n.* Where you put your foot when going up or down; a stair. **3** *v.* To move by taking steps. **4** *v.* To put your foot down.

stir /stûr/ *v.* **stirred, stir·ring,** *n.* **1** *v.* To move around with a circular motion: *Stir* the soup. **2** *n.* The act of stirring: Give the soup a *stir*. **3** *v.* To move or cause to move, especially slightly: The leaves *stirred;* The wind *stirred* the tall grass.

stitch /stich/ **1** *n.* What results when a needle and thread go through material and back again. **2** *v.* To sew.

stock /stok/ **1** *n.* Things for sale or future use. **2** *v.* To put in or keep a supply: That shop *stocks* games.

stood /stood/ *v.* Past tense and past participle of *stand*.

stop /stop/ *v.* **stopped, stop·ping,** *n.* **1** *v.* To come or bring to a halt. **2** *v.* To keep from doing something: She *stopped* him from taking candy. **3** *v.* To leave off doing something. **4** *n.* The act of stopping. **5** *n.* The place where something stops.

stor·age /stôr′ij/ *n.* **1** The act of storing or keeping for some future time. **2** A place for storing things.

sto·ry¹ /stôr′ē/ *n., pl.* **sto·ries** **1** An account of something that happened. **2** A tale that is usually made up.

sto·ry² /stôr′ē/ *n., pl.* **sto·ries** A floor in a building.

stove /stōv/ *n.* Something used for cooking or heating.

stream /strēm/ **1** *n.* A small flowing river. **2** *v.* To flow or move: Tears *streamed* down my face. **3** *n.* Any steady flow: a *stream* of traffic.

---

act, āte, câre, ärt;　　egg, ēven;　　if, īce;　　on, ōver, ôr;　　book, food;　　up, tûrn;
ə = a in *ago*, e in *listen*, i in *giraffe*, o in *pilot*, u in *circus;*　　yoo = u in *music;*　　oil;　　out;
chair; sing; shop; thank; that; zh in *treasure*.

197

streamline

stream·line /strēm′līn′/ *v.* **stream·lined, stream·lin·ing** **1** To shape something so that it offers the least resistance to air or water: to *streamline* a race car. **2** *adj. use:* a *streamlined* boat.

stress /stres/ **1** *n.* Accent in speech. **2** *v.* To accent a syllable. **3** *n.* Mental tension; worry.

strike /strīk/ *v.* **struck, strik·ing,** *n.* **1** *v.* To hit. **2** *v.* To cause to burn by friction. **3** *n.* In baseball, a swing that misses the ball. **4** *v.* To tell the time by sounding a bell: The clock *struck* midnight.

strug·gle /strug′əl/ *n., v.* **strug·gled, strug·gling** **1** *n.* A strong effort. **2** *v.* To try hard, especially to overcome something. **3** *n.* A fight.

stub·born /stub′ərn/ *adj.* Wanting to do things your way; refusing to give in.

stud·y /stud′ē/ *v.* **stud·ied, stud·y·ing** To work to learn something.

stum·ble /stum′bəl/ *v.* **stum·bled, stum·bling** **1** To trip. **2** To walk or speak in a shaky way.

stun /stun/ *v.* **stunned, stun·ning** **1** To knock unconscious; to make dizzy. **2** To shock; to astonish.

style /stīl/ *n.* The type of fashion popular at the present time.

sub·ject /sub′jikt/ *n.* **1** A word or group of words that names whom or what a sentence is about. **2** A course of study.

sub·scrip·tion /səb·skrip′shən/ *n.* An agreement that a person will receive a certain number of issues of a magazine or newspaper.

suc·cess·ful /sək·ses′fəl/ *adj.* Achieving a desired goal.

sud·den·ly /sud′ən·lē/ *adv.* All of a sudden; quickly and without warning.

suf·fix /*n.* suf′iks, *v.* suf′iks or sə·fiks′/ **1** *n.* One or more syllables added on at the end of a word to make another word of different meaning or function, as

swept

-*ment,* -*ness,* -*ible,* -*ful,* -*ous,* or -*ly,* or to make an inflectional form, as -*ed,* -*ing,* or -*est.* **2** *v.* To add as a suffix.

sug·ar /shŏŏg′ər/ *n.* A sweetener.

sug·ges·tion /sə(g)·jes′chən/ *n.* **1** The act of suggesting. **2** Something that is suggested.

su·per·sti·tion /sōō′pər·stish′ən/ *n.* An unreasoning fear or belief that certain objects, places, or actions have power over the normal course of events: The belief that a black cat crossing your path brings bad luck is a *superstition.*

sup·per /sup′ər/ *n.* An evening meal.

sup·pose /sə·pōz′/ *v.* **sup·posed, sup·pos·ing** To think or believe.

sur·plus /sûr′plus/ **1** *n.* The amount remaining above what is used or needed: The farmers' *surplus* of wheat was sold to other countries. **2** *adj.* Extra: *surplus* grain.

sur·round /sə·round′/ *v.* To close in on all sides; to encircle: An island is *surrounded* by water.

sus·pense·ful /sə·spens′fəl/ *adj.* Full of uncertainty; full of suspense.

swal·low¹ /swol′ō/ *v.* To make food or drink go from your mouth into your stomach.

swal·low² /swol′ō/ *n.* A small bird with a V-shaped tail.

swap /swop/ *v.* **swapped, swap·ping** To trade or exchange.

swarm /swôrm/ **1** *n.* A large group of insects. **2** *v.* To move together in a group: Bees *swarmed* around the hive.

sweep /swēp/ *v.* **swept, sweep·ing** **1** To clean, collect, or clear away with a broom or brush. **2** To move, go, or pass swiftly or with force: Fire *swept* through the house.

swell /swel/ *v.* **swelled, swol·len, swell·ing** To get bigger: *swollen* feet.

swept /swept/ *v.* Past tense and past participle of *sweep.*

swerve /swûrv/ *v.* **swerved, swerv·ing,** *n.* **1** *v.* To turn or cause to turn to get out of the way: The car *swerved* to avoid hitting the deer. **2** *n.* The act of swerving.

swim·mer /swim′ər/ *n.* A person who swims.

swirl /swûrl/ *v.* To move in a twisting or spinning motion: The fan made the dust *swirl* around the room.

swol·len /swō′lən/ *v.* Past participle of *swell*.

syl·la·ble /sil′ə·bəl/ *n.* A word part that has only one vowel sound.

T

tag /tag/ *n., v.* **tagged, tag·ging** **1** *n.* A small piece of paper; a label. **2** *v.* To attach or put on a tag. **3** *v.* To follow closely: He *tagged* after his sister.

tai·lor /tā′lər/ *n.* A person who makes or repairs clothing.

tan·gle /tang′gəl/ *v.* **tan·gled, tan·gling,** *n.* **1** *v.* To twist into a mass of knots. **2** *n.* A mass of knots; snarl. **3** *n.* A state of confusion; mess.

tar·di·ness /tär′dē·nis/ *n.* The condition of being tardy or late: We talked to Joel about his *tardiness*.

tar·dy /tär′dē/ *adj.* **tar·di·er, tar·di·est** Late; not on time.

tar·get /tär′git/ *n.* Something that is aimed or shot at.

tar·iff /tar′if/ *n.* A tax paid on goods coming into or going out of a country.

task /task/ *n.* A chore or job: My neighbor asked me to help her with the *task* of mowing the lawn.

taste·less /tāst′lis/ *adj.* Without flavor or taste: *tasteless* stew.

tax /taks/ *n., pl.* **tax·es,** *v.* **1** *n.* Money paid by people and businesses for the

support of their government. **2** *v.* To charge a tax: to *tax* property.

teach·er /tē′chər/ *n.* A person who teaches or helps others learn.

team /tēm/ *n.* **1** A group of people who work or play together. **2** Two or more animals that do work together.

tem·po·rar·y /tem′pə·rer′ē/ *adj.* Not lasting for a long time; not permanent: a *temporary* job.

ten·der /ten′dər/ *adj.* **1** Not tough; soft. **2** Gentle and loving. **3** Painful; sensitive to touch.

tense /tens/ *adj.* **tens·er, tens·est** **1** Stretched tight; stiff: The rope is *tense*. **2** Nervous; strained.

ter·ri·ble /ter′ə·bəl/ *adj.* **1** Causing terror or fear. **2** Extremely bad.

thank·ful /thangk′fəl/ *adj.* Grateful; full of thanks: a *thankful* friend.

thirst·y /thûrs′tē/ *adj.* **thirst·i·er, thirst·i·est** Needing or wanting something to drink.

thought·ful /thôt′fəl/ *adj.* **1** Full of thought: You seem *thoughtful* today. **2** Considerate; showing concern.

threat /thret/ *n.* **1** A warning that something will be done to hurt or punish. **2** A sign that something bad or unwelcome might happen: a *threat* of showers.

thrift /thrift/ *n.* The habit of not wasting anything; the saving of money.

throat /thrōt/ *n.* The upper part of the passage that leads from the back of the mouth to the lungs and stomach.

throne /thrōn/ *n.* The special chair on which a king, queen, or church official sits during ceremonies.

through·out /throo·out′/ *adv., prep.* In every part of; all through: The house is carpeted *throughout*. Thanksgiving is observed *throughout* the country.

---

act, āte, câre, ärt;   egg, ēven;   if, īce;   on, ōver, ôr;   boŏk, foōd;   up, tûrn;
ə = a in *ago,* e in *listen,* i in *giraffe,* o in *pilot,* u in *circus;*   yoō = u in *music;*   oil;   out;
chair; sing; shop; thank; that; zh in *treasure.*

199

thunder

thun·der /thun′dər/ **1** *n.* The loud noise that follows lightning. **2** *v.* To make or sound like thunder: The plane *thundered* down the runway.

tick·et /tik′it/ **1** *n.* A card that allows you to get on a train, bus, or airplane or into a theater. **2** *n.* A tag or label. **3** *v.* To attach a ticket to. **4** *n.* A written order to appear in court for breaking a traffic law.

tim·id /tim′id/ *adj.* Fearful or shy.

tis·sue /tish′oo/ *n.* **1** Light paper used as a handkerchief. **2** Tissue paper.

to·tal /tōt′əl/ **1** *n.* The whole amount. **2** *adj.* Complete. **3** *v.* To add: She *totaled* the bill.

tour·na·ment /toor′nə·mənt *or* tûr′nə·mənt/ *n.* A series of games or matches involving many players.

to·ward /tôrd *or* tə·wôrd′/ *prep.* **1** In the direction of; to: We are walking *toward* the library. **2** Near: We left for the beach *toward* afternoon. **3** For: This money is going *toward* your college education.

tow·el /toul *or* tou′əl/ *n.* A piece of cloth or paper used for drying.

traf·fic /traf′ik/ **1** *n.* The movement of people, cars, buses, etc., through an area or along a route. **2** *adj.* Having to do with traffic.

tramp /tramp/ **1** *v.* To walk with a heavy step: to *tramp* up the stairs. **2** *v.* To walk or wander: to *tramp* through the forest. **3** *n.* A person who wanders about and has no home; a hobo.

tram·ple /tram′pəl/ *v.* **tram·pled, tram·pling** To flatten by stepping on.

tray /trā/ *n.* A flat pan with a low rim used for holding and carrying food or other things.

trea·ty /trē′tē/ *n., pl.* **trea·ties** A written agreement between two or more countries regarding peace or trade.

trek /trek/ *v.* **trekked, trek·king,** *n.* **1** *v.* To make a long, slow, hard journey:

unbutton

to *trek* through the jungle. **2** *n.* A long hard journey: The *trek* across the desert took ten days.

trem·ble /trem′bəl/ *v.* **trem·bled, trem·bling** To shake with fear or cold.

trick /trik/ **1** *n.* Something done to fool or cheat. **2** *n.* Something clever or skillful: card *tricks*. **3** *v.* To fool or cheat.

trot /trot/ *n., v.* **trot·ted, trot·ting 1** *n.* The gait of a horse between a walk and a run. **2** *v.* To move at a trot: to *trot* around a track.

trou·ble·some /trub′əl·səm/ *adj.* Causing trouble: a *troublesome* person.

truth·ful /trooth′fəl/ *adj.* Honest.

tun·nel /tun′əl/ *n.* A long, narrow way under a river or through a mountain.

tur·key /tûr′kē/ *n.* A large North American bird, used as food.

turn·pike (tpk) /tûrn′pīk′/ *n.* A highway on which you must pay a toll.

tu·tor /t(y)oo′tər/ **1** *n.* A person who teaches or gives private lessons. **2** *v.* To give or receive private lessons.

twine /twīn/ *n.* Strong, heavy string.

twist /twist/ *v.* **1** To turn or wind around: The vine was *twisted* around the pole. **2** To turn: to *twist* off the cap. **3** To hurt a part of the body by turning: Tom *twisted* his ankle.

type /tīp/ *n., v.* **typed, typ·ing 1** *n.* A kind; a group of things that have something in common: a *type* of car. **2** *v.* To use a typewriter.

ty·rant /tī′rənt/ *n.* **1** An all-powerful ruler. **2** Someone who uses power unfairly or cruelly.

U

un·be·liev·a·ble /un′bi·lē′və·bəl/ *adj.* Not to be believed; incredible; an *unbelievable* story.

un·but·ton /un·but′ən/ *v.* To unfasten a button or buttons.

un·com·fort·a·ble /un·kum′fər·tə·bəl *or* un·kumf′tə(r)·bəl/ *adj.* Not comfortable; not at ease: an *uncomfortable* bed.

un·cov·er /un·kuv′ər/ *v.* **1** To take off the cover of: to *uncover* a pot. **2** To reveal: to *uncover* clues.

un·der·stand /un′dər·stand′/ *v.* **un·der·stood, un·der·stand·ing** **1** To grasp the meaning of: Do you *understand* the directions? **2** To accept as fact; to believe: I *understand* that you are moving. **3** To know well: Laraine *understands* fractions.

un·der·stood /un′dər·stood′/ *v.* Past tense and past participle of *understand*.

un·der·wa·ter /un′dər·wô′tər/ **1** *adj.* Found or done under the surface of the water: an *underwater* cave. **2** *adv.* Under the surface of the water: The treasure is buried *underwater*.

un·hap·py /un·hap′ē/ *adj.* Sad; not happy.

u·ni·ver·si·ty /yōō′nə·vûr′sə·tē/ *n., pl.* **u·ni·ver·si·ties** A school of higher learning consisting of more than one college.

un·kind /un·kīnd′/ *adj.* Cruel; not kind.

un·like /un·līk′/ *prep.* Different from; not like: This movie is *unlike* any other I have seen.

un·load /un·lōd′/ *v.* To remove or remove the load from: to *unload* the car.

un·lock /un·lok′/ *v.* To open or unfasten the lock of: to *unlock* a trunk.

un·luck·y /un·luk′ē/ *adj.* Having or bringing bad luck; not lucky.

un·pleas·ant /un·plez′ənt/ *adj.* Not agreeable; not pleasant: Cleaning the bird cage is an *unpleasant* task.

un·self·ish /un·sel′fish/ *adj.* Caring about others more than yourself; not selfish.

ur·gent /ûr′jənt/ *adj.* **1** Requiring quick action or attention: an *urgent* need to conserve water. **2** Insistent; pressing: an *urgent* request.

use·less /yōōs′lis/ *adj.* Having no use; worthless: a *useless* old stove.

V

va·ca·tion /vā·kā′shən/ *n.* A period of time for rest and recreation spent away from work or school.

val·ley /val′ē/ *n.* A low area between mountains or hills.

var·y /vâr′ē/ *v.* **var·ied, var·y·ing** **1** To change or alter: Dad *varies* his jogging route. **2** To be different in some way: My shirts *vary* in color.

vast /vast/ *adj.* Very large; huge; enormous: a *vast* desert.—**vast′ly** *adv.* —**vast′ness** *n.*

veg·e·ta·ble /vej′(ə·)tə·bəl/ **1** *n.* A plant or part of a plant used as food: Carrots and spinach are *vegetables*. **2** *adj.* Made with or from vegetables: *vegetable* soup.

verb /vûrb/ *n.* A word that shows action or being.

---

act, āte, câre, ärt; egg, ēven; if, īce; on, ōver, ôr; bŏok, fōod; up, tûrn;
ə = a in *ago*, e in *listen*, i in *giraffe*, o in *pilot*, u in *circus*; yōō = u in *music*; oil; out;
chair; sing; shop; thank; that; zh in *treasure*.

verse

verse /vûrs/ *n.* **1** Poetry. **2** A poem. **3** A stanza or line of a poem or song.

vic·to·ry /vik′tər·ē/ *n., pl.* **vic·to·ries** The defeat of an enemy or opponent.

vil·lage /vil′ij/ *n.* A small town.

vi·rus /vī′rəs/ *n.* Tiny particles that multiply in certain living cells, causing various diseases.

vis·it /viz′it/ **1** *v.* To go or come to see. **2** *n.* The act of visiting; a short stay as a guest.

vo·cab·u·lar·y /vō·kab′yə·ler′ē/ *n., pl.* **vo·cab·u·lar·ies** The words that people know and use.

vote /vōt/ *n., v.* **vot·ed, vot·ing** **1** *n.* A formal expression of choice: She received the most *votes* in the election. **2** *v.* To choose by a vote.

vow /vou/ **1** *n.* A promise or pledge: a *vow* of secrecy. **2** *v.* To make a vow: We *vowed* to love each other.

voy·age /voi′ij/ *n., v.* **voy·aged, voy·ag·ing** **1** *n.* A trip by water. **2** *n.* Any journey, as through air or space. **3** *v.* To travel on a voyage.

W

waist /wāst/ *n.* The part of your body between your chest and your hips.

ware·house /wâr′hous′/ *n.* A building where goods are stored.

warmth /wôrmth/ *n.* **1** The condition or feeling of being warm: the *warmth* of a fire. **2** A warm feeling: The *warmth* of my classmates made me feel welcome.

warn·ing /wôr′ning/ *n.* Something that tells you to expect danger.

wart /wôrt/ *n.* A small, hard lump that grows on the skin.

wa·ter·proof /wô′tər·prōof′ *or* wot′ər·prōof′/ *adj.* Able to keep out water: Wear your *waterproof* jacket when you go out in the rain.

weak·ness /wēk′·nis/ *n.* The condition of being weak or lacking in strength.

withdraw

week·end /wēk′end′/ *n.* Saturday and Sunday or from Friday evening to the following Monday morning.

wharf /(h)wôrf/ *n., pl.* **wharves** /(h)wôrvz/ A large dock where ships load or unload their cargo.

when·ev·er /(h)wen′ev′ər/ *adv., conj.* At whatever time: *Whenever* did you get a chance to knit this sweater? We'll leave *whenever* you want.

wher·ev·er /(h)wâr′ev′ər/ *conj., adv.* In or to whatever place: We'll have the picnic *wherever* you want. *Wherever* did you buy that hat?

whirl /(h)wûrl/ *v.* To spin or make to spin around very fast: The skater *whirled* around the rink.

whis·per /(h)wis′pər/ **1** *v.* To speak softly. **2** *n.* The act of whispering.

whis·tle /(h)wis′əl/ *v.* **whis·tled, whis·tling,** *n.* **1** *v.* To make a sharp sound by forcing your breath through your teeth or closed lips. **2** *n.* The act of whistling. **3** *n.* A device you blow to make a sound like a whistle. **4** *v.* To make a whistling sound: The kettle is *whistling.*

wife /wīf/ *n., pl.* **wives** A married woman.

wind·mill /wind′mil′/ *n.* A machine with sails or vanes that turn by the force of the wind, often used to pump water.

win·dow /win′dō/ *n.* An opening in a wall that lets in air and light.

wise /wīz/ *adj.* **wis·er, wis·est** Having or showing good sense: *wise* advice.

with·draw /with·drô′ *or* with·drô′/ *v.* **with·drew, with·drawn, with·draw·ing** **1** To take away or remove:

to *withdraw* money.   **2** To move back or to take back: to *withdraw* an offer.

with·drew /wi<u>th</u>·droo′ *or* with·droo′/ *v.* Past tense of *withdraw.*

wolf /woolf/ *n., pl.* **wolves** /woolvz/ A wild animal, like a dog, which hunts in groups and preys on other animals.

won·der·ful /wun′dər·fəl/ *adj.*   **1** Causing wonder; amazing.   **2** Very good.

wool·en /wool′ən/ *adj.* Made of wool: a *woolen* sweater.

word /wûrd/ *n.*   **1** A sound or group of sounds that has one meaning.   **2** The letters that stand for a word.

world /wûrld/ *n.*   **1** Earth.   **2** Everything; the universe.   **3** The people living on Earth.

worm /wûrm/ *n.* A small crawling animal having a soft, thin body and no legs.

wor·ry /wûr′ē/ *v.* **wor·ried, wor·ry·ing,** *n., pl.* **wor·ries**   **1** *v.* To be or make someone uneasy or upset.   **2** *n.* Something that makes you worry.

wor·ship /wûr′ship/ *n., v.*   **1** *n.* Honor and respect given to God: a house of *worship.*   **2** *v.* To give honor and respect to, especially to God.   **3** *v.* To attend services at a house of worship.

worst /wûrst/ *adj.* Least good or well: This was our *worst* harvest.

worth·less /wûrth′lis/ *adj.* Useless; without worth or value.

worth·while /wûrth′(h)wīl′/ *adj.* Having worth or importance.

wrap /rap/ *v.* **wrapped, wrap·ping**   **1** To put a cover around something.   **2** To wind around; to cover.

wreath /rēth/ *n., pl.* **wreaths** /rē<u>th</u>z/ A circle of flowers or leaves twisted together, usually displayed on windows and doors at Christmas.

wreck /rek/   **1** *v.* To destroy: Our boat was *wrecked* in the storm.   **2** *n.* Something that has been ruined.

wres·tle /res′əl/ *v.* **wres·tled, wres·tling,** *n.*   **1** *v.* To throw or force someone into a particular position on the ground.   **2** *n.* The act of wrestling.   **3** *v.* To struggle: to *wrestle* with a problem.

wrig·gle /rig′əl/ *v.* **wrig·gled, wrig·gling**   **1** To squirm or twist.   **2** To move by twisting: The caterpillar *wriggled* down my arm.

wring /ring/ *v.* **wrung** /rung/, **wring·ing** To squeeze liquid out by twisting.

wrin·kle /ring′kəl/ *n., v.* **wrin·kled, wrin·kling**   **1** *n.* A small fold, usually on cloth or skin: deep *wrinkles* on his forehead.   **2** *v.* To make wrinkles in; to become wrinkled: My skirt *wrinkled* when I sat down.

wrist /rist/ *n.* The place where your hand joins your arm.

wrist·watch /rist′woch′/ *n.* A small timepiece usually worn on the wrist.

write /rīt/ *v.* **wrote, writ·ten, writ·ing**   **1** To make or form letters and words.   **2** To make up stories; to be an author.   **3** To send a letter.

writ·ten /rit′ən/ *v.* Past participle of *write.*

wrong /rông/ *adj.*   **1** Not right; not true.   **2** Not working or acting properly: Something is *wrong* with my watch.

Y

yes·ter·day /yes′tər·dē *or* yes′tər·dā′/ *n.* The day before today.

---

act, āte, câre, ärt;   egg, ēven;   if, īce;   on, ōver, ôr;   book, food;   up, tûrn;
ə = a in *ago,* e in *listen,* i in *giraffe,* o in *pilot,* u in *circus;*   yoo = u in *music;*   oil;   out;
chair; si**ng**; **sh**op; **th**ank; <u>th</u>at; **zh** in *treasure.*

SPELLING THESAURUS

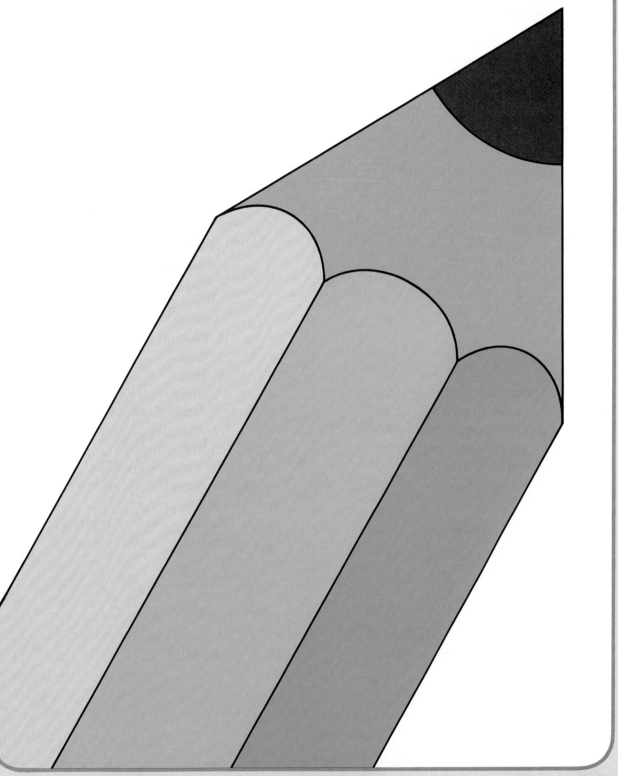

What Is a Thesaurus?

A **thesaurus** lists words and their synonyms. Like a dictionary, a thesaurus lists words in alphabetical order. Each of these words is called an **entry word**. A list of synonyms follows the entry word. Sometimes a thesaurus lists antonyms.

Look at the parts of this thesaurus entry for the word *customer*.

The **entry word** is in red letters. It is followed by the part of speech and a definition. An **example sentence** shows how the word can be used.

> customer *n.* A buyer of goods or services. Some store owners say that the customer is always right.

Synonyms for the entry word are in *italic* letters. Each synonym is followed by a definition and an example sentence.

> *buyer* A person who buys. The dealer is offering a discount to every car *buyer.*
> *consumer* A person who uses goods and services. We are all *consumers* of electricity.
> *shopper* A person who visits shops or stores to purchase or look at goods. The stores are filled with *shoppers* before holidays.
> *user* A person or thing that consumes or spends. Airplanes are among the largest *users* of fuel.

If an **antonym** is given, it is printed in dark letters.

> ANTONYMS: **merchant, provider, salesperson, seller**

How to Use Your Spelling Thesaurus

Suppose you are writing a business letter to a department store. You read over your work and see you have used the word *customer* too many times. You decide to use the Spelling Thesaurus to find some synonyms. Here are the steps you should follow.

1. Look for the word in the Thesaurus Index. The Index lists every word in the Thesaurus.

2. Find the word in the Index. This is what you will find:

   customer *n.*

   The red print tells you that *customer* is an entry word.

3. Turn to the correct page in the Spelling Thesaurus and read the entry carefully. Choose the synonym or synonyms that will make your writing clearer and stronger.

Remember: Not every synonym will have the meaning you want. Look at the sample entry for *customer* on page 206. Which synonyms for *customer* would fit best in your business letter?

- Sometimes you may find a word listed in the Index like this:

   shopper customer *n.*

   This means you will find the word *shopper* listed as a synonym under the entry word *customer.* Since *shopper* is not printed in red, it is not an entry word. If you look for *shopper* in the Spelling Thesaurus as an entry word under the letter *S*, you will not find it.

- You will also see some lines in the Index that look like this:

   seller customer *n.*

   This means that *seller* is listed as an antonym under the entry word *customer.*

A

abandon *v.*
absurd comic *adj.*
accept doubt *v.*
ache *n.*
acknowledge admit *v.*
admire regard *v.*
admit *v.*
adventurer explorer *n.*
advice *n.*
afraid *adj.*
afraid fearless *adj.*
agree disagree *v.*
agreeable enjoyable *adj.*
agreeable unpleasant *adj.*
agreement *n.*
aid hinder *v.*
aim goal *n.*
alarmed afraid *adj.*
alarmed fearless *adj.*
alert clever *adj.*
ally *n.*
alter change *v.*
ambition goal *n.*
amusing comic *adj.*
anchor fasten *v.*
annoy *v.*
annoying unpleasant *adj.*
answer question *v.*
answer reply *v.*
anxious nervous *adj.*
apprentice pupil *n.*
appropriate proper *adj.*
argue disagree *v.*
argument discussion *n.*
argument reason *n.*
article paper *n.*
assignment task *n.*
assist hinder *v.*
associate ally *n.*
assure promise *v.*
astonish shock *v.*
astound shock *v.*
astronaut explorer *n.*

attach fasten *v.*
attack v.
attractive beautiful *adj.*
average particular *adj.*
award prize *n.*

B

badger annoy *v.*
baffle v.
balanced even *adj.*
bare conceal *v.*
bare reveal *v.*
bargain n.
bargain swap *v.*
barter swap *v.*
bashful shy *adj.*
basic major *adj.*
battle struggle *n.*
beat defeat *v.*
beautiful *adj.*
begin stop *v.*
belief idea *n.*
betray conceal *v.*
betray reveal *v.*
bewilder baffle *v.*
bind fasten *v.*
bite *v.*
bitter enjoyable *adj.*
blanket wrap *v.*
blend *v.*
bliss happiness *n.*
block hinder *v.*
blunder *n.*
blur soil *v.*
bold afraid *adj.*
bold fearless *adj.*
bold shy *adj.*
boost *v.*
boring wonderful *adj.*
boss leader *n.*
bother annoy *v.*
brave afraid *adj.*
brave fearless *adj.*
break crack *n.*

break repair *v.*
brief short *adj.*
bright cheerful *adj.*
bright dim *adj.*
broad vast *adj.*
brook stream *n.*
bumpy smooth *adj.*
bunch *n.*
bundle parcel *n.*
bundle wrap *v.*
burden *n.*
business *n.*
busy quiet *adj.*
buy bargain *n.*
buyer customer *n.*

C

calm nervous *adj.*
calm quiet *adj.*
calm worry *v.*
can preserve *v.*
captain leader *n.*
capture catch *v.*
career business *n.*
careful careless *adj.*
careless *adj.*
carnival *n.*
carve *v.*
catch *v.*
cautious careless *adj.*
celebrate honor *v.*
central major *adj.*
challenge question *v.*
chance fortune *n.*
change *v.*
charge attack *v.*
cheerful *adj.*
cheerful unhappy *adj.*
cheerfulness sadness *n.*
chief major *adj.*
chisel carve *v.*
chore task *n.*
circuit direction *n.*
circus carnival *n.*

huge vast *adj.*
humorous comic *adj.*

I

idea *n.*
ignore notice *v.*
ignore overlook *v.*
immense vast *adj.*
immigrant settler *n.*
impolite civil *adj.*
important major *adj.*
important urgent *adj.*
important worthwhile
   adj.
improper proper *adj.*
improve damage *v.*
increase *v.*
incredible wonderful *adj.*
indecent proper *adj.*
individual particular *adj.*
industry commerce *n.*
inflate increase *v.*
inquire question *v.*
inquire reply *v.*
intelligent clever *adj.*
intense forceful *adj.*
intent goal *n.*
interrupt hinder *v.*

J

jam squeeze *v.*
jest joke *n.*
jingle slogan *n.*
job business *n.*
join fasten *v.*
joke *n.*
journey trek *n.*
joy happiness *n.*
joy sadness *n.*
joyful cheerful *adj.*
joyful unhappy *adj.*
jumpy nervous *adj.*

K

keep honor *v.*

kind tender *adj.*
kind unkind *adj.*
kingdom country *n.*
knead blend *v.*
knock strike *v.*
knot fasten *v.*

L

large short *adj.*
leader *n.*
league team *n.*
leave abandon *v.*
legend story *n.*
level even *adj.*
level smooth *adj.*
lift boost *v.*
light serious *adj.*
limit hinder *v.*
live occupy *v.*
lodge occupy *v.*
long desire *v.*
long short *adj.*
loose rigid *adj.*
lose defeat *v.*
lot fortune *n.*
loud *adj.*
loud silent *adj.*
lovely beautiful *adj.*
lower boost *v.*
loyal faithful *adj.*
luck fortune *n.*

M

magnify increase *v.*
main major *adj.*
major *adj.*
manner fashion *n.*
mark soil *v.*
marvelous wonderful *adj.*
mask conceal *v.*
meadow pasture *n.*
mean unkind *adj.*
meaningful major *adj.*
medal prize *n.*
meddle hinder *v.*
mend repair *v.*
merchant customer *n.*

merry cheerful *adj.*
method fashion *n.*
might force *n.*
minor major *adj.*
minor serious *adj.*
mischief joke *n.*
misfortune burden *n.*
mislead *v.*
miss notice *v.*
miss overlook *v.*
mistake blunder *n.*
mix blend *v.*
modest shy *adj.*
modest vast *adj.*
mold spoil *v.*
monarch ruler *n.*
motion move *v.*
motto slogan *n.*
move *n.*
mumble shout *v.*
mumble whisper *v.*
murmur shout *v.*
murmur whisper *v.*
myth story *n.*

N

narrative story *n.*
narrow vast *adj.*
nasty unpleasant *adj.*
nation country *n.*
navigator explorer *n.*
neglect notice *v.*
neglect overlook *v.*
nervous *adj.*
nervous quiet *adj.*
nibble bite *v.*
noisy loud *adj.*
noisy quiet *adj.*
noisy silent *adj.*
nonfiction story *n.*
normal particular *adj.*
note notice *v.*
note overlook *v.*
notice *v.*
notice overlook *v.*
notion idea *n.*

O

observe honor *v.*
observe notice *v.*
observe overlook *v.*
occupation business *n.*
occupy *v.*
officer leader *n.*
official leader *n.*
opinion idea *n.*
ordinary particular *adj.*
outfit team *n.*
outwit mislead *v.*
overlook *v.*
overlook notice *v.*

P

package parcel *n.*
paddle drift *v.*
pain ache *n.*
painful enjoyable *adj.*
panic horror *n.*
paper *n.*
parcel *n.*
particular *adj.*
partner ally *n.*
pasture *n.*
patch repair *v.*
path direction *n.*
pause hesitate *v.*
peaceful quiet *adj.*
peril danger *n.*
perplex baffle *v.*
pickle preserve *v.*
pioneer settler *n.*
plain beautiful *adj.*
plain pasture *n.*
pleasant enjoyable *adj.*
pleasant unpleasant *adj.*
pleasing unpleasant *adj.*
pledge promise *v.*
polite civil *adj.*
power force *n.*
powerful forceful *adj.*
prairie pasture *n.*
prank joke *n.*
preserve *v.*
press squeeze *v.*
pressing urgent *adj.*

principal major *adj.*
prize *n.*
proceed hesitate *v.*
profession business *n.*
profitable worthwhile *adj.*
promise *v.*
proof reason *n.*
proper *adj.*
protect guard *v.*
provider customer *n.*
pupil *n.*
purpose goal *n.*
puzzle baffle *v.*

Q

quake shake *v.*
question *v.*
question reply *v.*
quick clever *adj.*
quick short *adj.*
quiet *adj.*
quiet loud *adj.*
quiet silent *adj.*
quit abandon *v.*
quit stop *v.*
quiver shake *v.*
quiz question *v.*

R

raise boost *v.*
range pasture *n.*
rare particular *adj.*
reason *n.*
reckless careless *adj.*
recognize admit *v.*
reduce increase *v.*
refuse desire *v.*
regard *v.*
regard notice *v.*
reject desire *v.*
relaxed nervous *adj.*
relaxed rigid *adj.*
release catch *v.*
release fasten *v.*
reliable faithful *adj.*
repair *v.*
repair damage *v.*

reply *v.*
reply question *v.*
report paper *n.*
request reply *v.*
respect regard *v.*
respectful civil *adj.*
respond question *v.*
respond reply *v.*
responsibility task *n.*
restful cozy *adj.*
restful quiet *adj.*
restless nervous *adj.*
restore repair *v.*
retreat attack *v.*
return reply *v.*
reveal *v.*
reveal conceal *v.*
reward prize *n.*
ridiculous comic *adj.*
rigid *adj.*
risk danger *n.*
river stream *n.*
rot spoil *v.*
rough smooth *adj.*
route direction *n.*
route highway *n.*
rub skin *v.*
rude civil *adj.*
ruin damage *v.*
ruler *n.*

S

sad cheerful *adj.*
sad unhappy *adj.*
sadness *n.*
sadness happiness *n.*
sail drift *v.*
sail fly *v.*
sale bargain *n.*
salesperson customer *n.*
salt preserve *v.*
scared afraid *adj.*
scared fearless *adj.*
scatter splash *v.*
scholar pupil *n.*
scout explorer *n.*
scrape skin *v.*
scratch skin *v.*

A

abandon *v.* To give up completely; to desert or leave behind. May found a fawn that had been abandoned in the forest.

desert To leave a person, place, or thing, especially if one has a duty to stay; abandon. My friends *deserted* me when they learned that I had to mow the lawn.

leave To go or depart from; to abandon; desert. We had to *leave* before the ball game was over.

quit To give up a job. My father *quit* his job when he started his own business.

stop To leave off doing something. When the fire alarm rings, *stop* whatever you are doing and leave the building.

withdraw To move back or to take back. The candidate *withdrew* from the election.

ache *n.* A dull, steady pain. I had an ache in my shoulder after playing tennis.

cramp A sudden, painful tightening of a muscle, often in the leg or foot. Wearing proper shoes will help keep you from getting *cramps* in your legs.

pain An ache or soreness. A *pain* is often your body's way of telling you to rest.

smart A sharp, stinging sensation. The *smart* on my finger reminded me of where I had scratched it.

sore A place on the body where the skin is broken, bruised, or inflamed. The nurse put a bandage on the *sore*.

sting The wound or the pain caused by a sting. The bee *sting* on my leg bothered me all night.

admit *v.* To confess. I admit that I accidentally broke the window.

acknowledge To admit the truth or reality of. The opponent *acknowledged* the senator as the winner of the election.

confess To admit (guilt, love, shame, etc.).

My sister *confessed* that she really hadn't done her homework.

grant To accept as true; concede. I *grant* that you play the piano better than I do.

recognize To perceive as true; realize. Carol *recognizes* that it is good to read to children.

ANTONYM: **deny**

advice *n.* A suggestion made or an opinion given. Can you give me some advice about how to solve this math problem?

counsel Advice. The lawyer gave us good *counsel* before we signed the papers.

suggestion Something that is suggested. I followed your *suggestion*, and it worked.

warning Something that tells you to expect danger. The sound of cracking ice was a *warning* that the ice was too thin for skating.

afraid *adj.* Scared. The children were afraid of the old house.

alarmed Filled with fear; frightened. Though everyone was *alarmed* when the fire broke out, nobody panicked.

fearful Frightened; full of fear. There's no reason to be *fearful* of most of the animals in the forest.

frightened Filled with sudden fear; scared. The lightning *frightened* my baby brother.

scared Afraid. Many people are *scared* of the dark.

timid Fearful or shy. Rabbits are so *timid* that they run from any noise.

ANTONYMS: **bold, brave, courageous, fearless**

agreement *n.* A contract or treaty. The bosses and the workers signed a salary agreement.

contract A binding agreement between two or more parties, especially a written one. The rock group signed a *contract* with a record company.

settlement An agreement. The two sides reached a *settlement* without going to court.

treaty A written agreement between two or more countries regarding peace or trade. The United States and Japan signed a *treaty* that will increase trade between the countries.

ally *n.* A person or country joined with another for a purpose. France was an ally to the colonists in the Revolutionary War.

associate A person connected with another, as a fellow worker, companion, or partner. The company president had lunch with a business *associate*.

friend Someone on the same side, as contrasted with a foe. Mexico and Canada are important *friends* of the United States.

partner A person who is associated with another or others, especially in a business where the profits and losses are shared. My father and my aunt are *partners* in a computer company.
ANTONYMS: **enemy, foe**

annoy *v.* To bother. It annoys me when people talk in theaters.

badger To nag at; pester; tease. They *badgered* the star to sign their programs.

bother To annoy or trouble. The neighbor's barking dog *bothered* Pat all morning.

disturb To break in on or interrupt, especially with noise or disorder. I'll make sure that no one *disturbs* you while you study.

tease To pick on or fool with (another) for fun, in order to annoy or provoke. It is mean to *tease* other people.

trouble To make or become distressed,

annoyed, worried, or ill. I was very *troubled* until you called to say you'd been delayed.

attack *v.* To begin fighting, as in a battle; to hurt. The troops attacked the enemy at dawn.

charge To attack or rush upon violently. The soldiers *charged* the fort.

storm To attack or assault. The soldiers *stormed* the fort and captured it.

strike To attack or assault. The enemy *struck* when the troops were not expecting it.
ANTONYMS: **retreat, withdraw**

B

baffle *v.* To confuse completely; to bewilder. The tricky word problem baffled Otto.

bewilder To puzzle and confuse; baffle. Venice often *bewilders* tourists who don't know their way around all the islands.

confuse To perplex; mix up. The poorly written directions for the game *confused* the players.

daze To confuse or bewilder; stun. Everything she saw in Wonderland *dazed* Alice.

perplex To cause to hesitate or doubt; confuse; bewilder; puzzle. The riddle *perplexed* everyone in the class.

puzzle To confuse or perplex; mystify. Sherlock Holmes had solved the mystery, but it still *puzzled* Dr. Watson.

bargain *n.* Something sold at a lower price than usual; a good buy. I picked up some great bargains at the store.

buy Something bought or about to be bought, especially a bargain. This is a *buy* you can't afford to pass up.

discount An amount subtracted from the

real cost. Our school gets a *discount* on books for the library.

sale A selling of goods at bargain prices. In August stores have summer clothing *sales*.

See also **swap**.

beautiful *adj.* Lovely; pretty; full of beauty. San Francisco is one of the most beautiful cities in the world.

attractive Attracting interest; tempting; pleasing. The movie had some very *attractive* stars in it.

fair Beautiful. The young child's face was so *fair* that many people paused to admire her picture.

gorgeous Brilliant; dazzling; very beautiful. The sunset at the beach was *gorgeous*.

handsome Pleasing in appearance, especially in a stately or manly way. The governor and her husband were a *handsome* couple.

lovely Beautiful. The city park had a *lovely* garden.

ANTONYMS: **homely, plain, ugly**

bite *v.* To cut with the teeth. Don't bite off more than you can chew.

gnaw To bite or eat away little by little with or as if with teeth. The puppy got into trouble for *gnawing* the shoe.

nibble To eat or bite in a quick, gentle way. Sue *nibbled* celery and carrot sticks until dinner was ready.

snap To try to bite. The dog *snapped* at the mosquitoes that buzzed by it.

blend *v.* To mix. I blended the yogurt and the grated cheese together to make a salad dressing.

knead To mix and press dough with your hands. You have to *knead* bread dough before you let it rise.

mix To combine or add so as to blend. I *mixed* the butter and eggs, but I left out the milk.

stir To move around with a circular motion, as a fluid or group of dry particles, so as to mix thoroughly. I *stirred* the two colors together before I painted the floor.

whip To beat to a froth. *Whip* the egg whites before adding them to the batter.

ANTONYM: **separate**

blunder *n.* A stupid mistake. Spilling orange juice on the newspaper was my blunder.

error Something done, said, or believed incorrectly; a mistake. Thinking that the Earth was flat was a common *error* before Columbus's time.

fumble The act of handling or dropping clumsily. The football player's *fumble* caused the team to lose.

mistake An error or blunder. Barbara made three *mistakes* on the spelling test.

boost *v.* To push up or forward. Give me a boost up the tree.

hoist To raise or lift, especially by mechanical means. The builders *hoisted* the wood up to the roof.

lift To take hold of and raise to a higher position. My father *lifted* me up so I could see the parade.

raise To cause to move upward or to a higher level; lift. If you want to ask a question, *raise* your hand.

ANTONYMS: **drop, lower**

bunch *n.* A number of things of the same kind, growing or placed together. A bunch of grapes is always a good snack.

class A group of students who are taught together. We have some very bright students in our *class*.

community A group of people living together in one locality. Although people on farms may live miles from

burden

each other, they often form a close *community*.

crowd A large number of people gathered closely together. I sometimes get nervous in a *crowd*.

flock A large group of animals or birds; a large crowd of people. The man threw bread to the *flock* of pigeons.

herd A group of animals all of one kind. You can see *herds* of buffalo at a park in Oklahoma.

burden *n.* Something hard to carry or handle. Being part of a large family can be both a joy and a burden.

difficulty Something that is not easy to do, understand, or overcome; obstacle. Learning a new language can be a great *difficulty*.

hardship Something that is hard to endure. Spending a night in a tent is not a *hardship* for someone who enjoys camping.

misfortune Ill fortune; bad luck. It is a terrible *misfortune* to have your house burn down.

trial A cause of suffering, annoyance, or vexation. Illness can be a *trial* for the sick person's family.

business *n.* A job, profession, or trade. The computer business has prospered.

career A person's lifework; profession. My sister plans a *career* in law.

job A position or situation of employment. Jacob has a part-time *job* after school.

occupation Anything a person does, but especially what someone does for a living. Taking care of sick animals is an interesting *occupation*.

profession An occupation requiring a good education and mental rather than physical labor. Teaching is a noble *profession*.

trade A business or occupation, especially a specialized kind of work

carve

with the hands that requires training. My uncle learned the plumbing *trade* after high school.

C

careless *adj.* Reckless; done without care or effort. Randy's perfect composition showed that he is not a careless speller.

reckless Careless. *Reckless* driving is a major cause of accidents.

wild Not controlled or restrained, and often unruly or disorderly. The principal warned us not to be *wild* on the playground so no one would get hurt.

ANTONYMS: careful, cautious

carnival *n.* A fair or festival with rides and games. Jack rode the roller coaster at the carnival.

circus A traveling show, as of acrobats, clowns, or trained animals. My favorite acts at the *circus* are the clowns.

fair An exhibition, as of goods, products, or machinery. Mike's pig won first prize at the state *fair* this year.

festival A particular feast, holiday, or celebration, especially an annual one. Every year thousands of people come to the music *festival* at the beach.

carve *v.* To shape wood, marble, etc., by cutting. Mount Rushmore was carved by Gutzon Borglum and his son.

chisel To cut or shape with or as if with a chisel. The artist *chiseled* a swan out of the block of ice.

engrave To carve or cut letters or designs into. My grandmother gave me a watch with my name *engraved* on the back.

shape To give a shape to; mold; form. Clay can be *shaped* into many different objects, such as bowls and pitchers.

catch

catch *v.* To get hold of; to trap. Frogs catch flying insects with their long sticky tongues.

capture To catch; to take prisoner. Maria was able to *capture* my queen after five minutes of chess.

grab To grasp suddenly and forcefully; snatch. I *grabbed* the brass ring on the merry-go-round.

grasp To take hold of firmly, as with the hand. I *grasped* the reins to control the horse.

seize To take hold of suddenly and with force; grab; snatch. My brother *seized* my arm when the movie became scary.

snatch To grab or take hold of suddenly, hastily, or eagerly. I *snatched* the pencil away from the baby before she could hurt herself.

ANTONYMS: **free, release**

change *v.* To make or become different. The driver changed to a lower gear to go down the steep hill.

alter To make or become different; change. My father had to *alter* all his clothes after he lost some weight.

correct To change so as to make right; eliminate faults or errors from. I *corrected* my paper and handed it back to the teacher.

disguise To change in appearance or manner so as not to be known or to appear as someone else. Huckleberry Finn *disguised* himself as a girl so that he wouldn't get caught.

cheerful *adj.* Happy; full of cheer. Our teacher greeted us with a cheerful "Good morning!"

bright Full of gladness or hope. Andy's *bright* smile made us all feel better.

glad Having a feeling of joy or pleasure. I was *glad* to be home after the long trip.

happy Enjoying or showing pleasure;

clever

joyous; contented. I am very *happy* to see you.

joyful Glad; full of joy. Weddings are *joyful* occasions.

merry Full of fun and laughter; joyous; gay; zestful. Everyone at the New Year's Eve party was singing, laughing, and feeling *merry*.

sunny Bright; cheery. Mother's *sunny* greeting made all my friends feel at ease.

ANTONYMS: **gloomy, sad, sorrowful, unhappy**

civil *adj.* Polite. James was civil to Jane even though they didn't always agree.

courteous Polite and considerate. The *courteous* sales clerk listened to the customer's complaint.

gallant Courteous and respectful; chivalrous. The *gallant* young man helped the old woman cross the street.

polite Showing consideration for others; mannerly. Being *polite* means remembering to say "please" and "thank you."

respectful Courteous; full of respect. Most Asian societies are very *respectful* of old people.

ANTONYMS: **impolite, rude**

clever *adj.* Very smart; bright. The clever boy used a wagon to carry the packages.

alert Mentally quick and intelligent. The teacher was pleased to be teaching an *alert* class this year.

cunning Clever or tricky. *Cunning* Tom Sawyer got his friends to paint the fence for him.

intelligent Having or showing intelligence; smart; bright. She was so *intelligent* that she went to college at age fifteen.

quick Swift to learn, understand, or perceive; alert. The baby was *quick* to notice new things.

sharp Quick-witted, clever, shrewd. He has a *sharp* mind.

smart Quick in mind; intelligent; bright; clever. Some people think that pigs are as *smart* as dogs.

ANTONYMS: **simple, slow, stupid**

comic adj. Funny. Pearl made a comic face as she told her funny story.

absurd Unreasonable; ridiculous. My *absurd* Halloween costume was a ballet outfit with a gorilla mask.

amusing Causing amusement, fun, laughter, or merriment. The audience laughed during the *amusing* skit.

funny Amusing or comical. The circus clowns were very *funny*.

humorous Full of or using humor; funny; amusing. My father laughed at a *humorous* cartoon in the newspaper.

ridiculous Deserving ridicule or laughter because of its absurdity or silliness. The dog looked *ridiculous* wearing Mother's hat.

ANTONYMS: **serious, solemn**

commerce n. The exchange or buying and selling of goods, especially between nations; trade. Businesses were happy that the commerce between the countries had improved.

industry Manufacturing and business activity as a whole. The food *industry* plays an important role in America's economy.

trade The buying and selling of goods, at either wholesale or retail prices, within a country or between countries; commerce. Japan is one of America's most important partners in *trade*.

conceal v. To put out of sight; to hide. The lead actor concealed himself behind a couch for most of the first act.

cover To be put over or to put something over. Geraldo *covered* the ugly tabletop with a tablecloth.

disguise To conceal or give a false idea of. Hank tried to *disguise* his new haircut by wearing a hat.

hide To put or keep out of sight; conceal. We all *hid* in the bedroom to surprise my mother.

mask To hide or conceal; disguise. Karen was very upset, but she *masked* her feelings until she got home.

ANTONYMS: **bare, betray, reveal, show, uncover**

country n. A nation. The country to the north of the United States is Canada.

empire A country reigned over by an emperor or empress. Rome was once the main city of an *empire*.

kingdom A country ruled by a king or queen. The queen called together all of the people in the *kingdom*.

nation Country. Our *nation* is the United States of America.

state A nation. The head of the *state* of Israel is called a prime minister.

cozy adj. Warm and comfortable. That chair by the fire is very cozy.

comfortable Giving comfort and satisfaction. A good tent is *comfortable* in all kinds of weather.

homey Homelike. The friendly people made the country inn seem *homey*.

restful Full of or giving rest. A hot bath is very *restful* after a day of skiing.

snug Closely but comfortably covered or sheltered; cozy. The *snug* snowsuit kept the child warm and dry.

ANTONYM: **uncomfortable**

crack n. A narrow break. The car window had a long crack where the stone had hit it.

break A gap, crack, or broken place. My bicycle tire caught in the *break* in the crumbling sidewalk.

customer

fracture A crack, break, or rupture. The doctor said the bone *fracture* in my arm would heal quickly.

gap A crack or opening, as in a wall. The hikers made their way through a *gap* between the rocks.

customer *n.* A buyer of goods or services. Some store owners say that the customer is always right.

buyer A person who buys. The dealer is offering a discount to every car *buyer.*

consumer A person who uses goods and services. We are all *consumers* of electricity.

shopper A person who visits shops or stores to purchase or look at goods. The stores are filled with *shoppers* before holidays.

user A person or thing that consumes or spends. Airplanes are among the largest *users* of fuel.

ANTONYMS: **merchant, provider, salesperson, seller**

D

damage *v.* To do or cause harm. The hail damaged the paint on the car.

destroy To ruin completely; wreck; smash. The high waves pounded the shore and *destroyed* the dock.

harm To do harm to. The early frost *harmed* the tomato plants.

ruin To destroy, demolish, or damage. The cat pulled down the bird feeder and *ruined* it.

shatter To break into pieces; to damage; demolish; ruin. The vase *shattered* when I dropped it.

spoil To lessen the quality, value, or usefulness of; damage or destroy. The rain *spoiled* our weekend at the beach.

wreck To destroy. Dropping the model airplane *wrecked* it completely.

dim

ANTONYMS: **fix, improve, repair**

danger *n.* Something that can hurt or cause damage. The hole in the floor was a danger to everyone.

peril Danger; risk. Drivers who drink are a *peril* to other people.

risk A chance of meeting with harm or loss; hazard. Flying an airplane is a job that has many *risks.*

threat A warning that something will be done to hurt or punish. The heavy rains made us face the *threat* of a flood.

defeat *v.* To beat an enemy or opponent. The American colonists defeated the British in the Revolutionary War.

beat To defeat, as in a fight or contest. I finally *beat* Dad at chess.

conquer To defeat or win control of by use of force, as in war. The Greeks *conquered* the Trojans by hiding in a large, wooden horse.

triumph To win a victory; be successful. Even though he was slower, the tortoise *triumphed* over the hare in a race.

ANTONYMS: **fall, lose, surrender**

desire *v.* To wish; to want. Many people desire fame and fortune.

long To want greatly; yearn. The girl *longed* for a pet of her own.

want To feel a desire or wish for. Freddie *wanted* to go home from summer camp.

wish To want, desire, or be glad to have. I *wish* I could be a scientist when I grow up.

ANTONYMS: **refuse, reject**

dim *adj.* Not bright; not clearly seen. Because the sun is very bright, other stars look dim from Earth.

dull Not bright or clear. The whole world can look *dull* on a cloudy day.

faint Weak, slight, or dim. A *faint* light

flashed on the other side of the bay—the signal we had been waiting for!

gloomy Dull; dark. The sky looked *gloomy* on the morning of our fishing trip.

soft Not glaring, bright, or harsh. The *soft* lighting in the room was pleasant.

vague Not definite, clear, precise, or distinct. Tom saw a *vague* form moving through the fog.

ANTONYMS: **bright, clear, definite, distinct, glaring, harsh**

direction *n.* The line along which anything moves, faces, or lies. The storm was traveling in an easterly direction.

circuit A route that returns to where it began. The actors in the national touring group traveled in a *circuit* around the country.

course Something, as a path or ground, passed over; line of motion; direction. The explorers' *course* took them over three mountain ranges.

path A track or course along which a thing moves. The *path* of the comet passed near Earth.

route A road or course taken in traveling from one point to another. Many birds and animals migrate along the same *routes* year after year.

track Any regular path or course. The runners followed the leader's *track*.

disagree *v.* To fail to agree; to argue. People often write letters to newspapers when they disagree with the editors.

argue To disagree. My brother and my sister *argued* about whose turn it was to wash the pots.

debate To give reasons for or against; to argue; to consider. We *debated* over which movie to see.

ANTONYM: **agree**

discussion *n.* The act of discussing; an exchange of ideas. The class had a discussion about nuclear energy.

argument The act of arguing; quarrel. The hockey players were thrown out of the game because of their *argument*.

conversation An exchange of ideas by formal talk; talk. During my phone *conversation* with Grandmother, I told her I got an A on a math test.

debate The act of debating. The college held a *debate* between the candidates for governor.

dialogue Conversation involving two or more speakers, as in a book or play. Two actors in the play spoke so softly that I could not hear their *dialogue*.

doubt *v.* To be unsure or uncertain. I doubt that we are on the right road.

distrust To feel no trust for; suspect. I *distrust* people who say they can make you rich overnight.

suspect To have doubts about; mistrust. The detective *suspected* the butler's motive.

wonder To be doubtful or curious about something; want to know. I *wonder* if it will really snow tomorrow.

ANTONYMS: **accept, trust**

draw *v.* To make a picture with a pencil or crayon. Jerry can draw beautiful pictures of horses.

design To work out and draw plans or sketches for. My mother *designs* buildings for her company.

draft To make a plan, outline, or rough copy of. I *drafted* a plan for a model sailboat.

sketch To make a rough drawing. The artist made a *sketch* of the Eiffel Tower before she painted it.

drift *v.* To move or float along in water or air. The empty rowboat drifted away from the bank of the creek.

float To be carried along gently on the surface of a liquid or through the air; drift. The sound of distant music *floated* to us on the breeze.

flow To move steadily and freely. The rafts *flowed* down the river with the current.

paddle To move your hands and feet in water. The child *paddled* across the pool to his father's arms.

sail To travel over water in a ship or boat. It's my dream to *sail* across the Pacific Ocean.

swim To move through the water by using the arms, legs, fins, or the like. Ducks can fly, walk on land, and *swim*.

ANTONYM: **sink**

E

endless *adj.* Having no end; lasting or going on without stopping. The boring play seemed endless.

constant Happening over and over; endless; continual. My sleep was disturbed by the dog's *constant* barking.

continual Going on without a pause; continuous. The weather report calls for *continual* showers all weekend.

continuous Going on without any pause or interruption. The theater was offering *continuous* showings of old movies.

countless Too many to be counted. On a clear night, you can see *countless* stars in the sky.

eternal Seeming to last forever; continual. Although the tornado passed in just a few minutes, the time waiting for it to end seemed *eternal*.

ANTONYMS: **ending, finishing, stopping**

enjoyable *adj.* Pleasant; satisfying. We had an enjoyable visit with our

grandmother and our grandfather during the summer.

agreeable Giving pleasure; pleasing. Reading a good book is an *agreeable* way to spend a rainy day.

delightful Giving joy or pleasure. The evening breeze was *delightful* after the hot afternoon.

pleasant Giving pleasure; pleasing. The view from our room at the lodge was *pleasant*.

ANTONYMS: **bitter, harsh, painful, unpleasant**

even *adj.* On the same level; equal. My brother and I do an even amount of work around the house.

balanced Brought into or kept in a condition of equality, as between opposing forces, amounts, or values. It is important to eat a *balanced* diet.

equal The same in size, amount, or value. Two times six is *equal* to three times four.

fair Not favoring one above another; just. Each player received a *fair* share of playing pieces.

level Equal in height; even. The tabletop was *level* with the windowsill.

See also **smooth.**

ANTONYMS: **unbalanced, unequal, uneven, unfair**

explorer *n.* A person who seeks to learn or discover something. Many explorers in medicine are seeking cures for deadly diseases.

adventurer A person who looks for or takes part in adventures. Robert Peary, a famous *adventurer*, was the first person to reach the North Pole.

astronaut A person who travels in space. The *astronaut* Neil Armstrong was the first person to walk on the moon.

navigator A person who navigates. English *navigator* Sir Francis Drake traveled around the entire globe.

scout A soldier, plane, or ship sent out to observe and get information about the enemy. In the movie, the *scout* told the general that the enemy was ready to attack.

voyager A person who takes any journey, as one through air or space. Jules Verne wrote stories about *voyagers* who went under the sea, around the world, and to other planets.

F

faithful *adj.* Loyal; true. You can count on your real friends to be always faithful to you.

constant Faithful; true. Old Yeller was the boy's *constant* companion.

dependable Worthy of trust; reliable. Employers like to hire *dependable* workers.

loyal True; faithful. My father has been a *loyal* employee of his company for 30 years.

reliable Dependable; trustworthy. The man read a *reliable* newspaper for details about the President's meeting.

true Faithful, as to promises or principles; loyal; steadfast. The loyal dog is *true* to its owner.

trustworthy Worthy of confidence; reliable. The ship's *trustworthy* captain was an experienced sailor.

ANTONYMS: **disloyal, undependable, unfaithful, untrue**

fashion *n.* Way; manner. I like to do things in my own fashion.

convention The established way of doing things; accepted custom. Some people do not worry about following the *conventions* of modern clothing style.

custom A usual way of acting or doing something; habit. Our family's *custom* is to exchange gifts on New Year's Eve.

manner A way of doing, being done, or occurring. Peter holds his pen in a strange *manner,* but you can still read what he writes.

method A way of doing or accomplishing something. Researchers have discovered a new *method* of giving people certain kinds of medicine.

way A manner or method. There's more than one *way* to do most things.

fasten *v.* To attach. The driver asked us to fasten our seat belts when we got in the car.

anchor To keep in place with an anchor. The captain *anchored* the boat in the harbor for the night.

attach To make fast; fasten; connect. Connie *attached* a note to her report explaining why it was late.

bind To tie or fasten, as with a band or cord. We *bound* the newspapers to bring to the recycling plant.

join To bring or come together; to connect. The electrician *joined* two wires at the light switch.

knot To tie in a knot. Marcus *knotted* the two short ropes together to make one long one.

secure To fasten; make firm. We *secured* the window shutters before the hurricane struck.

ANTONYMS: **release, unfasten**

fearless *adj.* Brave; without fear. The fearless stunt man jumped from the bridge into the river.

bold Having or requiring courage; daring. It takes a *bold* person to jump from an airplane with a parachute.

brave Having or showing courage; not afraid. The *brave* firefighter rescued the baby from the burning house.

courageous Having or showing courage. Sometimes, people who seem shy turn out to be *courageous* when their help is needed in emergencies.

daring Brave and adventurous; fearless. The *daring* rock climber reached the top of the slippery cliff.

gallant Bold and courageous; brave. Many legends tell of *gallant* knights rescuing people in danger.

ANTONYMS: **afraid, alarmed, fearful, frightened, scared**

fly *v.* To go through the air. Carmel seemed to fly as she did her tumbling stunts.

flutter To flap the wings without really flying ; fly clumsily. The moth *fluttered* across the yard.

glide To move in a downward slant without using power, as an airplane. The model airplane *glided* softly to the ground.

hover To remain in or near one place in the air, as birds do. The hummingbird flaps its wings so quickly that it can *hover* above a flower.

sail To move, glide, or float in the air. Hundreds of balloons *sailed* into the air at the end of the festival.

soar To rise high into the air; fly high. The space shuttle *soared* into the sky early this morning.

force *n.* Power; strength. The force of the water broke the dam.

energy Lively force or activity; vigor; vitality. I don't have much *energy* after a large meal.

might Great power; force; strength. Davy Crockett fought with all his *might* at the Alamo.

power Physical strength or force. A rocket needs *power* to escape from the Earth's gravity.

strength The quality of being strong; force or power, especially of the muscles. Hercules could wrestle a lion because of his great *strength*.

vigor Active strength or force of mind or body; healthy energy. My grandfather has enough *vigor* to ride a bicycle an hour a day.

ANTONYM: **weakness**

forceful *adj.* Strong; energetic. That actor always plays forceful characters who get what they want.

intense Very strong, great, or deep. Peg was in *intense* pain before she had the operation.

powerful Strong; full of power. The boxer has a *powerful* punch.

strong Powerful or forceful. I'm not *strong* enough to lift this box myself.

ANTONYMS: **feeble, frail, weak**

fortune *n.* What is going to happen to a person; luck or chance. It was Max's good fortune to run out of gas near a gas station.

chance The unknown cause of the way things often turn out; fate; luck. Just by *chance*, his bus came as he arrived at the bus stop.

fate What happens to a person; fortune; lot. The *fate* of the boy's balloon depended on the wind currents.

lot A person's portion in life, ascribed to chance or fate. Ellen decided to improve her *lot* by taking college classes at night.

luck Something that happens by chance; fortune. I've had the good *luck* of meeting the President twice.

G

goal *n.* Aim. Charles Dickens's goal as a writer was to entertain people.

aim A purpose or goal. Helping other people is a noble *aim*.

ambition Something eagerly desired to be achieved. Reading about other people can help you choose an *ambition* for yourself.

end Aim; purpose. Doing a good job can be an *end* in itself.

grab

intent Purpose, aim, or intention. My only *intent* was to pass the test by studying hard.

purpose What one intends or wants to accomplish; aim. Jane Addams opened Hull House for the *purpose* of helping the poor.

target Something that is aimed or shot at. An advertisement's *target* is to get you to do or buy something.

grab *v.* To take hold of suddenly. I grabbed the small tree to keep from sliding down the cliff.

clutch To grasp and hold firmly. The child *clutched* the puppy to his chest.

grasp To take hold of firmly, as with the hand. Matthew *grasped* his little brother's hand as they crossed the street.

grip To grasp or hold on firmly. Few people can *grip* a basketball with only one hand.

seize To take hold of suddenly and with force; grab; snatch. Robin Hood *seized* the bag of money and rode off through the woods.

snatch To grab and take hold of suddenly, hastily, or eagerly. The dog *snatched* the sandwich right out of my hand.

See also **catch.**

guard *v.* To watch over or protect. The large dog guarded the baby while she slept in the carriage.

defend To protect. Police officers *defend* the community.

escort To accompany as an escort. Secret service agents *escort* the President wherever he goes.

protect To shield or defend from attack, harm, or injury; guard; shelter. Safe bicycle riders wear helmets to *protect* their heads.

shelter To protect; to give shelter to. A cave *sheltered* the skiers in the storm.

shield To protect or guard. An apron

hesitate

shields your clothes from stains while you are cooking.

H

happiness *n.* The feeling of gladness or joy. It gives me great happiness to see you again.

bliss Great happiness or joy. You could see the *bliss* on the young couple's faces as they looked at their baby.

delight Great pleasure or joy. It's a *delight* to spend a winter evening with hot food, a roaring fire, and people you like.

joy A strong feeling of happiness, contentment, or satisfaction. My mother's *joy* was obvious as she hugged my brother and me.

ANTONYMS: **grief, sadness, sorrow, trouble**

haul *v.* To pull or drag with force. The car hauled a small trailer behind it.

drag To haul or pull along. The little boy *dragged* his stuffed bear behind him.

draw To pull; drag. The settlers used horses and mules to *draw* logs to build their houses.

tow To pull or drag by a rope or chain. The motorboat *towed* a water skier over the lake.

helpless *adj.* Unable to help oneself. Most animals are completely helpless when they are born.

delicate Weak or easily injured. A fawn is a *delicate* animal.

feeble Lacking strength; weak. I felt *feeble* after being sick for a week.

frail Easily damaged in body or structure; weak. The injured bird looked very *frail.*

weak Lacking in strength or effectiveness. The small child was too *weak* to throw the ball very far.

hesitate *v.* To feel doubtful; to pause.

Don't hesitate to call if you need help fixing your bicycle.

delay To go slow; linger. The fire engines didn't *delay* in getting to the burning hotel.

pause To stop temporarily. The speaker *paused* to take a drink of water.

wait To remain or stay until something happens. I've been *waiting* for the bus for 40 minutes.

ANTONYMS: **continue, proceed**

highway *n.* A main road. An accident slowed up traffic on the highway.

expressway A highway designed for rapid travel. Ed traveled to the city in 30 minutes on the *expressway.*

route A road or course taken in traveling from one point to another. The Alaska Highway is the only land *route* to Alaska.

turnpike A highway on which you must pay a toll. We drove to Delaware on the New Jersey *Turnpike.*

hinder *v.* To interfere with; to block. Construction work hindered everyone who entered the building.

block To be in the way of. A fallen tree *blocked* the road.

delay To make late. Bad weather *delayed* Tex's flight.

interrupt To cause someone to stop doing something. It is impolite to *interrupt* people while they are talking.

limit To restrict; to set a limit to. Strict laws *limit* how fast you can drive.

meddle To interfere with something that is not your business. I never *meddle* in the problems of other people.

ANTONYMS: **aid, assist, ease, help**

honest *adj.* Truthful; fair. The honest girl pointed out she hadn't been charged for the sandwich she had eaten.

fair Following the right rules; honest. *Fair* play is important in all games.

frank Completely honest in saying or showing what one really thinks or feels. It is easy to be *frank* with someone you really trust.

honorable Fair; honest; upright. Admitting that you were wrong was the *honorable* thing to do.

truthful Honest. You must be *truthful* when you speak in court.

ANTONYMS: **crooked, dishonest**

honor *v.* To give or show respect and admiration for. We honor Abraham Lincoln and George Washington on President's Day each year.

celebrate To observe or honor in a special manner. Americans *celebrate* Independence Day with fireworks.

keep To be faithful to, observe, or fulfill. We *keep* Thanksgiving by having special dinners with our families.

observe To celebrate in the proper way, as a holiday. Different cultures around the world *observe* different holidays.

horror *n.* The feeling of dread or great fear. The witnesses watched with horror as the forest burned.

dread Great fear or uneasiness, especially over something in the future. Some people feel *dread* about going to see the dentist.

fright Sudden, violent alarm or fear. I always feel *fright* when I look down from a high window.

panic Sudden, overwhelming fear, often affecting many people at once. *Panic* struck everyone when the alarm rang.

terror Great fear; extreme fright or dread. Sharks can cause *terror* in anyone.

I

idea *n.* A thought or opinion. Does anyone in the class have any ideas about what the poem means?

227

increase

belief Something believed. Most societies share a *belief* in the value of life.

feeling An opinion. What is your *feeling* about working after school?

notion An opinion or belief. Mother had a *notion* that we might find you here.

opinion Something a person believes to be true but is not absolutely certain of. Good newspaper reporters keep their own *opinions* out of the news stories they write.

thought The result of thinking; idea or judgment. I am interested in hearing your *thoughts* on the subject.

view An opinion or judgment. In many people's *view,* the automobile is the best way to travel.

increase *v.* To make or become greater or larger. George slowly increased the number of sit-ups he did daily.

enlarge To make or become larger; to expand. The teacher *enlarged* the map in the book when he drew it on the chalkboard.

extend To increase in time or space. The dining table *extends* to make room for 14 people.

inflate To increase or expand a great deal. A balloon can *inflate* to many times its original size.

magnify To make something look bigger than its real size. My glasses *magnify* the words in a book.

swell To get bigger. My ankle *swelled* after I twisted it.

ANTONYMS: **contract, decrease, reduce, shrink**

J

joke *n.* Something that makes you laugh. My grandmother tied a ripe tomato to a young tomato plant to play a joke on my sister and me.

loud

jest A statement or action intended to cause laughter; a joke. When we didn't laugh, Frank tried to explain that his remark was really a *jest.*

mischief Pranks. The kitten's latest *mischief* was climbing up the curtains.

prank A mischievous, playful act or trick. I laughed even though I was the victim of the *prank.*

trick Something done to fool or cheat. April Fool's Day is a day to play harmless *tricks* on people.

L

leader *n.* A person who leads or directs. In the game "Follow the Leader" everyone does what the first person does.

boss A person who employs or is in charge of workers. My mother's secretary says she is a good *boss.*

captain A person in command; a leader. Theodore Roosevelt was *captain* of the Rough Riders in the Spanish-American War.

general A high officer in an army. Ulysses S. Grant and Robert E. Lee were opposing *generals* in the Civil War.

guide A person who conducts or leads others, as on a trip or tour. My brother is a *guide* on raft trips.

officer In the armed forces, a person who has the rank to command others. The Admiral of the Fleet is the highest *officer* in the United States Navy.

official A person who holds an office or job and has certain duties or powers. The mayor is an *official* of a city government.

ANTONYM: **follower**

loud *adj.* Not quiet; noisy. My uncle has a loud voice.

deafening Confusing or overwhelming

with noise. The whine of the chain saws was *deafening*.

noisy Making a loud noise. Our neighbor's *noisy* dog barks at every car that goes by.

shrill Having or making a high-pitched, piercing sound. The bird's *shrill* whistle warned of a nearby cat.

thunderous Of or like thunder. The drum's *thunderous* beat drowned out some of the other instruments.

ANTONYMS: **quiet, silent, still**

M

major *adj.* Important; greater or larger. Opposition to the extension of slavery was a major cause of the Civil War.

basic Forming the basis or most important part. Flour is the *basic* ingredient in bread.

central Most important; principal; chief. The *central* actors didn't appear for the movie's opening.

chief Most significant or important; principal. The *chief* crop of Iowa is corn.

important Having much significance, value, or influence. Benjamin Franklin was an *important* figure in American history.

main First or chief, as in size, rank, or importance. Paul and Maureen are the *main* characters in the book *Misty of Chincoteague*.

meaningful Full of meaning; important. Independence Day is a *meaningful* holiday for Americans.

principal Most important. The *principal* reason for the meeting was to elect a president.

ANTONYMS: **minor, small, unimportant**

mislead *v.* To cause someone to believe something that is not true. I was misled by incorrect information.

deceive To cause to take as true something that is not true; fool or mislead, as by lying. Don't let false advertising *deceive* you.

fool To make a fool of; deceive. Peggy and Angela *fooled* me into thinking they were sisters.

outwit To get the better of by being smarter or more clever. My little sister got me to do the dishes by *outwitting* me.

trick To fool or cheat. My brother *tricked* me into going to school on a holiday.

move *v.* To go or make go from one place to another. The traffic moved slowly down the street.

climb To go up. Few people have *climbed* to the top of Mount Everest.

dance To move in time, usually to music. The couples *danced* while the band played.

motion To signal; to make a movement that shows meaning. Mother *motioned* to the waiter to bring us our check.

sweep To move, go, or pass swiftly or with force. The raging river *swept* through the valley after overflowing its banks.

trot To move at a trot. The dog *trotted* behind its owner.

N

nervous *adj.* Tense; uneasy. The students were nervous during the test.

anxious Worried; uneasy. The mother was *anxious* for her children's safety.

jumpy Nervous; uneasy. The *jumpy* guard called out, "Who's there?"

restless Unable to rest or be still; nervous; uneasy. The *restless* tiger paced up and down.

tense Nervous; strained. The score was tied and the game *tense* when the home team's star player came to bat.

notice

uneasy Restless or nervous. The boy was *uneasy* as he stepped into the empty house.
ANTONYMS: **calm, relaxed, undisturbed**

notice *v.* To see; to pay attention to. I noticed that he was wearing a red jacket.
note To pay careful attention to. Be sure to *note* how the pieces go together.
observe To see or notice. The scientist *observed* that the mold was changing.
regard To look at closely or attentively. The sergeant *regarded* the soldier's dirty uniform with scorn.
stare To look steadily for some time, with the eyes wide open, as from surprise, curiosity, wonder, or bad manners. We all *stared* at the clown as he walked on his hands.
ANTONYMS: **ignore, miss, neglect, overlook**

O

occupy *v.* To live in. Nobody has occupied this house in a long time.
dwell To live or make your home. Bears *dwell* in dens.
live To reside. Marcel *lives* in Lyons, a city in France.
lodge To live temporarily, especially as a paying guest. That man *lodges* at my cousin's house.

overlook *v.* To fail to see. I overlooked a spelling mistake in my research paper.
excuse To understand and overlook. Lee's parents *excused* his falling asleep at the dinner table.
ignore To refuse to notice; pay no attention to. Everyone *ignored* the child's whining.
miss To fail to see, hear, notice, or understand. I *missed* the article about you in the paper.

particular

neglect To pay no attention to; ignore. If you *neglect* the plants in the garden, they will die.
ANTONYMS: **note, notice, observe**

P

paper *n.* Paper with writing on it. I handed in my paper on the results of our science experiment.
article A factual piece of writing on one topic, in a magazine, newspaper, or book. This magazine has an *article* about Henry Ford's first automobile.
composition A short essay, especially one written as an exercise for school. Dionne's *composition* was about Amelia Earhart.
essay A short composition, in which the writer gives his or her own ideas on a single subject. My *essay* on the importance of knowing how to do arithmetic won the school writing contest.
report An accounting or telling of something, often formal or in writing. Justin wrote a *report* on how Galileo developed the telescope.

parcel *n.* Something wrapped; a package. I received a parcel in the mail today.
bundle A package or parcel. My father took a *bundle* of laundry to the cleaners today.
package Something packed, wrapped up, or tied together. I would like a small *package* of raisins.

particular *adj.* Unusual; special. Most artists have a particular talent.
individual Characteristic of a certain person, animal, or thing. Whales have *individual* markings that allow people to tell them apart.
rare Not often seen or found; unusual. Wolves have become very *rare* in most parts of the United States.

special Out of the ordinary. Going to the ballet was a *special* treat for me.

unusual Not usual or ordinary; uncommon. Australia has many *unusual* animals.

ANTONYMS: **average, common, normal, ordinary, usual**

pasture *n.* A grassy field where cattle, sheep, and horses graze. The sheep all ran to the other end of the pasture.

field A large stretch of land with few or no trees, especially one set aside for crops or as a pasture. Farmers cut *fields* of hay by hand long ago.

meadow A tract of land where grass is grown for hay or for grazing. The horse and her colt trotted across the green *meadow.*

plain An expanse of almost level, nearly treeless land; prairie. American Indians who lived on the *plains* hunted buffalo for food and clothing.

prairie A large tract or area of more or less level, grassy land having few or no trees, especially the broad, grassy plain of central North America. Many wagon trains crossed the wide, empty *prairie* on the way to Oregon.

range A wide, grassy plain for roaming and grazing. Prairie dogs, hares, and many other small animals live on the *range.*

tundra A large, almost flat plain of the arctic regions, with no trees. A herd of reindeer roamed across the *tundra* for as far as the eye could see.

preserve *v.* To prepare food so it can be kept without spoiling. We preserved peaches in canning jars this weekend.

can To put in sealed cans or jars; preserve, as fruit. It's too hot to *can* vegetables today.

cure To preserve (meat), as by salting, smoking, or drying. A common way to preserve fresh ham is to *cure* it.

pickle To preserve or flavor in pickle. We *pickled* the ripe cucumbers from our garden.

salt To cure or preserve with salt. Before ice boxes were invented, people *salted* their meats.

smoke To cure or preserve (food) by treating it with smoke. We *smoked* all the salmon that we caught on our fishing trip.

prize *n.* Something won in a contest or game. Aunt Jean's quilt won a prize at the county fair.

award A prize. The teacher gave Raoul an *award* for being the best speller in the class.

medal A small piece of metal, sometimes attached to a ribbon, with a picture or writing on it. The mayor gave Soo Lee a *medal* for saving the drowning infant.

reward Money, praise, etc., given or received for working hard or doing something special. The woman gave Nat a *reward* for returning her lost wallet.

promise *v.* To give a promise. Hector promised Randy that he would keep his secret.

assure To convince or promise. I *assure* you that I'll be back in time for your birthday party.

pledge To promise to give. We *pledge* allegiance to the flag every morning at school.

swear To promise or cause to promise solemnly. Witnesses in court must *swear* to tell the truth.

vow To make a vow. My parents *vowed* to love each other when they were married.

proper *adj.* Correct for a certain occasion or situation. It is proper to stand when the guest of honor arrives.

appropriate Suitable; fitting. Jeans are not *appropriate* for dress-up parties.

correct Proper. People with good manners always know the *correct* thing to do or to say.

decent Proper; respectable. Please wear a *decent* jacket when we go out to dinner.

fitting Suitable; proper. Rude language is never *fitting*.

suitable Proper for the purpose or occasion; fitting. Light clothes are most *suitable* for hot weather.

ANTONYMS: **improper, indecent, unsuitable**

pupil *n.* A student. A tutor often teaches only one or two pupils.

apprentice A person who works for another in order to learn a trade or business; any learner or beginner. Johnny was an *apprentice* to a blacksmith.

scholar A school pupil or student. A cap and gown used to be the mark of a *scholar*.

student A person who studies, especially in a school or college. There are 23 *students* in my class.

Q

question *v.* To ask questions. We questioned the teacher about the science experiment.

challenge To question or dispute the truth or correctness of. The senator *challenged* his opponent's statement that there were no toxic waste dumps in the state.

contest To question or challenge. Amy *contested* the umpire's call.

examine To ask questions of in order to get information or to test a person's knowledge or skill. The lawyer

examined the witness for facts about the accident.

inquire To ask a question in order to get information. I forgot to *inquire* about the time the program starts.

quiz To examine by asking questions. The teacher *quizzed* the class after the geography lesson.

ANTONYMS: **answer, reply, respond**

quiet *adj.* Not busy; relaxed. I spent a quiet evening at home.

calm Quiet; peaceful; still. The air at the beach was *calm*.

peaceful Calm; quiet, full of peace. Lions are very *peaceful* after a large meal.

restful Quiet; serene. Our vacation at the lake was very *restful*.

See also **silent.**

ANTONYMS: **busy, nervous, noisy**

R

reason *n.* Explanation; excuse. The reason the moon shines at night is that it reflects sunlight.

argument The reason or reasons for or against something. A longer life span is a good *argument* for exercise and proper nutrition.

excuse A reason given to explain or justify. I have an *excuse* for missing school yesterday.

explanation A reason that explains. Science has provided *explanations* for many strange things.

ground (often pl.) A basic cause, reason, or justification. The people agreed to restrict building on the *grounds* that the town was becoming too crowded.

proof Facts that prove something is true or false. People used to believe the Earth was flat, even though they had no *proof*.

regard *v.* To show thoughtfulness toward; to respect. I always regard other people's feelings and opinions.

admire To regard or look upon with wonder, pleasure, and approval. I *admire* people who help those who don't have enough to eat.

honor To show or give respect and recognition. On Memorial Day we *honor* the people who died for our country.

respect To have or show high regard for; esteem; honor. People whisper in libraries to show that they *respect* the rights of others who are reading there.

value To regard highly; prize. We all *value* your friendship.

See also **notice.**

repair *v.* To fix or mend. Our car's dented fender is being repaired.

fix To restore to good condition; repair. Do you know how to *fix* a broken watch band?

mend To repair. I *mended* the hole in my jacket.

patch To repair or cover with a patch or patches. My sister helped me *patch* the tire on my bike.

restore To bring back to a former or original condition. The landlord *restored* the front of our building.

ANTONYMS: **break, damage, destroy, wreck**

reply *v.* To give an answer. The invitation asked us to reply as soon as possible.

answer To reply or respond to. Who would like to *answer* the question?

respond To give an answer or reply. The candidate did not *respond* to the critical editorial in the newspaper.

return To answer; respond. "That's not what you said before," he *returned.*

ANTONYMS: **inquire, question, request**

reveal *v.* To make known; to make visible. The last page of the magazine reveals the answer to the puzzle.

bare To make bare; uncover. I *bared* all my fears to my best friend.

betray To give away; disclose. Chung didn't want to speak to Cathy again after she *betrayed* his secret.

show To cause or allow to see or be seen. The map *showed* where the treasure was buried.

uncover To reveal. Nancy Drew *uncovered* the answer to the mystery.

ANTONYMS: **conceal, cover, disguise, hide**

rigid *adj.* Stiff; unbending. The cast kept his broken finger rigid.

firm That does not readily give in to touch or pressure. I like sleeping on a *firm* mattress.

fixed Firm; steady. A *fixed* mast was in the center of the boat.

hard Solid and firm; not easily dented or broken. The stale bread had a *hard* crust.

stiff Not easy to bend; not flexible; rigid. After exercising, cool down to keep your muscles from getting *stiff.*

tense Stretched tight; stiff. The student's neck and shoulders were *tense* from long hours of study.

ANTONYMS: **loose, relaxed, slack**

ruler *n.* A person who rules or governs, as a king or queen. King John was the ruler who signed the Magna Carta.

emperor The ruler of an empire. In the past, some European nations were ruled by *emperors.*

governor The chief elected official of a state. The *governor* signed a letter praising education in this state.

monarch A ruler, as a king or queen. Although Great Britain has a prime minister, the queen is considered its *monarch.*

tyrant An all-powerful ruler. Most *tyrants* do not treat their country's citizens kindly.

sadness

S

sadness *n.* The condition of being sad. The boy felt great sadness over his lost dog.

grief Deep sorrow or mental distress. Charlie shared Jiro's *grief* when their friend moved.

sorrow Great sadness or grief. The day Pearl Harbor was attacked was a day of *sorrow*.

trouble Distress, difficulty, worry, or suffering. Ellen's *trouble* started when her alarm didn't ring.

ANTONYMS: cheerfulness, delight, happiness, joy

serious *adj.* Thoughtful; grave. We discussed the serious problem of air pollution in our cities.

grave Very important; serious. I made a *grave* mistake by not studying for the test.

sober Solemn; grave. The jury looked very *sober* when they came back into court.

solemn Serious, grave, and earnest. Elected officials take a *solemn* oath.

thoughtful Full of thought. We spent a *thoughtful* moment in silence.

ANTONYMS: light, minor, unimportant

settler *n.* A person who settles or makes a home in a new country or colony. Many settlers in Minnesota came from northern Europe.

colonist A settler or founder of a colony. Some American *colonists* did not want the British government to rule them.

immigrant A person who comes into a country or region where he or she was not born, in order to live there. During the 1800's, many *immigrants* from Europe came to live in the United States.

pioneer A person who is the first to settle

shock

a new region. Lewis and Clark helped open the West to the *pioneers*.

shake *v.* To tremble. The building shook during the earthquake.

quake To shake or tremble, often with great force. The ground *quaked* as the plane flew over it.

quiver To make a slight trembling motion; vibrate. The frightened duckling *quivered* in my hand.

shiver To tremble, as with cold or fear; shake; quiver. I began to *shiver* as soon as I left the cabin.

shudder To tremble or shake, as from fear or cold; shiver. The thought of making a speech in front of the whole school made me *shudder*.

tremble To shake with fear or cold. The puppy was *trembling* when we found it in the snow.

vibrate To move back and forth rapidly; quiver. Piano strings make noise by *vibrating*.

shock *v.* Cause to feel surprise, terror, or disgust. Everyone was shocked that my grandmother could play the harmonica.

astonish To surprise very much; fill with wonder; amaze. It *astonishes* me that many people don't know how to read.

astound To stun with amazement. The Grand Canyon *astounds* people the first time they see it.

dismay To fill with alarm or disappointment. Margaret *dismayed* her parents when she forgot to call.

startle To frighten, surprise, or excite suddenly. The wrong note from the tuba *startled* everyone at the concert.

stun To shock; to astonish. The bad news *stunned* us all.

surprise To strike with mild astonishment, as by being unexpected or unusual. The students' high scores on the test *surprised* the teacher.

short *adj.* Not long; not tall. The child's legs were too short to reach the bike's pedals.

brief Not long; short. I need a *brief* description of your missing pet.

hasty Quick. We ate a *hasty* dinner to get to the show on time.

quick Done in a short time; fast. We took a *quick* trip to San Francisco for the weekend.

small Not large in size or amount. A guppy is a very *small* fish.

ANTONYMS: **large, long, slow, tall**

shout *v.* To make a sudden loud yell. The crowd shouted when the team scored.

howl To make a long, loud cry. Nobody is sure why wolves *howl* together.

scream To utter a long, shrill cry, as in pain, terror, or surprise. The baby *screamed* when its balloon popped.

shriek To make a sharp, shrill outcry, scream, or sound. The wind *shrieked* through the trees.

wail To make or utter a long, high cry. I'm not *wailing*—I'm singing!

whoop To make loud cries. The crowd of children *whooped* as they attacked the snow fort.

ANTONYMS: **mumble, murmur, whisper**

shower *n.* A short rainfall. The weather forecast calls for showers this afternoon.

cloudburst A sudden, heavy rainfall. A rainbow appeared after the *cloudburst.*

downpour A heavy fall of rain. We were soaked in a *downpour.*

drizzle A light, continuous rain; mist. It didn't rain hard, but there was a *drizzle* all day.

sprinkle A light rain. The plants did not get enough water from this morning's *sprinkle.*

See also **splash.**

shy *adj.* Quiet; not at ease with strangers. Because he was shy, Brian did not like to go to parties.

bashful Timid or uncomfortable with strangers; shy. The *bashful* child hid behind his parents.

modest Bashful; shy. My cousin is too *modest* to brag about her musical talents.

timid Shy. The *timid* boys and girls did not get up to dance right away.

ANTONYMS: **bold, confident**

silent *adj.* Remaining quiet; not speaking. The house is silent when everyone is asleep.

dumb Speechless for a time; silent. Many animals remain *dumb* when they are frightened.

quiet Having or making little noise. Everything was *quiet* just before the storm broke.

speechless Not speaking or unable to speak. The exciting movie left me *speechless.*

still Making no sound; silent. Everyone was so *still* that the cat's purr sounded loud.

ANTONYMS: **loud, noisy**

skin *v.* To scrape off skin. I skinned my knee playing football.

rub To move over the surface of with pressure or friction. I *rubbed* the edges of the shelf with sandpaper.

scrape To rub (a surface) with or against something edged or rough, so as to take off something stuck on. I *scraped* the ice off the car window.

scratch To tear or mark the surface of with something sharp or rough. I *scratched* the table top when I dragged the box across it.

slogan *n.* An expression or motto used in advertising or campaigning. The apple grower's slogan was "Eat an apple a day!"

expression A word or group of words used together. "I'll see you later" is just an *expression*.

jingle A catchy song or poem, especially for advertising purposes. I can't stop singing that store's *jingle*.

motto A word or phrase that expresses a principle or slogan, inscribed on a seal, coin, or other object. The *motto* of the United States, *e pluribus unum*, means "one out of many."

smooth *adj.* Without rough spots or lumps. A smooth layer of snow covered the football field.

even Flat and smooth. The car seemed to glide over the wide and *even* road.

flat Having a level surface; smooth. There was no wind, and the sea looked *flat*.

level Having a flat surface, with each part at the same height. The floors in the old house were not *level*.

ANTONYMS: **bumpy, coarse, rough**

soil *v.* To make or become dirty. Brooke slid in the grass and soiled her soccer uniform.

blur To smudge; to make messy or unclear. The dirty windshield wipers *blurred* the window so much that we couldn't see out.

dirty To make or become dirty. The spinning car wheels splashed mud and *dirtied* my clothes.

mark To make a mark or marks on. The students' shoes *marked* the gym floor.

smear To spread, rub, or cover with a greasy, sticky, or dirty substance. The baby *smeared* oatmeal in his hair.

smudge To blur, smear, or soil. Rain *smudged* the ink on the cover of Fran's book report.

stain To make or become dirty or discolored; soil; spot. Spots of paint *stained* the floors and walls in the artist's messy, cluttered studio.

ANTONYMS: **clean, scrub, wash**

sparkle *v.* To shine or glitter as if giving off sparks of light. His eyes sparkled with joy.

glisten To sparkle or shine. The water *glistened* in the sunshine.

shimmer To shine with an unsteady, glimmering light. The stars *shimmered* in the night sky.

shine To give off or reflect light. The moon does not *shine* as brightly as the sun.

splash *v.* To throw or scatter water or mud. The baby splashed the water in the tub.

scatter To throw about in various places; sprinkle. The dancers *scattered* flowers on the stage.

shower To rain. It *showered* all morning.

spray To send out (a liquid) in fine drops. I *sprayed* water on all the plants.

sprinkle To scatter in drops or bits, as of water or sugar. You should *sprinkle* water over that shirt before you start to iron it.

spoil *v.* To become bad. Milk spoils quickly if it's not kept cold.

decay To rot or cause to rot. The dead leaves *decayed* on the forest floor.

mold To become moldy. The two-week old cheese had *molded* in the refrigerator.

rot To decay, spoil, or decompose. The tomatoes in the garden *rotted* while we were away on vacation.

See also **damage**.

squeeze *v.* To press hard on or together. Squeeze the toothpaste tube at the bottom.

cram To push or stuff into a tight or crowded space. I think I *crammed* too many books into my pack.

crowd To fill too full; cram; pack. The people *crowded* into the gym to see the basketball game.

step

strike

jam To press or squeeze things or people together into a small space. Eight people *jammed* into the small car.

press To crush or squeeze so as to draw out juice. I think it's better to *press* garlic instead of chopping it.

stuff To cram, jam, or shove. We *stuffed* the turkey with a mixture of sausage and cornbread.

step *v.* To move by taking steps. Don't step on the broken glass.

stroll To walk in a slow, idle way. We *strolled* along the beach.

stumble To walk or speak in a shaky way. I was so tired that I *stumbled* up the stairs to bed.

tramp To walk with a heavy step. We *tramped* back to camp after the long hike.

trample To flatten by stepping on. That dog *trampled* everything in my garden!

trudge To walk wearily or with great effort; plod. The tired soldiers *trudged* uphill.

stop *v.* To come or bring to a halt. The wagon stopped at the river to let the horses drink.

flag To stop by signaling. I managed to *flag* a taxi.

halt To stop. The car race was *halted* because of rain.

quit To cease from; stop. The workers *quit* work early on the day before the holiday.

See also **abandon.**

ANTONYMS: **begin, start**

story *n.* A tale that is usually made up. Grandfather told my favorite story

fable A tale that teaches a lesson, especially one with animals that behave like people. One famous *fable* is called "The Town Mouse and the Country Mouse."

fiction Any story about imaginary people and events. Stories about people living on other planets in the future are science *fiction.*

legend An old story of strange or remarkable happenings that may or may not have some basis in truth. Most people have heard the *legends* told about John Henry.

myth A traditional story, usually about such creatures as gods and heroes, often offering an explanation of something in nature or of past events. According to one *myth,* Pegasus was a horse that could fly.

narrative An account, story, or tale. Mark Twain wrote an amusing *narrative* about his life as a riverboat captain.

nonfiction Any story about real people and events. Magazine articles are usually *nonfiction.*

tale A story, narrative, or account of real or imaginary events. In the *tales* of Paul Bunyan, Babe is a giant blue ox.

stream *n.* A small flowing river. This stream is a great place to catch trout.

brook A natural stream smaller than a river. A *brook* flowed through the farm.

creek A stream, especially one smaller than a river and larger than a brook. A *creek* connects the two mountain lakes.

river A large, natural stream of water, usually fed by smaller streams and flowing to the sea, a lake, or other body of water. The Nile is the longest *river* in the world.

spring A flow of water out of the ground. Water from *springs* tastes especially good.

strike *v.* To hit. The *Titanic*, a large ocean liner, sank when it struck an iceberg.

crash To hit making a loud noise. The jar *crashed* onto the floor.

struggle

knock To hit. My brother *knocked* the lamp off the table.

smash To hit with great force. A baseball *smashed* the kitchen window.
See also **attack.**

struggle *n.* A fight. The kittens had a playful struggle over the ball of yarn.

battle Any fight, conflict, or struggle. Many *battles* are fought in every war.

combat A battle or fight. Soldiers must always be ready to enter *combat* for their country.

conflict A struggle, fight, or battle. The two countries had a *conflict* over a spy.

contest A struggle, fight, or quarrel. A tug of war is a kind of *contest.*

swap *v.* To trade or exchange. The boys swapped baseball cards.

bargain To try to get a better price. I *bargained* with the owner before I bought the radio.

barter To trade by exchanging goods or services without using money. Many people in poor countries *barter* rather than pay for the things they need.

deal To do business; trade. That store *deals* only in records for children.

exchange To give one thing for something else; trade; swap. Can you *exchange* this shirt for a larger size?

switch To exchange. The twins *switched* hats, but no one noticed.

trade To exchange (one thing for another). My sister *traded* our cat for a puppy.

T

task *n.* A chore or job. Each scout had a task to do at camp.

assignment Something assigned; as a lesson. Our *assignment* was to look for political cartoons in the newspaper.

chore A routine task, as in housework.

team

Farmers have to begin their *chores* early in the morning.

duty Any work or task that is part of a particular job or occupation. It's a doctor's *duty* to try to save people's lives.

responsibility A person or thing for which one is responsible. Taking out the trash is my *responsibility.*

teacher *n.* A person who teaches or helps others learn. The teacher helped the students with a math problem.

coach A teacher or trainer, as for pupils, athletes, or actors. The speech *coach* taught the actors to speak with a British accent.

trainer A person who trains. The *trainer* had the boxer run and work out every day.

tutor A person who teaches or gives private lessons. Brian had a math *tutor* so he could pass the college test.

team *n.* A group of people who work or play together. Sharon and her cousin Scott were on the same baseball team.

club A group of people who join together. The library formed a *club* for people to discuss books they've read.

crew Any group of people working together. Andrea was on the cleanup *crew* after the party.

force A group of people who do a particular job. My mother is an officer in the police *force.*

league A number of persons, groups, or countries united for some common purpose. The United Nations replaced the *League* of Nations.

outfit Any organized group or team of persons who do some particular work, especially a military organization. My brother is in an *outfit* of marines.

society An organization. I belong to the American *Society* for the Prevention of Cruelty to Animals.

| tender | | unpleasant |

tender *adj.* Gentle and loving. Good
nurses are tender with their patients.
gentle Kind and tender. You must be
gentle when you play with a baby.
kind Willing to help; gentle; friendly;
sympathetic. The kind boy helped
carry Mr. Kelly's packages upstairs.
soft Tender, kind, and sympathetic. My
father may look stern, but he has a
very *soft* heart.
ANTONYMS: **cruel, hard, unkind**

trek *n.* A long hard journey. Lewis and
Clark made a trek across our country
from St. Louis, Missouri, to the
Pacific Ocean.
journey Travel from one place to another;
trip. The *journey* from the East to the
West by covered wagon took months.
tour A trip during which one visits a
number of places for pleasure or to
perform, as a theatrical company,
musician, or athlete. My family went
on a bicycle *tour* of Canada.
travel (pl.) Journeys or trips. One of John
Steinbeck's books describes his *travels*
across our country.
trip A journey or voyage. Our class saw
slides of the principal's *trip* to Egypt.
voyage Any journey, as through air or
space. Before the invention of the
steam engine, ocean *voyages* were
very slow.

twist *v.* To turn. I twisted my ankle while
I was running.
curve To bend. The road *curves* to the left.
swerve To turn or cause to turn to get out
of the way. Juanita *swerved* her bike
to avoid the pothole.
swirl To move in a twisting or spinning
motion. The dirty water *swirled* down
the drain.
whirl To spin or make to spin around very
fast. The dancers *whirled* around the
crowded ballroom.

wriggle To squirm or twist. The child
wriggled with delight.
wring To squeeze liquid out by twisting.
Wring out the mop before you put it
away.

U

unhappy *adj.* Sad; not happy. Flo was
unhappy when she missed the bus.
gloomy Sad. Why do you have such a
gloomy look on your face?
sad Unhappy or depressed; sorrowful. We
felt *sad* when we heard you were sick.
sorrowful Feeling, showing, or causing
sorrow. Susan felt *sorrowful* because
her dog was lost.
ANTONYMS: **cheerful, glad, happy, joyful**

unkind *adj.* Cruel; not kind. Paul was
ashamed of being unkind to his aunt.
cruel Eager or willing to give pain to
others; brutal; not caring whether
others suffer; pitiless. Many groups in
the community try to prevent anyone's
being *cruel* to animals.
heartless Cruel; without kindness. You
would have to be *heartless* not to love
a cute kitten.
mean Not noble in mind or character;
base. Some characters in fairy tales
are *mean* to the heroes.
spiteful Filled with bitter resentment.
Karen thought her brother was being
spiteful when he hid her teddy bear.
vicious Spiteful or mean. The child was
hurt by the *vicious* remark.
ANTONYM: **kind**

unpleasant *adj.* Not agreeable; not
pleasant. The weather was unpleasant
all weekend.
annoying Troublesome; irritating. The
insects are always most *annoying*
around sunset.
disgusting Arousing disgust; offensive.

Some of the scenes of polluted lakes were *disgusting*.

nasty Disgusting to smell or taste. Sour milk has a *nasty* smell.

troublesome Causing trouble. The teacher sent the *troublesome* student to the principal's office.

ANTONYMS: **agreeable, pleasant, pleasing**

urgent *adj.* Requiring quick action or attention. The secretary came in with an urgent message.

critical Of, related to, or causing a crisis. Getting a good education is *critical* to your future.

important Deserving special attention or notice. You received an *important* phone call while you were out.

pressing Needing immediate attention; urgent; important. I have some *pressing* business to discuss with the boss.

ANTONYM: **unimportant**

V

vast *adj.* Very large; huge; enormous. Australia has a vast desert stretching across much of the continent.

broad Of considerable size; large and spacious. The Snake River Canyon is not so *broad* as the Grand Canyon, but it is deeper.

enormous Very large; huge; vast. The blue whale is an *enormous* animal.

huge Very large; vast. A glacier is a *huge* river of ice.

immense Vast; enormous. Even from a distance, Mt. Hood looks *immense*.

ANTONYMS: **modest, narrow, small, tiny**

W

whisper *v.* To speak softly. Please whisper while the baby is sleeping.

grumble To complain in a mumbling way. My sister always *grumbles* about having to help out around the house.

mumble To speak in a low, unclear way, as with lips nearly closed. Tony *mumbled* something just before he fell asleep.

murmur To make a low, unclear sound. I can't understand you when you *murmur*.

ANTONYMS: **howl, scream, shout, shriek, wail**

wonderful *adj.* Causing wonder; amazing. Jim Thorpe was a wonderful Olympic athlete.

incredible So strange, unusual, or extraordinary as to be unbelievable. Many animals that live in the sea look *incredible*.

marvelous Causing wonder; amazing. Beethoven was a *marvelous* composer.

wondrous Wonderful; marvelous. The Lincoln Memorial in Washington, D.C., is a *wondrous* sight.

ANTONYMS: **boring, common, usual**

worry *v.* To be or make someone uneasy or upset. The whole town worried about the trapped miners.

distress To cause to suffer, worry, or be sorry. I *distressed* my parents by forgetting to call them.

fret To make or be cross, irritated, or worried. Don't *fret* if I'm late.

trouble To make or become distressed, annoyed, worried, or ill. It *troubles* me to see you looking so unhappy.

upset To disturb mentally. I *upset* my teacher with my bad grades.

ANTONYMS: **calm, soothe**

worthwhile *adj.* Having worth or importance. Reading is a worthwhile way to spend time.

important Having much significance, value, or influence. The ability to write well is an *important* skill to have.

worthwhile

profitable Bringing profit or gain. Ben's *profitable* lemonade stand helped him buy a catcher's mitt.

useful Having a use; giving service; helpful; beneficial. A dictionary is a *useful* reference book to have when you need to check a word's spelling.

valuable Being worth money or effort; having value. Any painting by the famous Dutch painter Rembrandt is *valuable*.

ANTONYMS: useless, worthless

wrap

wrap *v.* To put a cover around something; to wind around; to cover. *Wrap* the scarf around your neck to keep warm.

blanket To cover completely. Fog *blanketed* the bay and the surrounding hills.

bundle To make into a bundle. We *bundled* our important things together and ran from the flood.

envelop To wrap, cover, or surround. Thick clouds *enveloped* the mountaintop.

ANTONYMS: uncover, unwrap

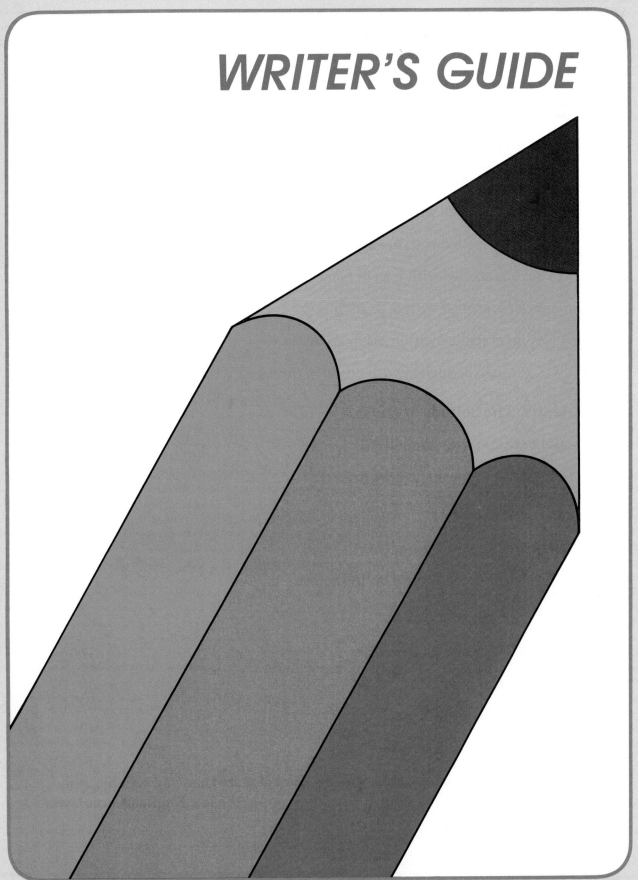

WRITER'S GUIDE

SPELLING RULES

Unit 1: The Sounds /a/, /e/, /i/, /o/, /u/

The short vowel sounds are often spelled with one vowel letter.

- /a/ is spelled with **a**, as in *snag*.

- /e/ is spelled with **e**, as in *chest*.

- /i/ is spelled with **i**, as in *twist*.

- /o/ is spelled with **o**, as in *flock*.

- /u/ is spelled with **u**, as in *dusk*.

- ☐ /e/ can be spelled with **ea**, as in *threat*.

Unit 2: The Sounds /ī/ and /ā/

Here are two ways to spell /ī/.

- with **i**-consonant-**e**, as in *strike*

- with **y**, as in *type*

Here are two ways to spell /ā/.

- with **a**-consonant-**e**, as in *spade*

- with **ai**, as in *fail*

Unit 3: The Sounds /ē/ and /ō/

Here are three ways to spell /ē/.

- with **ea,** as in *stream*

- with **ee**, as in *screen*

- ☐ When /ē/ comes at the end of a word of more than one syllable, it is usually spelled **y**, as in *city*. *Ski* is one of the few English words that has /ē/ spelled with **i**.

Here are two ways to spell /ō/.

- with **o**-consonant-**e**, as in *code*
- with **oa**, as in *coast*

Unit 4: **Words with *ed* and *ing***

- When *ed* and *ing* are added to most verbs, the spelling does not change.
  point—pointed   shout—shouting
- If a verb has a short vowel sound and ends with one consonant letter, double the final consonant before adding *ed* and *ing*.
  swap—swapped   grab—grabbing

Unit 5: **The Sounds /s/ and /z/**

Here are four ways to spell /s/.

- with **s**, as in *season*
- with **c**, as in *recite*
- with **ce**, as in *force*
- with **se**, as in *tense*

Here are two ways to spell /z/.

- with **z**, as in *cozy*
- with **s**, as in *closet*

Unit 7: **The Sounds /k/ and /kw/**

Here are four ways to spell /k/.

- with **c**, as in *comics*
- with **ck**, as in *deck*
- with **ch**, as in *ache*
- with **cc**, as in *occupied*

The sounds /kw/ are spelled with **qu**, as in *quit*.

Unit 8: **Plurals**

Here are the common ways to form plurals.

- Add *s*. Most plurals are formed this way.
  chair—chairs   pencil—pencils

- Add *es* to words that end with *ss*, *x*, *ch*, or *sh*.
  address—addresses   tax—taxes   stitch—stitches

- For some words ending in *f* or *fe*, change *f* to *v* and add *es*.
  shelf—shelves   knife—knives

- When words end with consonant + *y*, change *y* to *i* and add *es*.
  bakery—bakeries   diary—diaries

- Add *s* to words that end with a vowel + *y*.
  highway—highways   valley—valleys

- ☐ The singular of *movies* does not end with *y*. To make *movie* plural, just add *s*.

Unit 9: **Clusters and Digraphs**

- A **consonant cluster** is two or three consonant letters written together. You hear the sounds of all the letters.
  clamp   crust   traffic

- A **consonant digraph** is two consonant letters together that stand for one consonant sound.
  crunchy   shrub   thrift

- A **consonant digraph** can be part of a consonant cluster.
  shrub   thrift

Unit 10: **The Sounds /j/ and /ch/**

Here are three ways to spell /j/.

- with **j**, as in *jacket*

- with **g** before **e** or **i**, as in *agent* and *imagine*

- with **ge** at the end of a word, as in *range*

Here are two ways to spell /ch/.

- with **ch**, as in *checkers*

- with **t** before **u**, as in *fortune* and *nature*

Unit 11: **The Sound /sh/**

Here are four ways to spell /sh/.

- with **sh**, as in *shake*

- with **ss**, as in *issue*

- with **ci**, as in *special*

- with **ti**, as in *action*

Unit 13: **Words with *ed* and *ing***

- If a verb ends with *e*, drop the *e* before adding *ed* or *ing*.
  serve—served   excite—exciting

- If a verb ends with a consonant and *y*, change the *y* to *i* before adding *ed*. Keep the *y* when adding *ing*.
  study + ed = studied   study + ing = studying

- If a verb ends with a vowel and *y*, just add *ed*.
  employ + ed = employed   delay + ing = delaying

- Before adding *ing* to *lie*, drop the final *e* and change the *i* to *y*.
  lie + ing = lying

Unit 14: **The Sounds /oi/ and /ou/**

Here are two ways to spell /oi/.

- with **oi**, as in *soil*

- with **oy**, as in *annoy*

Here are two ways to spell /ou/.

- with **ou**, as in *doubt*

- with **ow**, as in *growl*

Unit 15: The Sounds /o͞o/ and /o͝o/

- The sound /o͝o/ is spelled with **oo**, as in *booklet*.

Here are four ways to spell /o͞o/.

- with **oo**, as in *boost*

- with **o**-consonant-**e**, as in *prove*

- with **ew**, as in *jewels*

- ☐ In *canoe*, /o͞o/ is spelled with **oe**. Only a few words in English have this spelling for /o͞o/.

Unit 16: "Silent" Letters

Here are four letters that can be "silent."

- **k** can be silent, as in *knob* and *kneel*.

- **w** can be silent, as in *wreck* and *wrist*.

- **h** can be silent, as in *honor* and *hour*.

- **t** can be silent, as in *castle* and *fasten*.

Unit 17: Double Letters

- **Double consonant letters** are two letters that are the same and stand for one sound. Usually double consonant letters come after a short vowel sound.

  dizzy   kennel   stubborn

Unit 19: The Sounds /ôr/ and /är/

- The sounds /ôr/ are often spelled with **ar**, as in *wharf*.

Here are two ways to spell /är/.

- with **ar**, as in *charm*

- ☐ In *sergeant*, /är/ is spelled with **er**.

Unit 20: The Sounds /ûr/

Here are four ways to spell /ûr/.

- with **ur**, as in *curve*
- with **er**, as in *verse*
- with **ir**, as in *whirl*
- with **or**, as in *worst*

Unit 21: The Sounds /ər/

Here are three ways to spell /ər/.

- with **er**, as in *clever*
- with **or**, as in *mayor*
- with **ar**, as in *collar*

Unit 22: The Sounds /əl/ and /ən/

Here are four ways to spell /əl/.

- with **le**, as in *ankle*
- with **al**, as in *pedal*
- with **el**, as in *barrel*
- with **il**, as in *pupil*

Here are three ways to spell /ən/.

- with **en**, as in *burden*
- with **on**, as in *apron*
- with **ain**, as in *captain*

Unit 23: Compound Words

- A **compound word** is made up of two or more words. The words are usually written together as one word.
      horse + back = horseback
      never + the + less = nevertheless

☐ Usually, the spellings of the smaller words do not change when they are combined to make a compound word. Sometimes, however, a letter is dropped.

where + ever = wherever

Unit 25: Synonyms and Antonyms

- A **synonym** is a word that has the same or nearly the same meaning as another word.

drowsy   sleepy

- An **antonym** is a word that has an opposite meaning.

victory   defeat

Unit 26: Social Studies Words

- Some social studies words come from Latin.

Latin	Meaning	Example
libertas	"freedom"	liberty
congressus	"meeting"	congress

Unit 27: Prefixes

- A **prefix** is a letter or group of letters added to the beginning of a base word. A prefix changes the meaning of the base word. Here is a chart of some prefixes and their meanings.

Prefix	Meaning	Example
dis-	"the opposite of"	*dis*obey
re-	"again"	*re*write
un-	"not"	*un*pleasant
	"the opposite of"	*un*cover
in-	"not"	*in*correct

Unit 28: Suffixes

- A **suffix** is a letter or group of letters added to the end of a base word. Here is a chart of some suffixes and their meanings.

Suffix	Meaning	Example
-ful	"full of"	power*ful*
-less	"without"	hope*less*

Unit 29: Noun Suffixes

The suffixes *-ion*, *-ness*, and *-ment* can be added to words to form nouns. The spelling changes when you add *-ion* and *-ness* to some words.

- Sometimes you must drop the letter *e*.
  educate + -ion = education

- Sometimes you must change the *y* to *i*.
  tardy + -ness = tardiness

☐ In *addition*, you add *-ition*.
  add + -ition = addition

Unit 31: Word Families

- A **word family** is a group of words that have the same base word. Here are some base words and their related words.

Base Word	Related Word
enter	entrance
move	movable
count	discount

Unit 32: Syllable Patterns

- When a word has two consonant letters between two vowel letters, divide the word into syllables between the two consonants.
  hunger   hun·ger   target   tar·get

WRITER'S GUIDE

- When a word ends with a consonant letter before *le*, divide the word before the consonant.

  sample   sam·ple   candle   can·dle

Unit 33: Syllable Patterns

Here are two ways to divide two-syllable words into syllables.

- If there is a long vowel sound in the first syllable, divide the word before the middle consonant.

  robot   ro·bot   basin   ba·sin

- If there is a short vowel sound in the first syllable, divide the word after the middle consonant.

  dragon   drag·on   petal   pet·al

Unit 34: Three-Syllable Words

- Some words contain syllables that are difficult to hear. When you spell these words, be sure to write each syllable.

  chocolate   favorite

Unit 35: Language Arts Words

- Some words are used in the study of grammar, composition, and literature. These words can help you become more skillful in using language: *predicate, paragraph, nonfiction.*

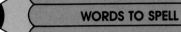
TROUBLESOME WORDS TO SPELL

about	have	quite	today
already	haven't	remember	together
am	hear	right	tomorrow
and	hello	school	tonight
anyway	her	sincerely	too
are	here	some	truly
awhile	hospital	sometimes	two
because	I'll	stationery	until
before	I'm	studying	very
birthday	isn't	suppose	want
cannot	it's	teacher	we
can't	know	Thanksgiving	well
close	letter	that's	went
couldn't	maybe	their	we're
cousin	Mr.	them	will
didn't	Mrs.	there	won't
don't	name	there's	would
down	now	they	write
everybody	off	they're	writing
for	our	think	you
friend	outside	thought	your
from	pretty	time	you're
grammar	quit	to	yours

LANGUAGE: A Glossary of Terms and Examples

Grammar

Sentences

- A **sentence** is a group of words that expresses a complete thought. It starts with a capital letter. It always ends with a punctuation mark.

- A **declarative sentence** makes a statement. It ends with a period (.).

  Gray storm clouds filled the sky.

- An **interrogative sentence** asks a question. It ends with a question mark (?).

  Where is the soccer ball?

- An **exclamatory sentence** shows strong feeling or surprise. It ends with an exclamation point (!).

  What a beautiful day!

- An **imperative sentence** makes a request or commands. It ends with a period (.).

  Be careful riding on that street.

- The **subject** of a sentence tells whom or what the sentence is about. It may be one word or a group of words.

  My mother studies Chinese on weekends.

- The **predicate** of a sentence tells something about the subject. It includes an action verb or linking verb and other words that go with it.

  She will be a translator someday.

Nouns

- A **noun** is a word that names a person, place, or thing.

- A **common noun** names any person, place, or thing. It is a general word that begins with a small letter.

  lantern   squirrel   roommate   cupboard

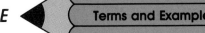

- A **proper noun** names a particular person, place, or thing. A proper noun begins with a capital letter.

    Mr. Chow   Tuesday   New Jersey   Arkansas River

- A **singular noun** names one person, place, or thing.

    parrot   Ohio   wagon

- A **plural noun** names more than one person, place, or thing.

    children   homes   cars

- To make most singular nouns plural, add *s*.

    sandal—sandals   hospital—hospitals
    coward—cowards   bicycle—bicycles

- If a singular noun ends with *s*, *sh*, *ch*, or *x*, add *es*.

    stress—stresses   couch—couches
    suffix—suffixes   splash—splashes

- If a singular noun ends in *y* with a vowel before it, add *s* to form the plural.

    turkey—turkeys   valley—valleys

- If a singular noun ends in *y* with a consonant before it, change the *y* to *i*. Then add *es* to form the plural.

    biography—biographies   country—countries

- Some nouns are not made plural by adding *s* or *es*.

Nouns That End in *f* or *fe*	**Nouns That Change Vowel Spelling**	**Nouns That Do Not Change**
scarf—scarves knife—knives	man—men goose—geese	trout—trout pants—pants

- Some singular nouns are made plural in other ways.

    child—children   ox—oxen

- A **possessive noun** shows ownership or possession.

- To form the possessive of a singular noun, add an apostrophe and an *s* ('s).

    editor—editor's   speaker—speaker's

- To form the possessive of a plural noun that does not end in *s*, add an apostrophe and an *s* ('s).

  people—people's   deer—deer's

- To form the possessive of a plural noun that ends in *s*, just add an apostrophe (').

  donkeys—donkeys'   wives—wives'

Verbs

- An **action verb** is a word or group of words that expresses an action. An action verb is often the key word in the predicate. It tells what the subject does.

  The waiter <u>dropped</u> the tray.

- A **linking verb** connects the subject of a sentence with a word or words in the predicate. It tells what the subject is or is like. The most common linking verbs are forms of the verb *be*: *am*, *is*, *are*, *was*, *were*.

  Alice <u>was</u> my swimming partner.   I <u>am</u> third in the line.

  Here are other common linking verbs.

  become   feel   seem   look
  grow   taste   appear   smell

  I will <u>become</u> an astronaut.

- A **helping verb** helps the main verb express an action or make a statement. These words are often used as helping verbs.

  am   was   has   do
  is   were   have   will   does
  are   had   did

  Matt <u>was</u> taking a picture.   They <u>have</u> gone away.

Verb Tenses

- The time expressed by a verb is called the **tense**.

- **Present tense** expresses action that happens now or regularly.

  He <u>purchases</u> the hat.   It <u>costs</u> ten dollars.

- Most present-tense verbs that follow singular subjects end in *s* or *es*.

  The necklace <u>gleams</u>.   The baby <u>reaches</u> for it.

- Present-tense verbs that follow plural subjects do not take an *s* or *es* ending.

  > The children <u>arrive</u> at noon.   They <u>enter</u> the building.

- **Past tense** expresses action that happened in the past. Many verbs use *ed* to show past tense.

  > I <u>bounced</u> the ball.   It <u>bumped</u> against a chair.

Irregular Verbs

- **Irregular verbs** are verbs that do not add *ed* to show past time. Some of these verbs are on the chart.

Verb	Present	Past	Past with *Have*, *Has*, or *Had*
bring	bring(s)	brought	brought
know	know(s)	knew	known
write	write(s)	wrote	written

Adjectives

- An **adjective** is a word that describes a noun.

  > An <u>enormous</u> mountain rises above the <u>ancient</u> village.

- Adjectives can describe by comparing.

- One-syllable adjectives use *er* or *est* to make comparisons. The letters *er* are added to an adjective when two things are compared. The letters *est* are added to an adjective when more than two things are compared.

  > A horse is <u>larger</u> than a dog.
  > The elephant is the <u>largest</u> animal in the animal preserve.

- Adjectives of two or more syllables usually use *more* or *most* to make comparisons. *More* is used when two things are compared. *Most* is used when more than two things are compared.

  > My picture is <u>more</u> colorful than Tina's picture.
  > This is the <u>most</u> colorful picture I've seen.

- Some words can become adjectives by adding *y*.

    crust—crusty   the crusty bread

Adverbs

- An **adverb** is a word that adds meaning to a verb by telling *how*, *when*, or *where*.

    The vase was broken accidentally. (how)
    It was knocked over yesterday. (when)
    It fell here. (where)

- Adverbs are used to compare actions.

- Adverbs that use *more* compare two actions.

    I exercise more frequently than Marcia.

- Adverbs that use *most* compare more than two actions.

    That skier glided the most swiftly of all.

- A few adverbs of one syllable use *er* and *est* to compare.

    I stayed at the party longer than Mel.
    Brit stayed at the party the longest of anyone.

- Some adverbs are formed by adding *ly* to words.

    total—totally

Vocabulary

Antonyms

- **Antonyms** are words that have opposite meanings. Here are some antonym pairs.

    victory—defeat   increase—decrease

Synonyms

- **Synonyms** are words that have the same or nearly the same meaning. Here are some synonym pairs.

    sorrow—sadness   drowsy—sleepy

Homophones

- **Homophones** are words that sound alike. They are spelled differently and have different meanings. Here are some homophones.

  sense—cents   creek—creak

Prefixes

- A **prefix** is a letter or group of letters added to the beginning of a base word. A prefix changes the meaning of the base word.

  obey—disobey

Suffixes

- A **suffix** is a letter or group of letters added to the end of a base word.

  peace—peaceful

Word Family

- A **word family** is a group of words that has the same base word.

  prove—approve, approval, disapprove

Analogies

- An **analogy** is a group of words that shows the relationship between things. An analogy is often presented as two pairs of objects.

  Finger is to *hand* as *toe* is to *foot*.

DICTIONARY: A Glossary of Terms and Examples

Alphabetical Order

- The order of letters from *A* to *Z* is called **alphabetical** order. Words in a dictionary are listed in alphabetical order. These words are in alphabetical order.

  apartment
  comet
  committee
  loaf
  product
  tailor

Guide Words

- There are two **guide words** at the top of each dictionary page. The word on the left is the first word on the page. The word on the right is the last word. All the other words on the page are in alphabetical order between those words.

imagine		jogger
im·ag·ine /i·maj′in/ *v.* **im·ag·ined, im·ag·in·ing** To have an idea or form a picture in your mind.		**in·ter·rupt** /in′tə·rupt′/ *v.* **1** To cause someone to stop doing something. **2** To stop an action.

Entry Word

- On a dictionary page, an **entry word** is a word in dark print that is followed by its meaning. Entry words appear in alphabetical order and are divided into syllables.

  jew·el /jōo′əl/ *n.* **1** A precious stone. **2** An ornament set with gems.
  jew·el·ry /jōo′əl·rē/ *n.* Objects worn for decoration, such as necklaces, rings, etc.
  jog·ger /jog′ər/ *n.* A person who jogs or runs regularly for exercise.

Entry

- An **entry** is an entry word and all the information about it.

Pronunciation

- A **pronunciation** follows each entry word. Letters and symbols show how the word is pronounced.

  > **is·sue** /ish′o͞o/ *n., v.* **is·sued, is·su·ing**
  > **1** *n.* Something sent out regularly: an *issue* of a magazine. **2** *v.* To send or give out.

Part of Speech

- A **part of speech** tells whether the word is a noun, a verb, or some other part of speech. The names are abbreviated.

Definition

- A **definition** tells what a word means. Many words have more than one definition. An example sentence may follow the definition.

  > **in·sect** /in′sekt/ *n.* A very small animal with six legs and often with wings.
  > **it·self** /it·self′/ *pron.* Its own self: The goat stumbled and hurt *itself*.

Example

- An **example** shows you how to use the word.

Word History

- A **word history** explains how a word and its meaning have developed. A word history usually gives the meaning of the older word that the modern English word comes from. In the **Spelling Dictionary,** this symbol ▶ indicates a word history.

  > **a·pron** /ā′prən/ *n.* A garment worn over clothes to protect them. ▶ *Apron* comes from the Middle French word *naperon,* "a small cloth."

Pronunciation Key

- A pronunciation key explaining the pronunciation marks appears at the beginning of a dictionary. A brief key is often found at the bottom of dictionary pages as well.

act, āte, câre, ärt; egg, ēven; if, īce; on, ōver, ôr; bŏŏk, fōōd; up, tûrn;
ə = a in *ago*, e in *listen*, i in *giraffe*, o in *pilot*, u in *circus*; yōō = u in *music*; oil; out;
chair; sing; shop; thank; that; zh in *treasure*.

Syllables

- A word is made up of several parts called **syllables.** Each syllable has a vowel sound.

- In a word with two or more syllables in the dictionary, the **accent mark** (') in the pronunciation shows which syllable is said with the most force.

- The syllable with the accent mark is called the **accented syllable**.

- A **secondary accent** is a lighter mark. It comes after a syllable you say with a little less force.

COMPOSITION

Guides for the Writing Process

Prewriting

Use this checklist to plan your writing.

- Choose a topic.

- Choose a purpose for writing.

- Ask yourself questions about your topic.

- Choose a prewriting plan that works best for the form of writing you have chosen.

- Add more ideas as you think of them.

- Read over your plan.

- Begin to put your ideas in order.

Here are some prewriting plans.

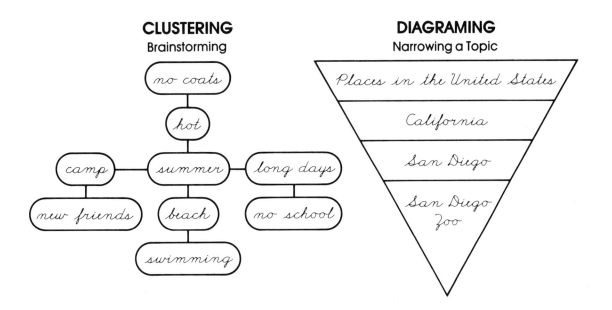

CLUSTERING
Brainstorming

no coats — hot — summer (camp, long days) — new friends, beach, no school — swimming

DIAGRAMING
Narrowing a Topic

Places in the United States
California
San Diego
San Diego Zoo

▶ WRITER'S GUIDE

CHARTING
Organizing Facts

Who	*What*	*When*	*Where*	*Why*
Anne	*mows lawn*	*week ends*	*local homes*	*to earn money*
Jose	*feeds horses*	*every day*	*the ranch*	*to help family*
Ray	*waters plants*	*once a week*	*in house*	*likes growing things*

OUTLINING
Organizing Research

Dinosaurs

Kinds of
A. Lizard-hipped
   1. Brontosaurus
   2. Tyrannosaurus
B. Bird-hipped
   1. Stegosaurus
   2. Triceratops

Living Habits
A. Lived in swamps
B. Got food from plants

MAPPING
Drawing a Plan

Beginning

Val wants to be on the U.S. Olympic Swim Team.

She starts to practice every day for hours at a time.

Middle

Val wins many local and state races.

Val signs up for a national race to qualify for the Olympic team.

One week before the race Val gets the flu.

Ending

Val must stay in bed. She cannot practice.

On race day Val does swim. She finishes third. She makes team.

Composing

Use this checklist as you write.

- Read over your plan.
- Think about your purpose and audience.
- Use your plan to put your ideas on paper quickly.
- Do not worry about spelling, punctuation, or grammar at this time.
- Remember that you may get more ideas as you write.
- Add more new ideas as you think of them.

Revising

Use this checklist when you edit and proofread your work.

Editing

- Read over your work.
- Be sure your audience has enough information.
- Be sure the order of your sentences makes sense.
- Check that each sentence is a complete thought.
- Be sure each paragraph has a clear topic sentence.
- Check that all the detail sentences support the main idea.
- Be sure the words are lively and interesting.

Proofreading

- Be sure you used capital letters correctly.
- Be sure you used punctuation marks correctly.
- Check the spelling of each word.
- Be sure you used each word correctly.
- Be sure the grammar is correct.
- Be sure the first line of each paragraph is indented.
- Be sure your handwriting is neat and readable.

Editing and Proofreading Marks

- Use **Editing and Proofreading Marks** when you revise your writing. These marks help you see the changes you want to make.

- Remember you can go back and change words or sentences as many times as you want or need to.

Editing and Proofreading Marks

☰	capitalize
⊙	make a period
∧	add something
⌄	add a comma
⌄⌄	add quotation marks
ℓ	take something away
◯	spell correctly
¶	indent the paragraph
/	make a lowercase letter
∼ tr	transpose

¶ The school fair will be held next *tuesday* afternoon. All students are going to attend⊙ There will be a ^writing contest and a crafts show. Science projects will also be displayed. Teachers⌄ families. and friends will be invited. The school band will play ⌄The Star-Spangled Banner⌄ Then the principal *and the coach* will give a speech. *Prizes* will be given for the best compositions and drawings⊙ ¶ The fair has always been a highlight of the /school year. Plans are already being made for the fair next year. It will *place take* in April instead of in May. tr

A Glossary of Terms and Examples
Kinds of Sentences

- A **sentence** is a group of words that expresses a complete thought. It always begins with a capital letter. It always ends with a punctuation mark.

- A **declarative sentence** makes a statement. It ends with a period (.).

    Grey storm clouds filled the sky.

- An **interrogative sentence** asks a question. It ends with a question mark (?).

    Where is the soccer ball?

- An **exclamatory sentence** shows strong feeling or surprise. It ends with an exclamation point (!).

    What a beautiful day!

- An **imperative sentence** makes a request or commands. It ends with a period (.).

    Be careful riding on that street.

Paragraph

- A **paragraph** is a group of sentences that develops one main idea.

- The **topic sentence** expresses the main idea of the paragraph.

- **Detail sentences** explain or tell about the main idea.

- The first line of a paragraph is indented.

Descriptive Paragraph

- A **descriptive paragraph** paints a picture with words such as colorful adjectives and adverbs.

- The **topic sentence** clearly tells what the subject is.

- **Detail sentences** give particular information about the subject.

Here is an example of a descriptive paragraph.

> I like summer evenings when the dark comes late. At seven the sky is still a dreamy purple-gray. The round white moon must be heavy, for it hangs as low as a street lamp. No one on our block wants to go indoors. I hear the squeals of little kids playing and the river-rush of skate wheels. Bicycles glide past as silently as deep-sea fish. Their tail lights gleam like orange eyes. The air is soft and warm, and I smell newly cut grass and wet cement.

How-to Paragraph

- A **how-to paragraph** explains how to do or make something.

- The **topic sentence** names the task that is being explained.

- The **detail sentences** name the necessary materials and the order of the steps required to do the task.

- The words *first*, *next*, *then*, and *last* help to show the order of the steps.

Here is an example of a how-to paragraph.

> You can use a trick to separate pepper and salt. First spill some salt on a table. Then sprinkle a little pepper on top. Tell your audience that you can remove the pepper from the salt. Yet you will not touch either! Now take out a pocket comb. Run it through your hair to give it an electric charge. Then pass it just above the mound of pepper and salt. The lighter pepper grains will rise and cling to the comb.

Opinion Paragraph

- An **opinion paragraph** states the writer's opinion about an issue or topic and gives reasons for that opinion.

- The **topic sentence** clearly states the writer's opinion.

- **Detail sentences** give reasons that support that opinion.

Here is an example of an opinion paragraph.

> The best vacation spot is at home. When my family stays home, I can do all the things I enjoy most. For example, I like being with my friends, listening to my tapes, making models, and playing softball. I can't do these things when we travel. When we go on trips, we spend long, boring hours in a car. We waste time looking for places to eat or sleep. The food is seldom as good as our dinners at home. Often motels are noisy or uncomfortable. Traveling makes us tired, and usually someone gets cranky. Very often that someone is me.

Comparison Paragraph/Contrast Paragraph

- A **comparison paragraph** shows the ways in which two things are alike.

- A **contrast paragraph** points out the ways in which two things are different.

- The **topic sentence** expresses the main idea and states whether the paragraph will compare or contrast. The qualities to be discussed are named in this sentence.

- **Detail sentences** explain each quality mentioned in the topic sentence in the order in which they are named in the topic sentence.

Here is an example of a comparison paragraph.

> Hills and mountains are similar in three ways: general appearance, plant life, and formation. Both hills and mountains rise above the level land below them. Both can support grass, trees, and many kinds of blooming plants. Both hills and mountains were formed long ago. Many took shape when Ice Age glaciers melted and left "folded" formations behind.

Here is an example of a contrast paragraph.

Old-fashioned typewriters were quite different from today's computers in appearance, in usefulness, and in printing ability. First of all, old-fashioned typewriters had no screens. Computers, however, have screens so that their operators can correct errors before the words are printed. Second, typewriters had no memory, and carbon paper was used to make copies. Computers hold information in their memories, and copies can be made simply by tapping a few keys. Finally, typewriters printed directly on paper from the keyboard. Computers, however, send signals to a separate printer, which can print the document in many different forms.

Friendly Letter

- A **friendly letter** has five parts.

- The **heading** contains the letter writer's address and the date. A comma is used between the name of the city and the state and between the day and the year.

- The **greeting** welcomes the person who receives the letter. The greeting begins with a capital letter and is followed by a comma.

- The **body** of the letter contains the message.

- The **closing** is the end of the letter. The first word is capitalized. A comma follows the closing.

- The **signature** is the written name of the person who wrote the letter.

Here is **an example** of a friendly letter.

1508 N.E. 49th St.	**Heading**
Gladstone, Missouri 64118	
September 28, 20--	
Dear Mike,	**Greeting**
Thanks for your letter. I'm glad you are having fun at your grandparents' house. Dad and I went fishing yesterday. I wish you could have been with us. See you soon.	**Body**
Sincerely,	**Closing**
Dave	**Signature**

Business Letter

- A **business letter** has six parts.

- The **heading** is in the upper right corner. It gives the address of the writer and the date.

- The **inside address** starts at the left margin. It shows the name and address of the receiver.

- The **greeting** begins at the left margin. It names the person to whom you are writing. The greeting begins with a capital letter and is followed by a colon.

- The **body** tells why you are writing the letter.

- The **closing** is in line with the heading. The first word of the closing is capitalized. A comma follows the closing.

- The **signature** is in line with the closing. The signature is the writer's full name.

Here is an example of a business letter.

> 6420 Peak Ave.
> Colorado Springs, Colorado 80917
> May 20, 20--
>
> Ms. Susan Fillmore
> 1600 Eighth St.
> Colorado Springs, Colorado 80917
>
> Dear Ms. Fillmore:
>
>   I am a student at the River School, and my class is sponsoring a career day. We would like you to come and speak to us about your career as a lawyer. Would you be interested?
>
>   Sincerely,
>
>   *Fred Varney*
>
>   Fred Varney

Heading

Inside Address

Greeting

Body

Closing

Signature

Journal

- A **journal entry** is a daily record of events. What someone writes in a journal each day is called an **entry.**

- Each journal entry gives the day and date and tells *who, what, when, where,* and *why* about events.

- A journal helps people remember events or things that have happened.

Here is an example of a journal entry.

September 13, 20--

Today went much better at my new school. Three of the girls in my class asked me to sit with them at lunch. One of them, Amanda, reminds me of my best friend Gina. She made me laugh. I still miss Gina and my friends in Ohio a lot. However, now I am starting to make friends here.

Story

- A **story** has a beginning, a middle, and an ending.

- The **beginning** of a story introduces the setting and main character(s) of the story.

- The **middle** of a story tells the problem or challenge the main character faces. It can also include conversation, or dialogue between the characters.

- The **ending** tells how the main character(s) solves the problem.

- A story has a title. The first word and each important word begins with a capital letter.

Here is the beginning of a science-fiction story.

Colony on the Moon

Michael spent the day staring out the round window of the rocket. The moon had grown so large that it filled the window. It looked like a pale, mountainous desert. Until now, Michael had been excited. Now his hands and feet were icy. He felt a little weak and shaky, as if he were getting sick. The moon was so vast and empty. Somewhere down there was a tiny dark shadow that was the Armstrong colony. It was too small even to be seen yet. Michael felt his mothers hand on his shoulder. "Well, Michael," she said, "there it is—our new home."

Conversation

- A **conversation** is a dialogue between two or more people. It sounds like real people talking.

- In a conversation the exact words of a speaker are enclosed in quotation marks.

- Each quotation begins with a capital letter.

- Use a comma between a quotation and the rest of the sentence unless a question mark or exclamation point is needed.
    "I'd like to buy a bunch of grapes," I said to the grocer.

- A new paragraph begins each time a speaker changes.

Here is an example of a written conversation.

> "I'm ready to go, Mom," said Shannon. "Shall I help you pack your things?"
> "Thank you, Shannon," called Mom from the back bedroom, "but I'm just about done. I'll be there in a minute."

Biography

- A **biography** is the true story of a person's life written by another person.

- A biography usually follows the events of a person's life in order.

- It often includes anecdotes, or short interesting stories about events in a person's life.

Here is an example of the first paragraph of a biography.

> In December, 1863, Annie Jump Cannon was born in Dover, Delaware. In the winter skies, the stars were at their clearest and brightest. To the infant Annie, those distant points of light meant nothing. Yet one day she would know the skies as well as her own town. Indeed, she would have classified more stars than any other astronomer, past or present.

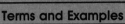
Book Report

- A **book report** gives a brief summary of a book.

- A book report gives the title and author of the book. It tells about the main characters and one or two important events in the story.

- A book report does not tell the ending of the story.

- A book report includes a reader's opinion of the book.

Here is an example of a book report.

Title *A Wrinkle in Time*
Author *Madeleine L'Engle*
Summary *Meg Murray is a young girl who finds herself on a trip through time and space. She is joined on her journey by her brother Charles and her friend Calvin. The three children discover some amazing things and meet some wonderful creatures along the way. They also have a big problem when the terrible Dark Thing captures Charles. Can Meg and Calvin save Charles? Read this book and find out.*
Opinion *I enjoyed this book because it is very exciting and full of wonderful creatures.*

News Story

- A **news story** gives readers information.

- A news story has a short **headline** with a strong verb. The first word and each important word in the headline begins with a capital letter.

- The first paragraph of a news story is called the **lead.** The lead paragraph includes the facts that tell *who, what, when,* and *where.*

- The **body** of the news story has more details about the lead.

Here is an example of a lead paragraph for a news story.

<u>Brave Pilot Sets Record</u>

A new flight record was set at the Oakland International Airport on Sunday, June 10. Donald Rodewald completed the first solo flight around the world by a pilot unable to use his legs. As "Flying Tiger" Rodewald brought down his specially built Piper Comanche, cheers rose from the waiting crowd.

Research Report

- A **research report** has several paragraphs that give facts about one subject.

- To begin research for a report, first take notes on the subject from two or more books. List the books you use in a bibliography.

- Make an outline using your notes.

- Follow your outline as you write your report.

Here is an example of paragraph from a research report.

> To the Hopi, keeping the past alive is as important as living in the present. They have a long history to remember. There have been Hopi in Oraibi, Arizona, for about 800 years. Today about 6,500 Hopi still live in that general region. Like their ancestors, many are farmers, herders, and artists. Some of their skills and crafts have been handed down over centuries. Yet the Hopi are also willing to adopt modern ideas and methods that seem useful and practical.

Poem

- A **poem** is a verse usually written in a regular rhythm and with a definite rhyme pattern.

- A **lyric poem** is usually short. It expresses what the writer sees, feels, hears, tastes, and smells.

- A **narrative poem** is a poem that tells a story. It has a setting, characters, and a plot. It has a beginning, a middle, and an end.

- Most narrative poems also have a strong rhythm and rhyme. They often tell about a great adventure.

Here is an example of the beginning of a narrative poem.

> Each month, when the moon was dark,
> Or so the town folk say,
> Old Whalen Buckley Butterworth
> Would saddle up his bay.
> Off he'd ride in the dead of night,
> Then back by noon next day.

Advertisement

- An **advertisement** is a public notice. Its purpose is to persuade people to buy something.

- A **commercial** is an advertisement used on radio or television. Like a written advertisement, its purpose is to persuade people to buy a certain product.

- A **classified ad** is a notice printed in a newspaper. It tells about a job opening, a service that is available, or something that is for sale.

Here is an example of a classified ad.

COOK WANTED FOR
POPULAR RESTAURANT
Good salary. Apply at
Sam's Cafe, P.O. Box 62,
Reston, CA 93940.
9:00 A.M. to 5:00 P.M. daily

Telephone Message

- A **telephone message** is a brief note given to someone who is not available to receive a telephone call.

- A telephone message should include the time and date of the call, the name of the person called, the name of the person calling, the message, and the name of the person who wrote the message.

Here is an example of a telephone message.

Monday, 3:30 P.M.

Chris,
Sharon called to ask about the concert
tonight. Please call her before you
leave for the grocery store if you can.
                              Debbie
Number (at her grandmother's) 555-1201
After 4:30 (at home) 555-4378

MECHANICS: A Glossary of Rules

Capital Letters

Names and Titles of Persons, Names of Pets, and *I*

- Begin each part of the name of a person with a capital letter. Capitalize an initial.

  Craig R. Rodman   Betty Miller

- Begin titles of people such as *Ms.*, *Mrs.*, and *Dr.* with a capital letter.

  Dr. Grace Olsen   Mr. Luis Flores

- Always capitalize the word *I*.

  Then I knocked on the door.

- Begin the name of a pet with a capital letter.

  Smoky   Ruff   Curly

Names of Places

- Begin each important word of the name of a town, city, state, and country with a capital letter.

  Durango, Colorado   New York City   Iceland

- Begin each important word in the names of streets and their abbreviations with capital letters.

  Third Avenue (or Ave.)   Jackson Boulevard (or Blvd.)

Names of Days, Months, and Holidays

- Begin the name of a day of the week or its abbreviation with a capital letter.

  Sunday   Sun.   Thursday   Thurs.

- Begin the name of a month or its abbreviation with a capital letter.

  August   Aug.   December   Dec.

- Begin each important word in the name of a holiday or special day with a capital letter.

  Lincoln's Birthday   Election Day   Labor Day

Titles of Books, Stories, Poems, and Reports

- Use a capital letter to begin the first, last, and all important words in the title of a book, report, story, poem, song, magazine, newspaper, record album, or television show.

  <u>Black Beauty</u> (book)
  <u>San Francisco Chronicle</u> (newspaper)
  "I Never Saw a Purple Cow" (poem)

Punctuation

Period

- Use a period at the end of a declarative or imperative sentence.
  Molly is getting on the bus.
  Please watch her.

- Use a period after an abbreviation.
  Sept.   Rd.   Sen.

- Use a period after an initial.
  Jason R. Eldridge

Question Mark

- Use a question mark at the end of an interrogative sentence.
  Will you take Ellie with you?

Exclamation Point

- Use an exclamation point at the end of an exclamatory sentence.
  Wow, what wonderful news!

Commas

- Use a comma in an address to separate the city and state or the city and country.

    Denver, Colorado   Kyoto, Japan

- Use a comma between the day and the year.

    April 15, 1901

- Use a comma after the greeting in a friendly letter and after the closing of any letter.

    Dear Elaine,   Best wishes,

- Use a comma between a quotation and the rest of the sentence unless a question mark or exclamation point is needed.

    "I'd like a dozen rolls," I said.

- Use a comma to separate three or more words in a series.

    Art, Sandy, and Eloise are swimming.

Quotation Marks and Underlines

- Place quotation marks before and after a speaker's exact words.

    "It looks like a haunted house," whispered Pedro.

- Use quotation marks before and after a direct quotation.

- Use quotation marks before and after the title of a story, poem, or song.

    "America the Beautiful" (song)   "Clara's Wish" (story)

- Underline the title of a book, newspaper, magazine, movie, or television show.

    <u>Heidi</u> (book)   <u>Washington Post</u> (newspaper)

Apostrophe

- Use an apostrophe to show that one or more letters have been left out in a contraction.

    would not—wouldn't   it is—it's

- Add an apostrophe and an *s* to singular nouns to show possession. Such nouns are called singular possessive nouns.

    <u>Maddie's</u> sneakers   <u>Tess's</u> house   <u>dog's</u> collar

- Add an apostrophe to a plural noun that ends in *s* to show possession. Such nouns are called plural possessive nouns.

    the <u>boys'</u> boats   the <u>horses'</u> corral

- Add an apostrophe and an *s* to plural nouns that do not end in *s* to form the plural possessive.

    the <u>children's</u> gear   the <u>oxen's</u> tails

Colon

- Use a colon after the greeting in a business letter.

    Dear President Hilyard:

HANDWRITING: Letter Forms

Uppercase and Lowercase Manuscript Letters

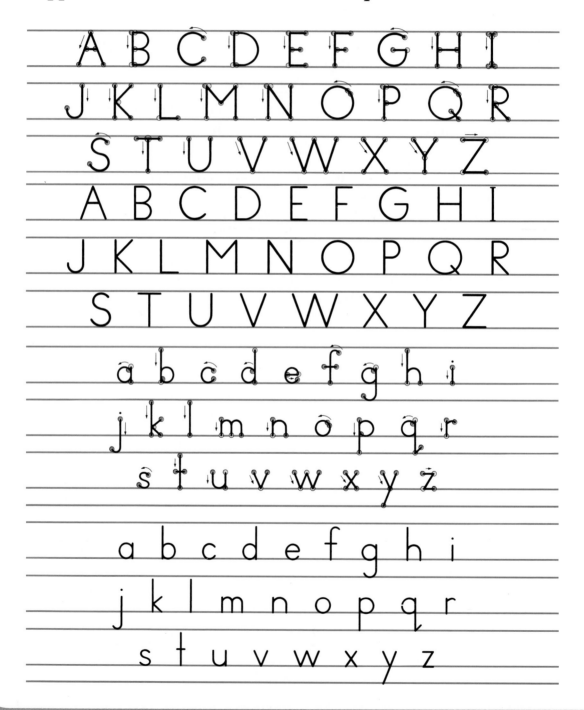

Uppercase and Lowercase Cursive Letters

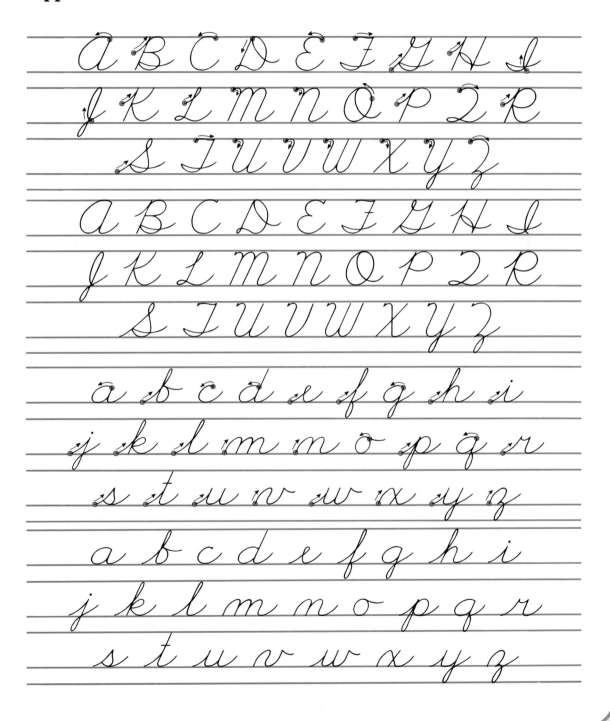